Little Legs,
BIG HEART

*One Girl's Journey of Acceptance,
Perseverance, and Growth*

Kristen E. DeAndrade

BALBOA.
PRESS

A DIVISION OF HAY HOUSE

Balboa Press books may be ordered through booksellers or by contacting:

Balboa Press
A Division of Hay House
1663 Liberty Drive
Bloomington, IN 47403
www.balboapress.com
1 (877) 407-4847

Because of the dynamic nature of the Internet, any web addresses or links contained in this book may have changed since publication and may no longer be valid. The views expressed in this work are solely those of the author and do not necessarily reflect the views of the publisher, and the publisher hereby disclaims any responsibility for them.

The author of this book does not dispense medical advice or prescribe the use of any technique as a form of treatment for physical, emotional, or medical problems without the advice of a physician, either directly or indirectly. The intent of the author is only to offer information of a general nature to help you in your quest for emotional and spiritual well-being. In the event you use any of the information in this book for yourself, which is your constitutional right, the author and the publisher assume no responsibility for your actions.

Any people depicted in stock imagery provided by Getty Images are models, and such images are being used for illustrative purposes only. Certain stock imagery © Getty Images.

Print information available on the last page.

ISBN: 978-1-9822-1899-7 (sc)
ISBN: 978-1-9822-1898-0 (e)

Balboa Press rev. date: 01/25/2019

Contents

for Grammie

Acknowledgments

There are an inconceivable number of people who have played a role in my journey. A mild fear of potentially leaving someone out prompted my thought of not including acknowledgments. Whether I name you or not, to each of you who has helped me along the way, I am forever grateful. Your support and encouragement over the years and willingness to keep the fire under my ass lit has led me to become the woman I am today.

First I would like to extend my deepest thanks, to Mom and Dad. Are you fucking shitting me?! Yes. It's true. My wicked awesome (possible bestseller?) memoir is complete. In addition to your monetary donations towards all of my beneficial medical torture, I also wanted to thank you for funding my temporary, childhood beanie baby addiction, extensive shoe collection and sophisticated palette. Lord knows these last thirty three years have not been easy and you have both handled every hurdle with choice phrases and grace. Your support and encouragement, since day one, means the world. I love you both deeply. When I make it big, you're brand new cars will be waiting in the driveway at 405 High Street. For now, can I just buy us all a round of Fireball to celebrate?

Derek, my not-so-little, younger brother, to you I say, Bumble Bee Tuna. I'm looking for an agent, maybe Ray Finkle and most definitely, a clean pair of shorts. For your consistent comic relief, sarcastic, witty (and sometimes unwelcome) remarks and never ending support; spank you helpy helperton. Your accomplishments, especially over the last year, are inspiring and I am so proud of you. It's been quite a ride, thank you for sitting shotgun with me. I love you.

I am indebted to, Kelly Valeri, the greatest teacher, friend, and confidant a woman could ever ask for. Kell, you will always be the only person I love to hear call me Krissy. Thank you for your countless kindnesses, consistent motivation, incredible generosity and for always strongly believing in me. You have been there for me from the moment I set foot in your classroom back in September of 1997. AJ, John, Emma and Grace, thank you for being like a second family to me. I love you all.

Deepest, glittering thanks to my fellow unicorn, Katherine Wilder. Simply put, you are a badass. Thank you for your understanding and willingness to help heal this little soul suit of mine. As a woman who has shown me how to deeply love every part of myself [titanium included], thank you for always listening, sharing, feeling and trusting, you inspire me every single day. Your brilliance is reflected throughout these pages and I am confident that we will toast appropriately (if we haven't already) with heart juice and tequila. I love you, the longest time, WildKat.

To Dr. Paley, Pam Wilson, Marilyn Richardson and all of the doctors and staff at the MCLLR at Kernan Hospital and the RIAO at Sinai Hospital, thank you, from the bottom of my heart, for EVERYTHING. I have abundant love and respect for each and every one of you.

Brenda O'Connell, Chris Coyne, Cyndi Amado, Flo MacDonald, Jayne Lipman and all of the staff at physical therapy, thank you for putting up with me over the years. You have seen me at my best and at my worst. It is because of your tough love and expertise that all three procedures yielded a successful outcome.

To my immediate and extended family, and my friends who have become my framily, I have abundant love and respect for each and every one of you. Maddie Cooke, thank you for your sisterhood and for talking me off of a ledge, on several occasions, when I thought I was crazy to publish this memoir. Thank you to the beautiful Chelsea Gates, especially for your incredible talent behind the camera. I had an idea for a book cover and you took it above and beyond. Amanda Robledo, thank you for your love, insight and feedback on this little memoir.

Without Dr. Feldman, Tiffany Brown, Miquele Smith, Dayle Federico, Mia and the entire Johnson Clan, and the unbelievable staff at The Paley Institute, I'm not sure my two feet would be on the ground nor my heart in the place to make this book possible. Your compassion, persistence, humor, support and love have been invaluable, especially over these last three years. Thank you so very much for believing in me.

Finally, my heart goes out to those I have had the honor of connecting with on this journey and all of you living in the face of adversity. Walking this path would not have been possible without each of you by my side. We are the lucky ones; the individuals who are strong enough, wise enough, to handle what we do. It takes a special soul with sheer strength and grace that cannot be understood by just anyone. Nothing is easy; easy doesn't last. At times, it is unbelievably difficult to the point where it's almost unfair. And we do it. Our different-abilities have given us tenacity that is envied. We love deeper, laugh harder and smile wider. What most view as a dead end street, is but a mere roadblock to us. We are warriors and we are in it together.

With the utmost love and gratitude, thank you, all.

Introduction

While all the other girls my age are concerned about what movie they're going to see at the mall with their friends on Friday, what's new on the rack at Limited Too, or how many times their Nano Baby pooped and peed while they were at school, my focus is elsewhere. I'm only twelve, and the best I can do right now is cultivate all the inner strength I possess. Strength, I didn't even know, hibernates deep down inside of me like a ferocious little black bear.

Why, you ask? I have fifteen pins and wires in each of my tibias, the bones in the lower leg. Both legs are broken, each supported on the outside by what looks to be a sort of futuristic birdcage. My new best friend is a wrench, my legs feel like they weigh ten pounds each, and no matter what position I'm in, finding comfort is nearly impossible.

It's the day after surgery. Here they are: my team of physical therapists. Merciless yet loving human beings, and two of them are standing at the foot of my bed. "You're getting out of bed and walking," one of them says to me. They have to be joking, I think.

They whip out the belt, put it around my waist, and practically drag me out of the hospital bed. It's clear they are serious.

My palms double their output in sweat, and the blood rushing through my veins creates an intensity in my body I'm sure the therapists can sense. Afraid of feeling pain, tears begin to fall onto my hospital gown. They haven't even screwed the footplates on the bottom of the external fixators yet. I'm scared. With wires going through each heel to suspend my foot in the middle of the Ilizarov device, I pull myself to standing with the aid of a walker beside my bed. It is impossible to describe the sounds escaping my mouth as a searing pain rips through my legs.

How is this fair? I can't even reason with them, although I do learn an excellent scare tactic: my volume level. All of those screaming contests Derek and I would have with our neighbors, starting practically inaudible and seeing who could shriek the loudest, usually in the form of the word "penis," have paid off. Hysterical, I scream until I have nothing left. My face is tear-stained, hot and red, my body trembling. An adolescent breakdown in the pediatric ward. That's what it takes to finally send the physical therapists the message that my little body can't take it. Not right now, anyway.

After all the excitement is over and I am resting comfortably, there is another knock on the door. In that moment, all I can think to do is hide under the sheets. But who am I kidding? I don't even have the energy to talk, let alone make myself invisible to the hospital staff. When the door opens, two nurses pop their heads in. Both nurses, who go by the name Pam, are here to help teach me the art of making new bone grow.

Gentle and kind, the Pams begin a bedside artsy-crafty project turned educational tutorial with me. Using nail polish, together we paint each face of the four-sided screws a different color: red, blue, purple, and green. This will make it easier to keep track of my "turns." My lengthening schedule is going to be one quarter turn, four times a day, at breakfast, lunch, dinner, and bedtime. One millimeter a day. Got it.

This is something I have been talking about since I was in third grade. Now, here I am. My only choice is to face my fears, find the strength, and take it one day at a time.

There is no turning back. For the next nine months, my legs are bone, flesh, and metal.

1

Unfamiliar with the word *achondroplasia*, the formal term for the most common form of short stature or dwarfism, my parents got a little surprise with me. My mom didn't find out that she was carrying a little, little girl until she was eight months pregnant. I was their one in forty thousand, a result of an autosomal dominant gene abnormality. Commonly characterized by a torso of normal size and disproportionately short arms and legs, achondroplasia is just one of more than two hundred types of dwarfism. Eighty-five percent of achondroplastic children are born to average-sized parents.

After gracing everyone with my presence in October of 1985, the world my mom and dad had known was turned upside down. They were the lucky ones. Not only were they new parents, their little girl was born a dwarf. Though it sounds more like a declaration of guilt, that is not the intention. I'm stating a fact. To use the term "birth defect" is too harsh. I was born different, yes, but my stature does not take away from who I am. It does not make me defective. In fact, it makes me the complete opposite, a beautiful individual. From day one, I made it clear that even though I was going to be little, I would do very big things. The urgency of my impending arrival forced my poor mother to be carried down the stairs, from the bedroom to the ambulance, in a kitchen chair by a couple of paramedics. No one else in my family had ever been diagnosed with short stature that we were aware of, so I was determined to make my first moments memorable.

Prior to my physical debut, Mom was desperate for more information and gathered all that she could. Being that the world wide web did not exist back in 1985, her research consisted of pamphlets, photocopied pages from library books, and magazine and newspaper articles. My parents' medical vocabulary expanded tenfold after I was born. Obstructive apnea, kyphosis, and varus deformity—what did it all mean for the future of their daughter?

While still in the hospital, our new little family of three got a visitor. A man named Jack came into Mom's hospital room. He lived a few towns over from us and was dad to a little girl, Becky, with achondroplasia. Jack, kind, reassuring, and confident, told Mom that all she and Dad needed to do was go home and love their little, little girl. And while there was some grief and a whole lot of uncertainty, that is exactly what they did. Dwarfism was not going to be the end of the road but the beginning of a beautiful journey. An obstacle to rise above.

Born with a New England Patriots jersey on my back, I required a tight ship and was sure to keep everyone on their toes at all times. Dad didn't miss a beat and documented a few very significant highlights of my infancy in my baby book:

> Kristen, or better known as "Puggy," refuses to let Dad have a decent night's sleep. She's like a human alarm clock. Every night promptly at two thirty and four thirty, Puggy makes her presence felt. She also likes to bob her head around to make sure that she doesn't miss anything going on. She likes to do liquid bombs in her diaper, which are real nice to clean up.

Like I said: tight ship. What he failed to mention was my sincere dedication to watching his beloved New England Patriots football games on Sunday afternoons and helping him read the *Boston Globe*.

Mom was also sure to document worthwhile memories.

> Kristen eats like a truck driver and cries when she's starving. She loves to be held, constantly. She loves her "nukie." She loves to be a busybody—nosy, very nosy. One of her favorite things to do is smile and eyeball Mummy while popping Kleenex in her mouth.

Who gives a "nuke" to their six-week-old? My parents, apparently. I'm hoping that Mom was actually referring to a pacifier. When the little truck driver was starving and there was no bottle in sight, she turned to Kleenex. Cue the eye roll.

Determined to find the right specialist, the DeAndrades, party of three, jumped around between a couple different doctors during my early infancy. Mom always knew there was someone out there who could give us answers and provide me with exceptional care. At the age of six months, my parents found an orthopedic specialist in Boston. Although that doctor provided some valuable insight, he was not an expert on short stature.

After some more intensive searching, the doctor my mother knew existed was discovered in Towson, Maryland. Dr. Steven Kopits founded St. Joseph's International Center for Skeletal Dysplasia. This was our guy. A consultation was immediately scheduled by Mom and Dad, and we packed up and took the train, eight hours, to Baltimore. More than five hours in the waiting room is a lot for anyone, but it is very long indeed for an infant. We waited first to be x-rayed. They took pictures my entire little body so Dr. Kopits could examine my arms, legs, back, and skull—all the major bones affected by achondroplasia. Escorted back into the waiting room, we sat some more. After a total of six hours in the clinic, we were finally called back into the exam room. At eight months, it was the first appointment with a specialist where my parents felt hopeful for answers to questions they had long anticipated.

Answers were exactly what they got. A man of expertise and compassion. Dr. Kopits discussed in detail my condition and the fact that I was affected to a mild or moderate degree. I had kyphosis, curvature of the thoracic spine, which was of some concern and would be monitored over the next couple of years. Dr. Kopits also told my parents about the possible development of bowleg deformities and recurring inner ear infections, both common among achondroplastic dwarfs. The six-foot-two Hungarian doctor not only answered their questions but promised my parents that I would thrive and lead a normal life. For that, my parents were eternally grateful. They took me back home to Massachusetts where I could cause trouble alongside my furry feline brother Spike.

As an infant, I was healthy and happy. My milestones were a little delayed, but not by much. At nine months of age, I finally learned to sit on my own. My biggest obstacle was my head being so large, a common characteristic of achondroplasia. In order to balance sitting, I had to gain further head and neck control. When I did eventually learn to walk at the age of fifteen months, I was all over the place.

My second checkup with Dr. Kopits came a little sooner than expected, after I caused my parents quite a scare. Since both Mom and Dad worked during the day, I had to be dropped off at the babysitter's house. Perhaps life seemed a little boring at the time, and I saw it as an opportunity to spice things up. While jumping on the couch under the sitter's "watchful" eye, I bounced off, hit the floor, and went comatose.

Obviously, she had never heard the story about the five little monkeys jumping on the bed. Thanks to one wee monkey, we were back on the train to Baltimore.

After close examination by Dr. Kopits at my checkup, it was evident that my neck was bothering me as a result of my fall. Mom explained that I was cranky and repeatedly trying to reach behind my head to hold my neck. Fracture and dislocation were ruled out.

Dr. Kopits decided that I had sprained my cervical vertebrae. Here's where things became rather unfortunate for the little monkey who enjoyed jumping on couches: as a precaution for my motor development and spine health, Dr. Kopits told my parents that now was a good time for me to be braced for kyphosis. This would also help with limb control and reduce the likelihood of future falls. Reluctantly, my parents agreed to the bracing to which I, at the age of almost three, had no say whatsoever. You can imagine how well this went over with a willful toddler. Trying to be fit with a hard, plastic, very restricting back brace was certainly not on my agenda. I don't remember much of that small portable prison aside from the fact that it got in my way whenever I had to wear it.

Bubbles. A little girl's favorite pastime. I could sit on the back porch, forever in awe and just blow bubbles. But when you're a tiny human in an overbearing back brace trying to pop bubbles on your own, unfortunate things can happen. With little legs that are already difficult to maneuver, mobility is hindered. One autumn day, while marveling over the magic of my bubbles, I wandered a little too close to the top porch step and took a digger, hitting my head on the cement at the bottom. This time, the result was a mild concussion.

As you can see, beginning early on in my lifetime, I kept things exciting. And this time, I wasn't even exhibiting my little monkey-jumping tendencies.

For two years, that brace and I formed a love-hate relationship. The little plastic prison impeded my swagger, so I learned to throw my legs out to the side when there were places to go and things to see, which was all the time. If there was an upside at all, it was that all of my tickle spots were inaccessible while wearing the baby corset of doom. With every removal and replacement period of that stupid thing, I showed more intolerance toward it.

As I grew older and wiser, my sense of independence clashed with the restrictions of the brace. After one year, too long, Dr. Kopits said it was no longer necessary.

2

As if the trauma of the brace wasn't enough, I soon faced the fact that I was no longer the only babe of the household. Derek Joseph, my little brother, made his appearance in August of 1988. Sharing the spotlight with another adorable human was not ideal.

Derek didn't know it yet, but I had every intention, from the beginning, of convincing him that my way of doing things was the best and only way.

After a few failed attempts, I managed to master the art of potty training, to the best of my ability. The duty of wiping my tushy proved to be a tad more challenging than anticipated. Little arms make reaching some places really difficult, okay? But in my own defense, I had the right idea. Besides, what was more exciting for a little girl than digging through her drawer full of big-girl undies and getting to choose whether it was a hearts or stripes kind of a day. I'll be honest, I was the rebel who wore her Friday undies on a Tuesday.

Making myself fashionably presentable was something else I also found to be mildly arduous due to my simple mobility limitations. Simple acts like getting dressed took a little bit more effort on my part since pants, tights, and shirtsleeves were always too long. It's a darn good thing that Mom was handy with a sewing machine. Working her magic, I was able to rock a pair of stirrup pants just like all the other little girls my age. God forbid I miss out on that fashion trend. You know what was the most difficult clothing hurdle? Snow pants. The whole getup, really. As if walking in the snow wasn't hard enough. Let's wrap Kristen in ten thousand layers, put puffy pants and a jacket on top of it all, and then watch her try to walk. Fun!

A sassy, wild little spirit from the start, I insisted on doing as much as possible on my own. Stools made tasks like brushing my teeth or reaching something out of a cupboard accessible. If someone told me something wasn't a good idea or said, "Kristen, you can't," it was a fantastic idea in my book—and Kristen can. Whenever I needed help, Mom and Dad were always there.

Checkups with Dr. Kopits were once a year to ensure that all was going well.

Toys overflow out of the toy box and spill onto the floor. It seems like every time I come for an appointment they have new and exciting things to play with. It makes waiting for hours not so bad. The tables have little chairs that I can sit in and have my feet touch the ground. It is the best feeling in the world because it never happens.

Kneeling on one of the big chairs in front of the giant fish tank, I get lost watching the fish swim around. They are all different and get along so well. Even the little hermit crab that hangs out in the sand. Every year, new aquatic friends appear in the tank. It's a fun mental game I play to see if I can pick out the new guys.

You know what's strange? Seeing other kids who look just like me. It is not something I am used to. And yet, even though I question if I really look like that—my hands, the way they walk, or how their legs stick straight out off of a normal chair—I find comfort in knowing that I am not alone. Every visit with Dr. Kopits begins with a set of standing and sitting x-rays. They take me back into this large room with gigantic machines and a strange humming noise. The technician puts a very heavy jacket on me for some of the "pictures" and tells me to be very still and hold my breath. Are they kidding? This sheath of death weighs more than I do. Not only can I not move, I can hardly breathe. A job well done laying lifeless on the table and standing still warrants some stickers and a lollipop of my choice.

When I am called into Dr. Kopits's office to see him, the nurse leads us into the big room with a black grid on one wall and the exam table covered in tissue paper on the other. Using various stools, I climb my way up onto the table and move around as much as possible to create as much unnecessary noise as I can.

Dr. Kopits comes in and immediately gives me a big bear hug, kisses me on the forehead, and bathes me in compliments. Spotlight on Kristen? Yes, please. He has me stand on a scale and records my weight and then, standing in front of the grid on the wall, he measures how much I have grown. Examining the numbers, he holds his chin in one hand, nods his head, and comments on how wonderful my quarter of an inch of new growth is.

I hop back up on the examining table, and Dr. Kopits uses a yellow tape measure, like the one in Dad's toolbox, to assess the circumference of my head and then takes measurements and range of motion in my legs. "Look at these beautiful little legs," he says in his gentle, Hungarian accent. "Now let me see you walk. Lovely walking!" There is something about him that makes him different from other doctors. Coming to see him does not instill a sense of fear in me. I love making this trip to Baltimore every year. What really wins me over is his humor and kindness. He takes the time to answer every question and truly gets to know me as a girl not just as a patient. How am I doing at home? Am I getting around okay? Any pain? We cover all the bases. The end of every appointment is my favorite part. Pulling a red or black flare pen out of the pocket of his white coat, Dr. Kopits meticulously draws little kitties on the tops of my feet. It tickles, and I try my best to stay still so he doesn't mess up. It's our thing. And in my eyes, those little kitties are ten times better than any sticker.

During one of my visits with Dr. Kopits, Mom, Dad and I met another family with a little girl who also had achondroplasia. While eating at a Howard Johnson's in Towson, Maryland, Mom noticed a little bebop, like me, with her parents at an adjacent table. She too was bouncing up and down in her high chair at the table. Mom couldn't help herself. Walking over to their table, conversation immediately led to friendship. There were striking similarities between little ol' me and Monica: not just our good looks, but our personalities. Monica and her family were also in Maryland to see Dr. Kopits, and we were all staying at the same hotel.

A door opened for my family and me that day; we had found a support system, a family who understood everything. Gerri and Frank invited Mom, Dad, and me up to their hotel room to talk and visit, allowing Monica and me to play together. Gerri had compiled as much information as she could on achondroplasia, just like Mom had done. Newspaper clippings, magazine articles, and informational packets—there wasn't much due to the scarcity of information and lack of the internet, but the moms did a great job of keeping up to speed with everything they could.

Monica and her family lived in New York. We vowed to keep in touch by phone calls and Christmas cards. If Monica and I were lucky, our annual checkups with Dr. Kopits would coincide with one another.

3

As I continued to grow, ever so slowly, my little legs didn't move as fast as the average child's, but they got me where I needed to go. Gymnastics, I learned early on, was something I was effortlessly good at and adored. Miss Cathy helped me hang from the uneven bars and balance on the balance beam. On special days, we took turns bouncing with her on the big trampoline, which ended with a kiddie cannonball into a black hole of foam shapes. The cartwheels and somersaults did not just happen in my leotard at the local gym. I found it necessary to bust them out at home or in the middle of the grocery store. Mom tells me that it did not take long before I began to instill some fear in Dad and her, but there wasn't much that scared me. What I lacked in inches, I made up for in my energy levels and sass, running circles around anyone who moved slower than me.

Like a rogue little duckling who cared less about following the crowd, I took my own path, at my own pace. My "run" was quite comical—or so I've been told. There were a couple variations that rotated. The windmill arm involved throwing one arm in circles at my side as I ran with a little pep in my step. In my mind, I clearly must have thought it would propel me faster forward. And then there were times when putting my arms outstretched behind me and legs thrown out to the side seemed aerodynamically successful. In actuality, I looked more like a little duck as I speedily ran about.

Like any big sister would, I showed Derek how much fun causing trouble could be. When we went to a department store with Mom, hiding in the clothing racks was much more fun than looking at prospective outfits. Although, there was one time when Derek and I may have taken it a little too far in a Caldor. Amidst a game of hide-and-go-seek, Mom called for us, saying that it was time to go. By the third or fourth time, she beckoned for us and hearing the level of annoyance in her voice rising, I made my presence known. Derek, however, did not. Even I, being much lower to the ground, couldn't find him. With frustration quickly turning to fear, Mom frantically went to the customer service desk. It wasn't until a store clerk made an announcement over the loudspeaker about a missing little boy with dark hair that Derek surfaced thanks to another store patron. After that, we put our department store hide-and-go-seek games on hold for a while. You know those little monkey backpacks for children where the tail of the monkey is actually a leash? Did those exist in the early nineties? Those would have been a blessing to Mom and Dad, for sure.

While it was obvious that I was born to be a little bitty free spirit, my mermaid fins were a little more inconspicuous. Unless you put me in water, of course. A pool, the ocean, rain, the bathtub, or a puddle—I never met a water source I didn't like. Well, actually, the machine that they used at the doctor's office that squirted water in my ears to clean them out—I hated that. I don't think any mermaid would care for such a thing. Despite most pairs of swimmies taking up my entire arm, it didn't matter, once they were on, I was in the water with no intention of coming out. Ariel was my inspiration. After *The Little Mermaid* came out in theaters, I knew I was a mermaid in my past life.

Caution did have to be taken with my love for an active lifestyle. It did not take much before I became tired. Too much walking caused me to complain of cramping in my lower legs, forcing me to stop and rest or be carried. Frequent pain in my joints, especially my elbows, occurred more often than I would have liked. On the days that my tenacity levels were unusually high, frustration would often follow with the accompanying discomfort preventing me from keeping up with other kids. In an effort to cast a positive light on my disappointment, we labeled the achiness in my joints "growing pains." If that isn't ironic, I don't know what is.

4

As if the discomfort I dealt with in my arms and legs wasn't enough, I suffered from several ear infections. Let me put emphasis on the word *several*. In fact, let's just use the phrase "too many." The anatomy of an achondroplast's ear canal does not allow fluid to drain; instead, it settles in the middle ear and causes a raging infection.

If anyone caught the brunt of my auditory battle, it was Dad. Like the one of many times he came home from work, and I told him my ear really hurt. Mom, who was working the four-to-midnight shift with the telephone company, instructed him that it was probably a good idea for me to be taken to the after-hours medical center. Poor guy had just gotten home from work, so that was the last thing he wanted to do. In somewhat of a huff and amidst a cloud of expletives, Dad put Derek and me in his gray Dodge pickup truck. Throwing it in reverse and putting his lead right foot to the gas, we were all quickly reminded that Mom carpooled to work with her friend Bill. Everything came to a screeching halt before we had the opportunity to reach the end of the driveway. Far too young to be thinking about my driver's license, that evening I learned the value of a rearview mirror. In the heat of the moment, Dad had neglected to glance into his and slammed right into Billy's car. Seatbelts, everyone!

Derek and I froze, eyes fixated on the windshield. We didn't need to look over at Dad's face to know that the whole situation had just gone from a two to a ten on the no-good-really-bad scale. The choice curse words, including but not limited to, "Are you fucking shitting me?" deafened my good ear and were concrete evidence that Daddy was not happy.

After a quick damage assessment, Dad got back into the truck and drove silently to South Shore Medical Center. After close examination by Dr. Cox, there was no evidence of an infection, which, under normal circumstances, would be a good thing. That night, however, it was not the case. My lack of infection just made matters worse. The doctor described it more along the lines of an irritation and suggested some drops to prevent a full-blown ear infection. When we got home, I escorted myself to bed and listened to Dad break the news of Billy's car to Mom over the phone. It was not a good night for any of us.

On another "let's take Kristen to South Shore Medical Center" occasion, Derek and I were fighting over God knows what while waiting in the truck for Dad. Things got a little physical. One of us, and I'm 87 percent sure that it wasn't me, kicked the stick shift into reverse. Suddenly, the truck began to roll backward down the driveway, stopping us cold in our tracks. We didn't know what the hell to do. The only car I had ever driven was the neighbor's Power Wheels Barbie Beach Cruiser. It was automatic and battery-operated, and even with that, reverse wasn't my forte. Panic-stricken and rolling closer to our very busy street, Derek and I started screaming for Dad. Like a bat outta hell, Dad flew from the house and managed to stop the truck before his two bickering children rolled out into the middle of High Street.

I don't think I could count on two hands—I'd need more—how many times I had ear infections as a kid. Thankfully, amoxicillin was the medication I was prescribed by the doctor and also one I would graciously accept via one of those little plastic cups. Not only was it my favorite color—pink—but it tasted like bubble gum. That glory was short-lived after my tenth raging infection. The pink stuff was no longer functioning as an antibiotic but simply as liquid candy. The doctors had no choice but to switch my medicine to something stronger—and more gag-worthy. My parents found themselves stuck with a child who was no longer a fan of taking medicine.

My ear feels like there are a thousand little gremlins taking revenge on my eardrum, and it is getting really old. This new white medicine the doctors gave me is disgusting. I would rather lick a New York City sidewalk than drink this crap. Mom and Dad try too hard to convince me that mixing it with applesauce will make it easier to take. Lies! Pudding isn't even an option. Why would I sacrifice the chocolatey decadence for some stupid medicine? Stuffing crackers in my mouth doesn't work either. I feel like Iago from Aladdin, compelled to laugh simply for the pleasure of spitting Ritz cracker crumbs all over the floor. It's much easier to create a scene and throw a fit. I don't know what a drama queen is, but apparently, I am one.

Once I feel as though my feelings of hostility toward the revolting white potion have been validated, I give in and chase it down with the largest cup of apple juice. And that isn't the worst part. Drops. After Mom puts two in one ear, she has to squish it around and put a piece of cotton in. Repeat on the other side. And I have to do this every day? Why can't I have normal ear canals like everyone else? No more fear of swimming underwater, no more disgusting medicine, and no more ear drops. Please? Although, I will say, walking around with cotton in your ears makes for a great excuse to not being able to hear when you're asked to pick up your toys.

At the advice of my pediatrician, Mom and I went into Boston Children's Hospital to see an ENT specialist, Dr. McGill, to discuss having tubes inserted into both ears. At the age of five, this would be my first surgery. Sitting in the appointment at the doctor's office, Dr. McGill handed me what looked like a small plastic brick with the so-called tubes displayed in it. They looked like the little backs to Mom's earrings. Why and how were these silly objects, when put in my ears, supposed to stop my ear infections? I was skeptical and far from thrilled about the whole situation. We, and by we, I mean Mom, agreed that this was the right thing to do and scheduled surgery for a few weeks later.

Sitting in the pre-op holding area in my fancy gown, two nurses walked up and began sweet-talking me. Something was up. I knew I was cute, but they were hiding something. They were buttering me up to prevent me from melting down. While one of them began to shower me in compliments, I noted the other pulling up a silver table to the bedside and laying out a bunch of needles and other paraphernalia on it. Preparation for an IV. I wasn't an imbecile. No amount of sweet-talking was going to convince me to lay still and play the role of kiddie pincushion. No way, Jose. My legs may be short, but my sass and attitude were a tall drink to sip on. Trying with fear of failed attempts just was not an option. Sassy was boss, and she demanded a new plan. The anesthesiologist agreed, probably dreading a potential disaster, and allowed me to go to sleep using a mask. They would stick me once I was asleep.

Mom signed her daughter's life away and a team of people stood at my bed ready to whisk me out of pre-op. You know those foolish hairnet things the people behind the meat counter wear at the supermarket? They look like one of Mom's shower caps, in a way. Well, they slapped one of those on my head, told me to say goodbye to Mom, and then wheeled me back into the operating room. For a minute, I thought I had been cast in the sequel to *E.T.* There is no denying that I would make a great Gertie. Bright lights and a sickening yet clean smell filled the room. Everyone was dressed like the strange men who locked E.T. in the cooler, masked and gowned. And for some reason, I trusted this group of strangers to take care of me.

Lying flat on my back, staring up into the blinding light, nurses were sticking things to my chest and covering me in warm blankets. Another masked face held a mask over my nose and mouth. Whatever was flowing through the mask, the smell made me want to gag, but I was too sleepy to care. The people around me began to get fuzzy, and sounds were echoing.

Next thing I knew, I was awake. The procedure was over, and I felt like poop. The anesthesia gave me horrible nausea, and my ears, stuffed with bloody cotton, were ringing. My throat felt like sandpaper, and I hated everyone who came within a one-foot radius of my bed.

Stop touching me—and don't talk to me.

Not even an orange popsicle could make me feel better, and usually anything with more than twelve grams of sugar in it was a guaranteed source of bribery.

After resting for an hour or so, agreeing to a popsicle, and screaming when they finally took out my IV, I got over the ringing and discomfort in my newly excavated, tubed ears and was sent home. *Success* would not be the word to describe the surgery. The tubes helped the infections subside in a timelier manner, but they did not cure anything. It wasn't long before the tubes fell out and warranted another surgery to place a second set. Still, the results were subpar. The pesky, painful infections became something I learned to live with. Over the years, recurring, raging infections caused scarring on my eardrum. In one case, I had an ear infection that was so bad in my right ear, the eardrum ruptured. I found myself with permanent 80 percent hearing loss on my right side.

Tiny, sassy, and nearly deaf in one ear.

But that still didn't stop me.

5

My childhood was just like that of any other kid growing up. Things rarely bothered me, aside from the occasional—okay, frequent—tiffs I found myself in with Derek. Listen, I was here first, and in my book, that meant I made the rules in our siblinghood.

Still, inclusivity was important to me, especially when it came to dance parties. Don't get me wrong, I had no problem cutting some rug solo with The New Kids on the Block cassette blasting in the background, but it was always better to have a partner. With my black leotard on, I let Derek wear my "more masculine" orange and yellow striped one. Together, with our mean moves, we put any sibling duo to shame in the exquisite maneuver category. Our beanbags made for excellent dance props.

Dad was the king of nicknames. Under the roof at 405 High Street, it was rare that our first names were ever used—unless Mom and Dad were angry. First names were a telltale sign that we were in serious trouble. *Banaka*, as unattractive as it sounds, is Portuguese for "little doll." Yes, it is also the name of a minty fresh spray that people suffering from bad breath use. I can assure you that while I fully supported fresh breath, it was more my adorable, I-can't-get-over-how-sweet-that-little-girl-is characteristics that warranted the name. The origin of Derek's nickname is a little unclear. Google has told me that Buckmeister, aside from being a surname, has no real lineage behind it. Maybe that's why it evolved into Bucky Beaver and eventually, simply Bucky. Yes, Bucky and Banaka, wreakers of havoc. It has a nice little ring to it, don't you think?

When we weren't doing our rightful duty of arguing, as siblings do, Buck and I enjoyed hunting for salamanders under the rocks in Mom's garden, throwing the baseball and football with Dad in the front yard, keeping the playroom as messy and disorganized as humanly possible, using the swing set as a pirate ship, playing manhunt and loud games of "Penis" with the neighborhood kids, and rescuing the little mice that Dad trapped in old coffee cans in the garage.

At such a young age, I never saw myself as living with a disability. I knew that my body was "different" from other kids,' but to me, it wasn't a cause for concern. The simple fact that my limbs were shorter did not limit the integrity of me being Kristen. From what I can remember, through my eyes, there were no boundaries. I never walked down the street or through the halls at school thinking of myself as the little girl with achondroplasia. I was just me. There were more important things that I had to worry about, like convincing my parents that smothering my Honey Nut Cheerios with honey was indeed a complete breakfast.

Everywhere I went, I attracted public curiosity—mostly stares—but I was usually oblivious to the negative connotation. Wasn't it obvious? The general public was jealous of my angelic face and bouncy personality. Paying attention to, let alone acknowledging, the public stares, though it was something my parents, especially Mom, detested, was at the bottom of my to-do list.

Making friends in school came very easy to me. I was still pretty close in height with other kids. What I lacked vertically, I made up for with my vocal volume, and ability to outplay anyone in hide-and-go-seek. Most kindergarteners aren't concerned about each other's cosmetic abnormalities. Most of our time was spent fighting over who was going to change their name to Ariel first, after *The Little Mermaid*, or which one of us was going to be the first to get their ears pierced. It wasn't until elementary school that other children my age began creating aesthetic standards for their friendships.

Every morning while waiting for the school bus, I assumed position on my little rock, my home base. Along with the neighborhood kids, I played tag while waiting for the school bus. Unable to run as fast as everyone else, I managed to cut corners and made great use of small spaces to elude my friends with longer legs. My initial thought when I walked into my first grade classroom was not, *Everyone is going to make fun of me because I am different."* Carrying a backpack, allowing it to hang all the way down to my rear end with a packed snack and lunch money tucked away inside, turning in schoolwork, and racing around at recess like all the other kids gave me a new sense of independence. However, for the first time in my life, I was made aware of the teasing my parents feared. It hit hard, but I refused to let it have a lasting effect on me. No words from a seven-year-old were going to take me down.

I'm sitting at my desk and the two boys are looking at me and laughing. Not just looking, actually. They are turned completely around in their seats, pointing and laughing so hard that they are holding their bellies like it hurts. Why they are snickering doesn't quite register. Looking around and behind me to see if I am in fact the person they are making fun of, I can't be sure. And then I hear the word that would soon become something I hated and caused my stomach to lurch.

"Midget."

If there is one thing I know, it is the negative connotation and humiliation I feel in hearing the word. Digging around in my seven-year-old mind, I try to think of a comeback. Pee-brain and fart-sniffer won't do justice. It being my first day in the first grade, I don't want to be known as a tattletale, but I am so upset that my face feels warm and my body tense. Without saying a word, I scoot to the edge of my chair until my feet touch the floor. Part of me feels guilty for what I am about to do. Then I hear them laughing again, the feelings of doing wrong are now a distant memory as I walk up to the teacher's desk.

Mrs. Black pulls the three of us out into the hallway. Kneeling down to be eye to eye with us, she looks directly at the boys. "There will be no tolerance for this behavior."

The boys look confused. Stupid boys, isn't it obvious?

She explains to them that it is hurtful to make fun of someone because they are different. "And there is to be no name-calling. Period."

I find myself puffing out my chest as the conversation continues. Suddenly I feel invincible.

The boys apologize to me; whether or not they mean it, I will never know.

What I learned that day went far beyond my spelling list or simple addition. There were people, kids and adults, aside from my immediate family, on my side. A small army in defense of different being beautiful and the general in command was a girl with little legs and a big heart.

6

Now seems like a convenient time to broach my favorite subject: What do you call a little person? How about simply utilizing their first name? Surely, I speak for a lot of people in the dwarfism community when I say that "midget" is a definite no-no. Often referred to as the "M-word," just saying it used to make me cringe. Personally, I would like it if everyone omitted the term from their vocabulary completely. Knowing well that will never happen, I do my best to not attach to the word. Allowing it to spark reaction gives power to the word and its speaker.

We are not oompa-loompas, elves, or mini-mes. Dwarf is the preferred medical term. As for everyday lingo, I prefer little person. Better yet, like I said before, call me Kristen. Introduce yourself, know our names. We are people, not fantasy creatures. Though, along with my mermaid lineage, I'm pretty sure there's some fairy and unicorn mixed in. Regardless of my enchanted side, it isn't respectable that any one person should have to put up with being made to feel ridiculous by those in this society who would call themselves "normal." No one is normal: we are all different. I would never, in my life, behave in a way to belittle individuals who have a physical handicap, those mentally challenged, or people otherwise different. We are people with the same emotional needs and desires as everyone else.

Persons with short stature are also not armrests. I cannot stress how annoying it is to have someone walk up to you and rest their arm upon your head while carrying on a conversation. One's arm is meant to be rested on an inanimate object, like the arm of a chair, perhaps. Play it safe and just keep your hands in your pockets if you don't think you can withhold from the degrading gesture. Even though my cuteness level as a child was comparable to that of a puppy, patting me on the head … no thank you. It too was frowned upon. This went along with having the urge to pick me up. It blows my mind that, as a grown woman, the head patting and need to try to get my feet off the ground is still something people do. Strangers, at that. Unless I ask for a piggyback, back off.

Oh, the stares. With young children, I understand, they don't know any better. They are extremely curious upon seeing something or someone different, and they have very little filter when it comes to asking questions. Usually it is innocent, honest inquisition. Parents should discourage their kids from laughing or jeering. Ignoring their curiosity is not going to better the situation either. When in doubt, just be honest. Kids are sponges; tell them that a different-ability is not a disease, and they will listen. For some teenagers and adults, well, I have a few words: insensitive, ignorant, rude, disrespectful, and plain old mean. They think it is acceptable to laugh, stare, point, make comments, and generally ensure that everyone around them has noticed. I consider myself a very strong and rational person, but there are times when I either want to immediately lock myself in a closet and cry or flat out clothesline a complete stranger.

When I was in college, I was browsing in a Target—minding my own business—and a middle school-aged girl came up behind me, so close I could feel her breathing down my back, and began mocking every move I was making. When I turned around, she ran away laughing at her apparent hilarious mockery. I immediately assumed she didn't dare do it again since I had seen her, but when I heard snickering moments later, I turned back around to find her acting as my shadow. She was crouched behind me with her arms tucked in her shirtsleeves.

In the heat of the moment I got angry. Quickly walking after her, I yelled, "Is something funny?"

Her response was, "Yeah. You!"

My heart was crushed. She might as well have dropped an anvil on my chest. Knowing that stooping to her level was not the answer, I allowed it to be what it was. She found the attention I had given her amusing too, but I had to do something. Creating the small scene was enough to get another store patron to intervene. The older gentleman told the birdbrained teenager and her posse to get lost. A few other bystanders began sympathizing and apologized for her. You can try to act macho during an incident like that, but let's get real: it cuts deep, and it sucks. That shit fucking hurts. While in the checkout line, I hung my head to hide the tears welling in my eyes. My mind wanted to know why. What kind of person does that? What was she so insecure about that she had to take it out on me? The dam eventually broke, and tears just kept coming the entire drive home. Society's cruelty toward those with noticeable disparities is real. Nevertheless, for those of us affected, despite public ignorance, we learn to let it go. Yes, I know—easier said than done.

When people see someone physically different, it can lead them to believe that intellect is also affected—not at all true. We are immediately aware of anyone's attempt at belittlement and mockery. It isn't a secret. Even when you think that you're being discreet, you're not. We know. And individuals with dwarfism or any different-ability for that matter, lead happy, healthy, successful lives. I consider myself living proof.

Excuse me while I toot my own horn for a hot moment. By the end of first grade, I was reading bigger chapter books like *Stuart Little* and *The Trumpet of The Swan*, while some kids my age were still learning to read. Constantly on top of my work and earning As and Bs, in the fifth grade, I was accepted into the Extended Learning Program (ELP). Boasting about my scholastic intelligence is not my point here. I worked my butt off in school to be little miss smarty pants. The bottom line is that someone's outward physical appearance doesn't determine what kind of person they are on the inside or their intellectual abilities. It's so cliché, but it's not what is on the outside that matters. Persons living with short stature work today as actors, lawyers, and orthopedic surgeons. Despite the fact that society may still associate tallness with physical prowess or intelligence, the possibilities are endless when you have the drive and mind-set to achieve what you desire.

7

Little legs allowed me to maintain a great perspective throughout my childhood because I was always looking up: figuratively and quite literally. I was constantly craning my neck so that my eyes met whoever I was talking to. Short stature was never something I despised when I was a little girl; it was a part of me. Being little Kristen, I accepted all of myself and did my best to educate others about my condition. It was simple: I was a normal girl who enjoyed tormenting her little brother, Barbie dolls, cheerleading, Disney princesses, and blowing bubbles in my chocolate milk. I just happened to be tiny for my age. At nine years old, I was no taller than a kindergartener. An exceedingly positive attitude served as my defense mechanism. Theoretically, the way I saw it: if everyone knows me, then they won't make fun of me.

In third grade, our class read a story about a little girl named Jaime who had achondroplasia, just like me, called *Thinking Big*. My teachers at the time, Ms. Whiteley and Mrs. Labadie, saw this as the perfect opportunity for me to speak up and share my story. Excited for the freedom to show my classmates who I really was. Liz, my best friend, agreed to costar in a homemade educational production. Together, we wrote out our scripts and practiced endlessly in Liz's living room after school in the week leading up to our debut. In our thick Boston accents, we detailed the trials and tribulations of one little girl with short stature and her best friend of average height. We demonstrated how I was unable to reach higher objects—light switches, countertops, the freezer, and the bathroom sink to name a few.

Getting in and out of cars, especially sport utility vehicles, was no easy feat either. We recalled a particular time when Liz's mom drove me home from school. Mrs. Sadler had a big red Isuzu Trooper, a car very high off the ground for any little legs. In order for me to get in, I had to climb my way up the side of the door. Before successfully seating myself inside the vehicle, on this respective day, Liz's mom began to pull out of the parking lot with me desperately clinging onto the still-open door. Panicked yet stricken with a severe case of the giggles, I started screaming, "Wait!" in an attempt to signal that I hadn't yet found my seat let alone buckled my seat belt. Mrs. Sadler stopped the car, and I safely hoisted my way in. Though a little frightening in the moment, we couldn't help but laugh hysterically at the situation.

With the camera continuing to roll, we sat cross-legged and then kneeled next to each other to show that the disproportion was only in my arms and legs and not in my torso. When Liz and I sat on the floor next to each other we appeared to be the same height. However, when kneeling or standing next to each other I was visibly much shorter. In order to remain seated comfortably during class, I was given a much smaller chair, my own table, and some boxes to rest my feet on. Sitting in one of the normal classroom chairs made it clear why I needed the special accommodations. My legs stuck straight out from the end of the chair, making sitting at my desk uncomfortable. When I moved to the smaller chair, taken from the kindergarten classroom, my knees bent, and my feet rested comfortably on the boxes.

Saving the best for last, the spotlight moved onto why being little was awesome. Not that I needed any reasons at all. With a wide smile, I showed off my acrobatic talents, things I could do that most people could not: a full split without hesitation, "the worm," which came to me as naturally as it would to one of The New Kids on the Block, and, how could I forget, the move that I still have to verbally explain more than once, hence why it was dubbed "the human rocking chair." No one I knew could master the art of sitting down and then standing up without bending their knees, like me. Trust me when I say, you'd have to see it to believe it. (Disclaimer: The last maneuver was fun while it lasted and I don't advise trying it at home.)

Not only did our movie allow me to talk about the ups and downs of living with dwarfism and show my peers that despite my physical differences, I was just like them, it also opened a new window of discussion and opportunity. It was the first time I started talking openly about "the operation." Briefly brushing over the topic of limb lengthening and giving some very skewed facts from the eyes of a third grader, I had very little knowledge of what I was actually talking about. Somehow, in the eyes of a nine-year-old girl, lengthening one arm and one leg at a time sounds like a great idea. Still, in the back of my mind and with the general conceptual idea, I did know that this was something I wanted to delve deeper into and possibly pursue. The more I learned about the extravagant surgeries, the more confident I became in knowing it was the right decision for me.

Dressed to the nines in my stirrup pants and high-tops, my little snaggletoothed-smile self stood in the art room in front of the camera alongside Liz while the rest of our class was at recess. With our teachers guiding us, we filmed our very own production of *Thinking Big*, tying it all together by ending with, "It doesn't matter if you're tall or small, you can still be friends."

Mic drop.

8

Determined to put meaning to the phrase, "big things come in small packages," I tackled anything and everything with excitement and determination. If an opportunity to try something new presented itself, I took it.

Skiing, both on snow and water, came rather naturally to my little legs. Sometimes it can be nice when you're closer to the ground with a lower center of gravity. Being covered in layers and wearing boots that, not only took up most of my lower leg but also restricted ankle motion, made it extremely difficult to walk. Once my skis were on, I was fine.

It's Storybook Day at Shawnee Peak. The mountain isn't far from our house on the lake. We wake up super early and dress in a gazillion layers. My Hot Chilly fleece pajama pants and wind pants are layered under my snow pants along with my long underwear turtleneck, wool sweater, and vest are making me sweat like a piglet while I try to scarf down some breakfast. Mom says that we can stop at Dunkin' Donuts on the way to the mountain. Mmm, Dunkaccino. Mom, Derek, Aunt Suzutte, and I are meeting Ray, Betty, Lianna, and Natalie at the mountain.

Over the past week, Maine has gotten slammed with snow. That means great skiing conditions and not-so-great driving. Sitting in the back seat, clutching my Dunkaccino, which is way too hot to drink, I look out the window and think about what a great day it's going to be. My daydreaming is cut short when Mom's Jeep hits a frost heave and my Dunkaccino cup flies out of my hands, hits the roof of the Jeep, and then lands on the floor, its scalding chocolatey contents all over my person. Derek, of course, thinks it is hilarious. I do not. Mom, the prepared woman she is, pulls over and digs a roll of paper towels and some baby wipes out of the back. Resembling Gloppy from the game Candyland, I can't decide whether I am more upset about my new appearance or the loss of my drink. Post clean-up attempt, I look a little less like I pooped myself.

Standing in line for the chairlift, I make sure to take the inside corner closest to the lift attendant while Mom flags him down to ask for his help in getting me on the lift. Gladly, he agrees and throws a wink my way. When it's our turn, he hits the button to slow the chair way down, grabs me under my arms and after a three count, hoists me up onto the seat. Success!

After a few runs, we approach the same lift and fail to notice that the attendants had switched. Mom starts yelling at the guy to slow the chair and help get me on as it comes barreling around the corner. The thrilled look on his face told me that this was not going to end well. He half-asses his attempt to help by grabbing my left arm, nearly ripping it out of the socket, while Mom takes my right. With only one butt cheek on the seat as the chair speeds up out of the terminal and over a snow-covered frozen pond, Mom lets go of my other arm to put the bar down, and I slide off. What a spectacle this must be. A small child falling from the chairlift into a frozen pond. Thank goodness the snow is higher than I am tall so it feels like I've landed in a cloud, unscathed. The ski patrol dudes come and fish me out. My friend Meaghan's family skis Shawnee Peak every winter. When they catch wind of the not-so-helpful lift attendant, they go to management. Word on the mountain is that the dude is no longer working here.

Pooped from an eventful morning, we break for lunch. There are all kinds of storybook characters parading around outside the lodge. There are big tables set up next to a grill where you can buy hot dogs and hamburgers. With the sun shining, we opt to eat our PB&Js we brought from home at a picnic table. After we are done eating, a DJ gets on the mic to announce that they are going to start playing some games. Derek, Lianna, Natalie, and I get up from the table to check it out. They start playing the chicken dance over the speakers—I know these moves well. As we do-si-do in little circles, my arm locks with Lianna's. Spinning around, the toe of my ski boot catches a crack in the cement, sending me forward at a rather alarming speed. Unlocking her arm from mine, Lianna watches as I sail straight into the long table and then onto the ground, taking the plastic tablecloth and condiment spread with me. After that stunt, I wave my white flag. That was enough excitement for one day.

With nothing ever labeled too difficult, in my mind, I was competitive in anything I took interest in, never placing myself in a separate category due to my vertical limitations. In fact, sometimes my itty-bitty frame ended up working to my advantage.

Cheerleading became a true passion of mine—not for the popularity but for the competition, the dancing, and the gymnastics. Ask my parents, and they will both tell you that I had found somewhere I could put my big mouth to good use. My petite size and flexibility of a rubber band made me an ideal uniformed loudmouth. Mom and Dad weren't too fond of the idea, other kids tossing me in the air like a little rag doll, but I adored it. The older girls would seek me out at the end of evening practice to get a few basket tosses in. Physically I soared—and so did my spirit. Finally, I was accepted for my abilities and not rejected for my differences.

Running into 7-11, Derek and I grab our fuel for this evening's practices. I opt for my go-to strawberry-kiwi Gatorade, and he goes with grape. When the babysitter drops us off behind the high school, Derek, clad in his practice pads, makes a run for the fields, and I go find the girls. It isn't hard to figure out where they are; all I have to do is listen for Val's booming voice. I like her. She laid it out for me in the very beginning: the cheerleading squads and coaches aren't worried about outward appearances or medical conditions. As long as you are dedicated, loud, and proud to be a Warrior, you fit right in. I'm convinced that I am one of the loudest ones on my peewee squad. My big mouth is free to be without risking detention.

We are cheering our last game of the football season this weekend. That means one thing: competition. The competitive aspect of cheering is what I enjoy most of all. In it to win it. The discipline and intensity of practices are something I look forward to after sitting at a desk all day. We are all there for one reason: to exceed expectations. Whether it is practice, a game, or a competition, I am totally immersed. After running through our halftime dances and some new cheers, we start learning our competition routine. As part of our first dance to "Candyman" by Aqua, I am one of the flyers for the opening stunts. Situated in a split, held up in the air by my teammates, a smile screaming confidence permanently on my face.

At the end of practice, all the squads meet by the back gate for a cheer-off. Whoever is loudest wins. Each group has an A squad and a B squad; the mites are the youngest group, then peewees (that's me), and the older girls are the midgets. Looking forward to cheering as I get older, declaring that I am on the midget A or B squad will not pain my esteem. The word midget, used in this context, is positive. It doesn't pain me to hear or say the word. It is a privilege to wear a uniform and stand alongside my teammates.

Our squad, peewee A, wins. And I no longer have a voice. Before leaving, some of the older girls ask if I am willing to do a couple of basket tosses. Heck yeah. If there is a way to possibly touch the clouds, this is it. These girls give me wings, and I'm not sure who is more excited—me or them.

Climbing into the back of Dad's gray Dodge pickup truck, Liz and I sit as far away from her brother Ben and Derek. They are muddy and gross from practice. The open air is completely necessary. Is this legal? I'm not sure, and we could care less.

Softball was also fast becoming a competitive favorite. It wasn't that I had difficulty running; my legs simply did not carry me at lightning speed. Throwing and batting were not a problem. Despite my shorter arms, with immense upper-body strength, I often pitched for my team. To our opposing team, I was a deceiving little thing. Up to bat, the outfielders would move in assuming my hits were weak. They were wrong. I was a wild card. Once they finally learned my capabilities and began backing up in the outfield, I came out of nowhere with a bunt. Take that, suckas!

9

Appointments with Dr. Kopits are always something I look forward to. It has become a tradition for Mimi to come with Mom and me—ladies only. Dad has the privilege of staying home with Derek to do manly things. This time, we are flying. As we board the plane, the stewardess hands me a set of Continental wings to pin to my shirt. Then the pilot and copilot ask me if I want to come and sit in the cockpit. Heck yeah, I do! All of the lights, levers, and switches are dizzying. I imagine myself as George Jetson sitting in front of his control panel at Spacely Sprockets, but I don't dare use my pointer finger to press any buttons. Moments like this make me feel like one special little lady.

The entire flight down to Baltimore, we laugh. Yes, I am the excited child who is walking up and down the aisle, insisting on having to go to the bathroom for the seventh time, flashing my cute smile at anyone who will pay attention, wriggling in her seat, and causing the person's drink in front of me to slosh all over their tray table. My backpack houses several items to keep me occupied. Best of all is my deluxe container of Gak. That's right, straight from Nickelodeon Studios. Propping my feet up on my tray table, I allow one ball of Gak to slowly ooze down over my feet and in between my toes while making juicy farting noises with the other pieces in the container. The flight attendants are intrigued and a little grossed out, and I would not be surprised if some people are becoming mildly annoyed by my presence on the flight.

Dad was kind enough to reserve a car for us at the airport, but I'm not sure that "car" is the right term, it resembles more of a lawnmower. We get around and then get lost. We always get lost. If there is one thing that Mom and Mimi do really, really well, it's getting turned around even with a map in hand. I can barely contain myself when we arrive at the Holiday Inn in Timonium, Maryland. The indoor/outdoor pool is any kid's fantasy. I love the manager who works here. He goes by "Buddy" and every time I see him, he has a new outlandish tie on. This time is like every other; upon arrival, I am beyond impatient to get to the pool. The same pool where, over the years, I have learned to swim. Mom bought me this sweet swim getup from a catalog to keep me from sinking to the bottom of the pool like a sack of rocks. It has little Styrofoam bricks that insert into the suit around my waist. It improves my floatation and gives me an incredibly muscular physique. Slowly but surely, I become more confident with each brick we take out of the suit until I am treading water and swimming. Now that I have achieved official mermaid status, I am sporting a sweet new two-piece adorned in glitter. My royal blue muscle suit is a thing of the past.

Usually while here at the hotel, it is an opportunity to meet other kids with dwarfism and their families who are also in town to see Dr. Kopits. It is a valuable fortuity for nonjudgmental play and interaction between us kids, and our parents are able to talk amongst each other regarding concerns and questions. My favorite visits are ones that we coordinate with the Taddeos. Monica and I continue to be childhood friends even though we rarely see one another.

The following day, we have a delightful breakfast at Denny's. My argument that I can finish an entire plate of pancakes myself is convincing enough and complete with a large glass of chocolate milk that I can blow bubbles in, immediately eliciting Mom's attention telling me to stop. Next stop is St. Joseph's Hospital in Towson for our appointment. After waiting for what seems like forever, Dr. Kopits is ready to see me. And I am really excited to see him! So much has happened over the past year, and I cannot wait to share everything with him.

At a recent visit to the eye doctor, I got my first pair of glasses. Now I can see the board in school and continue to excel in my scholarly ways. Dr. Kopits thinks they make me look very grown-up and sophisticated. During my cheerleading banquet, I won two trophies: one for most valuable cheerleader and the other for most spirited, and a plaque for our first-place win in competition. Additionally, I joined the swim team; the butterfly is my favorite stroke, and I pull out a handful of colorful ribbons from my backpack to show him.

"Just wonderful, my little doll," he asserts in his gentle Hungarian accent.

I am sure not to forget that last winter, at Shawnee Peak, in Maine, I won a gold pin doing a NASTAR downhill ski race! Sharing all of my accomplishments with Dr. Kopits is something I love because he appreciates everything I tell him, and he praises me for doing what I love. He certainly doesn't see the boundaries that some people have created for me based on my stature.

Tonight, we are going to Red Lobster for dinner and then stopping at the Inner Harbor to walk around. Pulling out of the hotel parking lot, we see a man walking with something perched on his shoulder. A monkey?! It's a monkey wearing a diaper. We drive closer to inquire about the gentleman and his companion. With my window rolled down, I stand on the back seat and lean the majority of my body out of the car. I need to meet this little primate. The man walks over to us and mom starts talking to him. Curiosity is about to kill me, I have never been this close to a monkey before. Come to find out, the little monkey's name is George. How fitting. Too bad his human friend isn't wearing yellow. George starts trying to groom my head and I am tickled with laughter. This is the best day ever! The man hands George a bottle of what appears to be beer and the monkey takes a big old swig. A beer drinking monkey? This day is a definite win.

After the idea of extended limb lengthening made its way into my life, I toyed with it for a while—as early as the third grade—when I mentioned the thought of the operation in the movie Liz and I made for our classmates. Somehow, in my elementary mind, lengthening one arm and one leg at a time made sense? The hopeful buzz must have traveled to my brain causing my facts to be skewed. The more I talked about it, the more enthusiastic I became about the procedures.

Mom was definitely the pioneer in finding all the information. The green folder labeled "Limb Lengthening" became thicker and thicker over the years. Booklets, newspaper articles, journals, and internet information sat atop a stack of VHS tapes with documentaries on dwarfism and limb lengthening. You name it, that folder contained anything and everything Mom could get her hands on. My dedication to the limb-lengthening surgery never rested solely on the detail of adding inches to my height. My focus was to shine a light on my future and the impending pain and difficulties I would ultimately face.

By the time I was eleven, I began to think about what it meant to be a little person, in regard to my future, understanding the difficulties I would face in the years to come. I'm not talking about looks, height, or name-calling. Medical problems commonly seen in achondroplastic dwarfs like arthritis, obstructive apnea, knee instability, and spinal stenosis, to name a few, were of real concern. Deep thoughts for a young girl, huh?

At my annual visit to Dr. Kopits, he informed Mom, Mimi, and me that surgery was inevitable. My lower legs were becoming severely bowed. It was interfering with my sassy strut and proved to be a potential danger to my long-term joint health. Knowing something had to be done in order to prevent further damage to my knees, I was okay with this news. However, when he explained how he planned on correcting the deformity—by removing a piece of the fibula bone to make the leg straighter—my mind-set quickly changed. Something about taking bone out of my legs just didn't sit right with me.

At that same appointment, we also discussed the limb-lengthening procedures that had begun to surface on television specials and magazine articles in great detail with him. Dr. Kopits explained that it was not a surgery he performed, and in the past did not support, but he understood if it was something I wanted to consider. Out of respect, I told him that I wanted to look into the surgery a little more and asked his permission to do so. I had very high regard for the man who had so compassionately taken such good care of me over the years, and I wanted his best wishes before I did anything. Holding me in a tight embrace, he kissed my head and told me that he wanted me to do whatever was going to make me happy.

Little did I know that would be the last time I would ever see Dr. Kopits. In 2001, he had a recurrence of a brain tumor and was forced to close his practice at St. Joseph's Medical Center. On June 18, 2002, Dr. Kopits passed away. I will always remember the kind, caring, and gentle man he was. He was a specialist who helped so many people, and I know his lifetime passion of healing will live forever on in the hearts of many.

10

With a permission slip tucked away in my heart from Dr. Kopits, further research on extended limb lengthening began. Articles, books, and television programs—whatever Mom could get her hands on for more information. Two large green folders still exist to this day: one with information on achondroplasia and the other with information on extended limb lengthening. Since before I made my grand entrance into this world, Mom always knew there were other options out there. A few years earlier, she had come across an article in *People* about a little girl named Gillian. Gillian was born with dwarfism and underwent the application of external fixators on her arms and legs to correct specific deformities, consequently making her taller. Rediscovering this article was a game changer.

My first thought is, *No way, Jose. This is nuts. Some crazy operation is actually going to make me taller and straighten me?* The more I read about limb lengthening, the more I realized how valuable this procedure could really be to me. Length is not going to be everything. For me, this is also a corrective surgery. I want to say goodbye to my bowed legs and constant achiness. I know pain throughout the procedure will be a given. However, looking at the pictures of kids with the Ilizarov frames on I notice one thing: they look happy and hopeful. If they can do it, then so can I.

Through one of my teachers at Hobomock Elementary School, we learned about the Shriners Hospital in Springfield, Massachusetts. We were told that they were using the Ilizarov method to lengthen limbs. Immediately, Mom was on the phone to schedule an appointment with one of the orthopedic surgeons there. I could not wait for that day to come. Containing my angst and excitement was difficult. Everyone in school knew about my appointment, and they were hopeful for me. Three hours in the car could not have gone by any slower. My best efforts to impress the doctors even included a cute little blue dress that Mom and I bought for the occasion. Excited, nervous, unsure, hesitant, eager—I was all the feels sitting in the back of Mom's Jeep. A laundry list of emotions three miles long. This could possibly be a huge turning point in my life.

Sitting in the waiting room, I see a little boy in a wheelchair with a futuristic contraption on one of his legs. I recognize it is an Ilizarov frame from one of the pamphlets we have at home. At first glance, it doesn't look that bad. Then my eyes find the wires going into one side of his leg and out the other. Um, ouch? Seeing it in person is far different than on glossy paper, even from a distance. He doesn't seem to be in pain, but he doesn't look overly thrilled to be relying on wheels either. There are other kids walking around on crutches with casts and braces of all types. Shriners Hospital seems to be helping so many. Am I one of the lucky ones? Obviously there has to be hope for me, right?

We wait six hours, yes, six hours, during which I sample all the options in the vending machines, until a nurse calls me back into the examination room. Sitting across from Mom and Dad, I choose to act interested in the pictures on the wall behind them. No eye contact, I am too nervous for that right now, a shaking in my britches, should have worn a diaper, I think I am going to be sick kind of apprehension. The nurse takes my vitals, height, and weight, and asks me a few questions.

"Do you smoke?"

Is she seriously asking me this right now? Yes, I smoke about a pack a day and prefer Virginia Slims. When I'm feeling frisky, a cigar will do.

No, dummy. I'm eleven.

That's what I want to say but I reply with a simple, "No."

She leaves. Ten or so minutes later, I hear muffled voices from a team of doctors conversing outside the door. My stomach feels like I ate one too many Oreos. There's a click of the handle, the door opens, and at least six people in white coats walk in. One look at them, and the huge smile residing on my face immediately vanishes. None of them seem delighted or impressed with my presence. The attending orthopedic surgeon steps forward, looks directly at me, and without introducing himself, in a very harsh, serious tone asks, "Why are you even here?"

Cue the orbital faucets. Slowly, painfully, visible tears well in my eyes.

What the hell does he think I am doing here? He's a doctor—he went to medical school. Seriously? Oh, you know, just came by to check out the facilities and maybe dabble in a little thing called surgery. No biggie.

Words fail me. All I can do is sit completely still on the exam table, tears falling from my eyes, pooling in my hands, which are resting in my lap. My gaze falls down to my feet. The voices become foggy and almost distant in my ears. With my eyes closed in an effort to put a stop to the tears, I indistinctly hear Mom trying to explain that we are here seeking more information on the limb-lengthening procedures.

The doctor says, "Why? We don't offer that type of surgery for people like her."

I have a name, you uncaring jerk.

And that is it. The whole team walks out. I break down. Mom is sobbing. Dad looks confused and let down. We leave.

At eleven years old, the cacophony of disturbing emotions resulting from that one appointment ripped me apart. It was true hurt, letdown, and heartbreak. That man called himself a doctor? The entire drive home, I cried. Curled in a ball against the door, gazing out the window, I dreaded going to school the next day for fear that people were going to ask me how the doctor's visit went. How do you explain to your teachers and friends that a health care professional pulled the rug out from underneath you without warning?

11

For what seemed like weeks, maybe even months, hope had wandered to hide down a deep, dark hole. As much as I wanted to resent the Shriners, I could not find the capacity to do so because I knew how many other people they helped. They just weren't going to make me one of those individuals. Some things are meant to be. What I had to come to terms with was that I was not meant to be treated by doctors at the Shriners Hospital. I did not want a person capable of being that heartless in charge of my care either. Bearing in mind the emotional letdown I had suffered, continuing the search for a doctor no longer became a priority.

The summer after fifth grade began like any other: sunshine, beach trips, lemonade stands, and late nights out with the neighborhood kids playing flashlight tag for hours. It is said that things come the moment you stop looking for them, and that is exactly what happened. A family friend stumbled upon the Maryland Center for Limb Lengthening and Reconstruction through an internet search. Our home team support system with assistance from the world wide web pulled through for the win.

Upon immediate request for information from MCLLR, we received a letter from the center, along with a plethora of informational packets. Dr. Dror Paley and Dr. John Herzenberg were codirectors of the Maryland Center for Limb Lengthening and Reconstruction in Baltimore. Their program at Kernan Hospital, a branch of the University of Maryland, was created to provide the most technologically advanced treatment for children and adults with limb length discrepancies and limb deformities, defects, and infections. They were the leaders in this field and had performed more than two thousand lengthening procedures. Oddly enough, Dr. Paley was the surgeon who had operated on Gillian, the young lady from the *People* article Mom had saved a while back. My hope was restored.

Mom, Mimi, and I are off for Baltimore once again. It is the summer before sixth grade, June 1997. We have made this trip a hundred times, but this time is different, this time I have an appointment with Dr. Paley at the Maryland Center for Limb Lengthening and Reconstruction. Baltimore is feeling more like a home away from home.

Our appointment is not scheduled until later in the afternoon. Figuring the earlier we get there, the earlier we can leave and be on our merry way, we show up around ten o'clock in the morning. Then we wait and wait and wait. When we initially got here, I'm pretty sure I was the only patient. The clinic was deserted. After an hour or two, the waiting room is overflowing with people, and the staff is running around like crazy. Finally, a tech calls me in for x-rays, which take no time at all, and then back out into the waiting room I go. Considering the majority of the patients are children, they have a great playroom: crafts, books, video games, you name it. I had the feeling we would end up waiting a long time to see Dr. Paley, so I have lots of things, including my summer reading, to keep me occupied as well.

While in the waiting room, twin girls arrive in a stroller with fixators on both of their legs. They are at least eight or nine years younger than I am, and they are both perfectly happy when their mom hoists them out of the stroller and onto the floor to play. It seems crazy to me that they have all these pins and wires going through their legs, and they are still smiling and laughing, crawling around on the floor, hardware snagging the carpet as they go. There are other kids with fixators, casts, and colorful braces on their arms and legs. Though I have yet to see anyone with achondroplasia in the clinic.

After another hour or so of waiting, a receptionist escorts us back into an exam room. My x-rays are displayed on illuminated boxes mounted on the wall. I sit on the paper covering the exam table, trying not to make too much noise as I impatiently rustle about.

Dr. Paley walks in with an entourage, introduces himself, and immediately begins explaining that I am a fantastic candidate for the procedure. My heart is racing, my hands are balmy, and my eyebrows are raised so high I could be mistaken for the first eleven-year-old having gone through Botox. He just said yes!

Dr. Paley explains that limb lengthening works by taking advantage of the body's natural tendency to heal itself. In my first surgery, he will cut the tibia and fibula, the bones in the lower leg, in two places and stabilize them on the outside with wires, pins, and a titanium Ilizarov frame. By turning the nuts on the fixator, the ends of the bone are slowly pulled apart, creating a gap that will naturally fill in with brand-new bone. Recovery will be an extended test of mettle and will with physical therapy being of utmost importance. In addition to bone, the muscles and nerves are also stretching to meet the demands of new growth. Once the desired length is achieved, the bone must solidify before the frames are removed.

A smile three feet wide creeps across my face. He shakes my hand and even though I'm more of a hug person, I didn't want to scare him off so I give him the firmest handshake my little hand can summon. This process is not going to be a walk in the park. I have only known Dr. Paley for a mere seven minutes, and I am confident that this is my guy. Finally!

Dr. Paley went into great detail about how the entire process would work specifically for me. The adolescent method would be used in my case with the tibias being lengthened first using the Ilizarov apparatus. The use of the Ilizarov frame would allow for the correction of my bowleg deformity. This was huge. Even though I would be allowed to bear weight with the frames on my legs, they would be heavy and cumbersome. A wheelchair would be necessary. Anticipating an inch of new bone growth a month and a goal of six inches, the first phase, of lengthening and consolidating, would take nearly a year.

Once I fully recovered from the first phase of surgery, Dr. Paley planned to operate on my upper arms, the humerus bone between the shoulder and elbow, using an orthofix fixator. This stage of surgery was much less invasive and would offer me a lot more freedom since it does not interfere with mobility. Upon completion of the second lengthening, the simple act of sticking my hands in my pockets would be possible. Dr. Paley also said that as a result of the four inches he foresaw me getting, the flexion deformity in my elbow would no longer be an issue, and my arm would extend closer to straight. Since there was less growth involved with this phase, it was not going to take nearly as much time to complete.

The final operation would be on my femurs and also required the orthofix device. This would be the most difficult of the three procedures. Over the course of five months of lengthening, Dr. Paley explained that weight bearing would not be possible. After I gained my goal of five inches and moved into consolidation, I could gradually begin to bear weight on my legs. In addition to new height, Dr. Paley sought to decrease the flexion deformity in my hips, allowing me to stand up straighter.

There he was, standing before me: I had found my guy. After hearing Dr. Paley lay the foundation for the next few years of my life, our next step was to schedule surgery. My magical day, the day everything in my life would change, was going to be in a year: June 3, 1998. In the end, my decision to go through with the surgery did not solely rest on a taller life, but on one that would be proportionate and full of independence.

12

All of my teachers in grade school nurtured my tenacity for life. They didn't treat me any more or less special than my classmates. Well, except for the time in third grade when I fractured my collarbone and had to wear a sling. All of the kids were told to imagine a ring of orange cones around me and not to set foot within that boundary.

Upon entering the sixth grade, it became a harsh reality: I was different. Really, very different. Not just short, disproportionately tiny. My dwarfism impacted how some of my peers saw me. I was no longer Kristen, the twelve-year-old, driven girl who freely embraced her inner tomboy and loved a game of flag football. In their eyes, my disability fiercely overshadowed my drive to tackle anything thrown my way, and I was more easily seen as the small fry who couldn't run fast enough or throw as far.

In my early elementary school years, it never really bothered me, aside from the occasional isolated incident, but by the sixth grade, my peers were hitting their growth spurts—and it was obvious how short I really was. Girls my age started hanging out with the boys, and I never felt included. It felt like none of the boys liked me—at least not like that—because I was a dwarf. You know what I mean. Just as before, I did not want to be emotionally rocked by my omnipresent label and resulting exclusion; suppressing was easier than expressing. In the end, my willing and bubbly personality was inexorably trapped in a dwarf body that others saw as incapable, funny, and inferior. It was a strike to my self-esteem.

Despite the emotional difficulties, I kept my small circle of friends close and remained determined to be on top of my schoolwork. That year, I was blessed with a teacher who drastically changed the way I had begun to look at myself. Kelly Valeri was far from oblivious on the days that I struggled with the aggressive voice of negative self-talk that seemed to be getting louder and louder as the school year moved on and surgery loomed.

"They're right, Kristen. You can't. You are not good enough. It doesn't matter how hard you try. No one is ever going to look past the fact that you have achondroplasia. You suck at math. A boyfriend? You'll never have one of those."

And so on and so forth. Yes, those voices surfaced more often than I preferred, and I gave my best effort to quiet them.

In a valiant attempt to prove I was good enough and an individual who had no limitations, I ran for vice president of Mrs. Valeri's class. Our election was held in the school cafeteria. Each candidate was required to get up on stage in front of the class and give a speech explaining why we would be a good candidate for the position we sought to fill.

Nervous? I'm not nervous. I know exactly what I am going to say. I have known these kids since I was seven. Piece of cake.

Walking up on stage, my palms are sweating, and my heart feels like the drum of that stupid Energizer bunny. I'm lying. I might be a little panicky. Turning to face my adolescent audience and Mrs. Valeri, I realize the microphone is over my head and begin struggling to adjust it lower. After what seems like two minutes too long, the mic drops with a loud, metallic clunk to the lowest setting. Comic relief? Absolutely. If there is one thing I have learned? Laugh with them. I manage to get a hesitant giggle or two out of the situation as I feel my face flush.

Eye contact, Kristen. Look at them. Smile. Stop holding your breath. Nothing good comes from a VP who goes blue in the face. God gave you a big mouth for a reason—be louder.

The words effortlessly roll off my tongue ... are they words or gibberish? I can't be sure. Too late to worry. Done. The class is clapping, and I hear Mrs. Valeri yell, "Way to go, Krissy!" Thank God that is over with. A little wave of pride washes over me, I step away from the microphone and toss in a little curtsy before stepping off the stage. And it's happening—I'm in midair. One of my feet is caught the mic cord. I am doing my best superwoman impression as I fly over the steps and land in a heap in front of my classmates. Welp. Good thing I decided not to wear a dress this morning! Standing up, initially wanting to cry, I hear the laughter of my classmates and a few cries of, "Kristen! Are you okay?" I continue to play along in my role as superwoman. I stand up and simply take another curtsy because that's what super ladies do.

Whether it was my speech or my surprising ability to become airborne, I will never be sure, but I won the vice presidential election.

It's easy to say that my sixth and final year at Hobomock Elementary School was my most memorable. We changed classrooms to prepare us for middle school, had exciting projects like Sugar Babies (or were they eggs?) and created television ads for our inventions, and played rowdy games of silent ball. Mrs. Valeri's homeroom class was a cohesive one. There was always time for laughter amidst hard work, and sometimes attempting to stifle it, especially when Mr. Bigglesworth, Jason's alligator pen was involved, proved unsuccessful.

Still, at twelve years old, reality had sunk in. I was having a difficult time dealing with the stress of being little. This was not a new revelation or something that constantly affected me. Every once in a while, something would happen and my emotions would flare up. Sometimes it felt as if I was being put on the back burner by my friends, especially the boys. Feeling upset about issues that were out of my control was hard to come to terms with and not something I was particularly proud of. How was I going to get through my upcoming surgeries if I could barely handle being ... me?

Buck up, Kristen. This is life.

Seriously, though. As children, when we cry, the response is typically "Shh" or "Don't cry." Therefore, we learn that showing sad, scared, or angry emotions is a sign of weakness, and I certainly did not want people to see me as a weakling. Add that right under small fry on my resume, and things weren't looking too good.

There was one particular day that served to be a nearly unbearable challenge for reasons I don't recall, and it didn't go unnoticed. Mrs. Valeri pulled me aside later that morning and asked if I would stay in from recess and come back to class after lunch. She was sure to reiterate that I was not in trouble since most kids who stayed in were usually headed to detention. Knowing all too well that she wasn't going to elaborate on her request, I agreed, and after lunch that day, I went back to her classroom. She wasn't back from lunch duty yet, so I sat down at my desk and opened up *The Slave Dancer*, the book we were reading in class. If I had done something wrong, maybe my scholarly ways would ease any potential impending discipline.

"Krissy!" Mrs. Valeri yelled rather excitedly as she walked into the room. "What's up, kid?"

Hmmm. Maybe I wasn't in trouble. She seemed awfully happy prior to bringing the hammer down on me.

Mrs. Valeri took a seat at the desk next to me and scooted a bit closer. "Krissy, what's going on?" she asked, now in a more serious yet uncomfortably gentle tone.

Shit. I mean, crap. She's good. She knows.

Sitting across from me, I'm getting a look of genuine concern and with that all-knowing look that some adults are just so good at that you have no choice but to divulge everything. Yeah, you know what I'm talking about—that. There is no fooling her with my half-hearted smiles and laughs. She knows that they are incognito for the sad, scared, and angry feelings that I have been suppressing and trying to ignore. At this point, it's clear that my butt won't be leaving my seat until I come clean. And I want to tell her everything, I do, but there is a piece of me that is so concerned about what she will think of me after I tell her.

Sympathy was hard to receive. I never wanted people to feel bad for me; that's why discussions like these were avoided. Deep down, I knew that Mrs. Valeri understood that and would respond to my story with compassion. I opened up, and we talked about it all. From how much I hated math and how bad I was at it, to feeling excluded more often than usual and the fact that this life-changing surgery lay ahead of me in June. I felt overwhelmed, and I wasn't quite sure how to even put it into words. None of the other kids my age seemed remotely perturbed by little events in their life, so why was I? This whole "being different" thing was getting out of hand and reaching emotional levels that I couldn't seem to control and certainly did not want to admit to.

Mrs. Valeri says my favorite phrase: "You can." And apparently, it's okay to talk about when things get hard. "Krissy, so many people love you and are rooting for you. If there are friends who aren't doing that, then they aren't friends, are they?"

And math. Ugh. She is willing to help me in any way she can. A lot of the problem rests in my head and my confidence. If I think that I'm terrible at it, then I am going to struggle. It is not going to be easy, but right now, I choose to change my thoughts. Mrs. Valeri also knows that I made a huge decision, opting to follow through with limb-lengthening surgery. It might not be a life-threatening decision, but it is a life-changing one. She doesn't even realize what it entails and is shocked when I tell her. "You can do this, Krissy. I see it in your eyes, as you're talking about it, that this is what you want—and I support you 100 percent."

Buoyed by the fact that I had compassionate support from a person I had an immense amount of respect for allowed me to ride the waves of adolescence in my last year of elementary school. When it came to math, I did my best to change my thoughts and insert confidence into the crevices of uncertainty. Hard work and positivity paid off—and my name went up on the white board holding the second-fastest time for our multiplication time sheets.

With Mrs. Valeri's assurance that disrespect of any kind was not tolerated in her classroom, I felt my confidence taking root. Anytime I had a problem, I hesitated less and less before seeking her guidance. Together, we decided it would be helpful to give the rest of the class an opportunity to understand the procedures I would undergo at the end of the school year. One afternoon, our entire homeroom class stayed in from recess to watch a documentary that had recently aired about Dr. Paley and his amazing work.

The whole class is sitting on the floor of our open-area classroom watching as the 20/20 documentary begins. If the graphic nature of this show doesn't familiarize everyone with the procedures I will undergo, I don't know what will. The opening scene is of Dr. Paley in the operating room, with the largest power tool I have ever seen, drilling pins into a patient's leg. Mrs. Valeri and my classmates sit, mouths agape, as Dr. Timothy Johnson explores the incredible medical phenomenon of limb lengthening with an Ilizarov external fixator. As the screen again shows Dr. Paley in the operating room now using a hammer to break a patient's bone, I catch a glimpse of a few kids wincing. Turning around, Mrs. Valeri gives me a look like, "Kristen, you are crazy." Turning back to the television, I think, maybe I am. There still isn't a doubt in my mind that this is the right decision. It makes me happy to know that my friends, classmates, and other teachers support my decision to embark on this journey.

That year, I learned a few things that have stuck with me. For one, Bounce dryer sheets are best for static cling. Especially when your skirt catches on your tights so everyone catches a glimpse of your underwear as you write an answer on the board. So beyond embarrassing. Second, don't let someone tell you that you can't. Not even that little voice in your head. Ever. You need to believe that you can with every ounce of your being. Positive thinking must be met with positive doing. At twelve years old, I'd found my courage: being okay with the emotional hardship that parallels living as a differently-abled young human and asking for help when necessary. Something I knew that I would need moving forward with surgery. Lastly, there are people in this world who go above and beyond their teaching role in the classroom.

Kelly Valeri remains one of my closest friends and greatest confidantes to this very day. She continues to embrace my strengths and struggles either on the phone or over a glass of wine.

Only a few days prior to embarking on the big journey to Baltimore, some of my closest friends threw me a "good luck" party, a last hoorah of sorts, as I would not be on my feet again for a while. Opening up gifts of stationery, stamps, and cute little envelopes caused the reality of everything to really hit. Cards with best wishes and messages implying that I could do anything made me a ball of smooshy sentiment. No way would I have admitted it then, but I felt moved by the outpouring of support from family and friends.

Today is my last day of sixth grade. Whoa baby! No more elementary school. How did that happen? This weekend we leave for Baltimore with my pre-op appointment Monday and surgery on Tuesday. Who doesn't love an excuse to have a party at school even if the reason is saying goodbye? Well, see you later, really.

Mrs. Valeri's husband, AJ, brought in cupcakes for our class, and we are staying in for recess to play silent ball. Typically, we play when it's raining and are forced to have indoor recess, but since it's my last day, Mrs. Valeri says that we can play a farewell game. If all goes well after surgery, I will be back to Hobomock for promotion night where we get our yearbooks and end-of-the-year awards. No perfect attendance certificate this year. Oh well, it's for good reason. Before Mom picks me up from school, I give hugs and high-fives to my friends. One of the teachers in the open area, Mrs. Vilagi, hands me a gift bag. Inside is a stuffed dog. I give her a big squeeze and say thank you. (To this day, I still have the dog—Patches—and he has been in the operating room with me for every surgery I have undergone.) With my purple L. L. Bean backpack clad in hordes of keychains slung past my little bum, lower than any doctor would recommend, I walk up to Mrs. Valeri and give her a huge hug.

"See ya, Krissy! You got this, kiddo. I'll be praying for you."

13

When I think about my childhood, I don't think of dwarfism plaguing life and making things hard. Not at all. My mind is flooded with memories and tradition. Girl Scouts and convincing Dad to take my cookie-selling sheet to work with him because those telephone company guys were a gold mine. Sports—watching and playing them—football, swimming, softball, skiing on snow and water. The time Derek hid in the dryer during a game of hide-and-go-seek in the basement, and our babysitter came downstairs to finish laundry and almost "dried" him. The same babysitter who told us that she was thirty-nine years old as she shmeared Fixadent all over her dentures and secured them back in place … multiple times a day. Trips to Maine with my friends who thought it was a stellar idea to read ghost stories about the Wolfman in the back of Mom's old Jeep, and upon arrival, walk in a huddle through the dark, down the steps to Camp, only to find that the electricity was out, so two of us start crying, and we all sleep piled on top of each other on the pull-out couch. Playing *Super Mario Brothers 3* with Derek for hours up in the spare bedroom, until we nearly went cross-eyed. Climbing in bed with Mimi when she stayed at our house so she would scratch my back (I called it "bees" because it felt like little bumble bees buzzing on my back.) Providing evidence to support my assertion that I needed to add that Beanie Baby to my collection and then going home to fashion new clothes for said growing collection out of scrap fabric with Mom's sewing machine. (The same collection that sits in two very large Tupperware bins in Mom and Dad's attic gathering dust. Are they actually worth a fortune? If you know something I don't, please tell.) Pretending to communicate with my paternal grandparents who only spoke Portuguese, which I understood none of—the love was felt through pinched cheeks, a full belly, and enough soda to fuel a jetliner. Building sick jumps out of plywood and bricks in the driveway and channeling my inner BMX biker who was lucky to get her bike tires both in the air at the same time. Going to the Charlie Horse with the Sadlers and Roses, ordering Shirley Temples and buffalo wings, and blowing Mom and Dad's dollars on arcade games and the candy crane. Hitting up Blockbuster on a school night, and Dad flipping a coin to see who got to watch their movie first. Winning first place in the science fair with Liz for our "Life Cycle of a Chick" project and keeping the baby chicks as pets for too many days too long according to Mom and Dad. Watching *20,000 Leagues Under the Sea* while Dad set up his new "in-home gym" in the living room and then having nightmares about a giant squid for the next five years of my life. Actually, I'm still terrified. And no, you can't pay me to watch that movie again. Kicking ass during our neighborhood games of Manhunt. I couldn't run super-fast, but was I phenomenal at hiding. Swimming in the rain up at the lake. Getting egg beaters, full of brownie batter, stuck in my hair because I tried to sneak a taste while mixing at the same time and my newly braided hair from Florida got in the way. Laughing my ass off at Derek who idolized Ace Ventura as he got up from the dinner table, on a nightly basis, went into the downstairs bathroom, flushed the toilet and came back out exclaiming, "Do *not* go in there! Whew!" Mom bribing me to stop biting my nails by offering to pay me two dollars a finger, which never happened. Playing the part of Pocahontas in fourth grade. Popping in the Richard Simmons workout video and jazzercising solo in the living room wearing my leotard and tights; I was only missing an afro. Standing on the starting block alongside teammates and competitors of average height and diving into the pool to be the fiercest butterfly and coming away with a first-place finish. Playing outside in the snow, refusing to wear a hat, and then giggling hysterically as Derek and I carried armfuls of snow up the front porch and threw them at Mom who was videotaping. Climbing into Dad's lap in the driver's seat while on the back roads of Maine and learning how to operate a vehicle like a true Masshole far earlier than any state trooper would ever prefer. Taking family trips to Siesta Key, Florida, to see Uncle Frank, Aunt Sue, and cousins Kimberly and Matthew—trust me when I tell you that the home movies are Hollywood worthy, especially the one of everyone smoking cigarettes, including three-year-old Derek, and Uncle Tom using the pool as an ashtray. Spending the night at Grammie and

Grampie Dick's house up in Maine and experiencing the delight that was Limburger cheese on toast for breakfast. Doing school reports on Wild Bill Hickok, Amelia Earhart, and the black-footed ferret. Derek and I learning how to paddle a canoe up at Camp by Mom tying said canoe to a tree and leaving us and our two paddles to our own devices. Most of the time, we ended up sideways on the neighbor's beach tangled in our nautical leash. Celebrating many a birthday party and taking roller skating lessons at Skatetown USA … and the time the roof collapsed. Convincing Mom that I just had to spend the snow day over at Kate's house only to have Mom's Jeep hit a patch of ice in Kate's treacherous driveway and hit a tree. Whoopsie. Venturing next door to Ruth's house up at Camp with Meaghan for glasses of cream soda. Obsessing over Jonathan Taylor Thomas and covering my walls with posters from *Tiger Beat* magazines. Watching the Patriots on one particular Sunday, situated in Dad's lap, when Drew Bledsoe made a monumental error, and in order for Dad to properly and fully express his distaste, he threw me off his lap in the direction of the woodstove, which was indeed burning. Spending a week at Camp Wind in the Pines with a bunch of Girl Scouts and learning what it meant to be homesick. Christmas caroling with the DeAndrade clan on Christmas Eve and being slipped moonshine in my Coke can at one of our caroling stops. Climbing Rattlesnake Mountain with Mom, Sue, Derek, and Sammy-dog and bearing witness to Mom making to most epic of faceplants into a gigantic mud puddle on the way down. Eagerly awaiting to see what highly inappropriate gag gifts Grampie Dick was given on Christmas morning—it's a tie between the apron concealing a larger than life penis and the chock blocks and helmet to prevent his Mercedes from rolling down the driveway. Being employed as a personal masseuse to walk on people's backs during family gatherings where all the adults had a few too many libations. Dad's constant need to video everything with his new camcorder, including Derek and my first experience with an outhouse at Barbie and Tom's. Playing (getting in the way of) rousing games of football at Grandma and Grandpa's house. Leaving swim practice at the Percy Walker pool in the middle of winter and sporting a headful of icicle dreadlocks. Standing out at the end of the dock at night and learning the names of stars and constellations from Suze.

If that isn't evidence supporting the fact that my life was full of adventure, love, and learning and that Mom and Dad always nurtured my fiercely independent spirit, I'm not sure what is. I was your typical kid—out to have fun and live life the best way I knew how. It was a semi-equal balance of trouble and fun. The only thing I can truly think of that they ever said no to was my request to play youth football. Now, I completely understand their concern for my safety, but back then, I saw no reason why I couldn't. Even though I was denied the opportunity to play football on the field, it didn't stop me from dressing up in Derek's practice gear and throwing the ball with Dad and him in the yard.

Was I crazy? Maybe. And I did not care one bit how people reacted when they saw me. I never walked around in public, through the mall, for example, taking note of others staring and pointing; it rarely caught my attention. I had more important things to worry about, like bathing myself with every tester body spray from Bath and Body Works. My friends and I walked out of that store smelling like vanilla cupcakes that had rolled in a field of strong smelling flowers; our suffocatingly sweet essence having a much stronger effect on my psyche than any stranger's rubbernecking. My innocence of the unknown impact of harsh words or actions was a beautiful thing—and it didn't last forever.

In youth cheerleading, the squads were divided into three different age groups: the mites, pee-wees, and midgets. Yes. There's that word. I never thought twice about it. In fact, when I became a part of the midget squad for the Warriors, the seniority made me feel important. I didn't care what we had been labeled. Eventually, that all changed. As that purity of mine slowly eroded, I faced numerous hurdles. And the life-changing decision of limb-lengthening surgery. That is a lot for a twelve-year-old to handle. It was almost as if a switch flipped one day, and I immediately began to notice the stares and hear the snickering and remarks. The word *midget* meant something. Hearing or seeing it written began to strike a nerve as I held the understanding that *midget* carried an unbelievable negative connotation for any individual with short stature.

As a child growing up with what most saw as a disability, I experienced a rapid onset of emotional maturity. Taking the ridicule like bullets, it became clear that different was intolerable in the eyes of society. The fierce tendencies of singling individuals out with any disparity, whether physical, emotional, or spiritual, caused immense hurt for me and so many others fighting their own battles. There was always going to be that person who was going to discount me because of my height. That time that I went home, closed the door to my bedroom, and cried because an ignorant human being made others laugh at my expense was not going to be the last. Acquaintances, even strangers, were going to force the phrase "you can't" into my vocabulary because my adapted way of doing something was incorrect in their book. My short stature, always warranting name-calling, laughing, pointing, and staring. Why? Simply because I look different. Evidence to support society's ever evolving standards stating that I would never be good enough were stacking against me.

As children, we are coddled and shushed when crying and told everything will be okay. It was something that I had become very familiar with. My parents, family, and friends did their very best to shield me from this portrayal of "different" as undesirable. Whenever people gave me a hard time in public, whether with their eyes or words, Mom had a most difficult time with it. It hurt me to know that she felt sad about something I couldn't control. Pretending that it never happened and suppressing my emotions seemed like a surefire way to make it all disappear. So, I put on my brave face, appearing on the outside unscathed, but deep down, the feelings slowly began to pile up. Somehow, I'd hoped that if I suppressed them long enough, they would evaporate into thin air.

We all know it doesn't work that way.

Eventually, there came that time when I looked at myself in the mirror and wished that I was someone else, that I had a body that was proportionate and beautiful in the eyes of everyone. I looked at my life and told myself, "That will never happen no matter how hard I try. It's just a dream. Not all dreams come true." After Mom and Dad tucked me in at night and closed my door, I threw back my covers, got onto my knees, and prayed. Every night. I prayed hard. I would have one-sided conversations with God, "Why was I born this way? Why was I dealt such a difficult hand?" Was he listening?

When you're growing up, everything matters. You have to be like everyone else. Why does it matter? Because your "friends" say that it does. If they don't like you, who will? Fear steps in. The fear that we won't have any friends. We will be alone. We aren't good enough. So, what is left? We have to change. Sadly, I started to believe what I once promised myself I wouldn't. "Kristen, you can't." "No."

Fear told me not to own my emotions—that they would only make me weaker. When I was hurt, I hid my anger and sadness. The wall I was building in front of the real me was so high that I could no longer scale it. Fear was wrong; it always is. Why else would it stand for *false emotions appearing real*?

While some people continued to confirm what fear had instilled in me, there were those who weren't so resistant to my dreams. People fought for me. My parents. My brother. My family. My teachers. My friends. All of them. They reintroduced and consecrated the phrase "you can," into my vocabulary. When I said, "I can't," they retaliated. "Kristen, you can."

It came down to two choices. I could give up and let others dictate my life—or I could keep going and fight for what I wanted. I was not going to let anyone hold me down. No one was going to extinguish my flame—no matter how much it hurt. June 3 was fast approaching, and I was ready.

It has always been important to me that people know: my parents left me standing on an open field. They assured me support in any decision that I made, no matter which side I ran to. Honestly, Dad was pretty hesitant at first. He feared the possible complications of the procedure and arthritis as a result. Still, my internal compass was pointing to Dr. Paley in Baltimore. At twelve years old, when most of my friends were deciding whether or not to go to a private middle school, I came to stand at a crossroads. The surgeries were not a Band-Aid or cure for my dwarfism. The promise of correcting complications I was already experiencing and preventing future ones was my primary motivation. The added inches would make independence in an average height world accessible. There wasn't a question or doubt in my mind that I was making the right decision. As one window closed, a very large door opened—and my strength of will was soon to be tested to the max.

14

There are two things that I have never seen Dad do in all my moments here on planet earth: cry or shave his moustache.

As of this morning, I can cross number one off of that list. Sitting in the passenger seat of Mom's gold Jeep, in the driveway, with the door ajar, Dad stands there with tears in his eyes before hugging me goodbye. I'm twelve. What am I supposed to do when my Dad starts to cry? Start crying? Oh good, that's exactly what is happening. Of course when I say "see ya" to Derek, the tears have to be gone. Siblings do not cry when bidding farewell to each other. Don't get me wrong—I'll miss him.

No food after midnight; that's what I was told at my preoperative appointment. So at 11:30 p.m. on June 2, 1998, I sat up in bed at the Comfort Inn and indulged in a small bowl of Cheerios. My nerves were so electrically charged that I could only force down a couple bites. Rather than returning to sleep, I wrestled with my dreams, wondering if I was still making the right decision or not. Every time a negative thought entered my head, I immediately tried to contradict it by telling myself I was in the best hands possible and everything was going to be just fine—but what would people really think of me for going through with this? It seemed like I had so much support, but was it real?

Driving on the highway to Kernan Hospital at five o'clock the next morning, it was still dark. Mom and I were both silent. Awkward silence. Yuck. My body was shaking, and my heart felt like it was ready to race down the beltway ahead of us. I knew that if I attempted to utter one syllable I would either throw up or burst into tears. That's not what I wanted to feel, but it was uncontrollable. I reached forward and turned on the radio. My jam was on: "Believe" by Cher. I turned the volume up loud enough to drown out my audible sniffs as I turned my head to gaze out the window and wipe the tears on the sleeve of my sweatshirt.

"Well, I know that I'll get through this. 'Cause I know that I am strong," Cher sang. Hell, yeah. I didn't care if she was singing about life after love. That line right there gave me goosebumps.

We pulled up outside the front of the James Lawrence Kernan Hospital, and Mom dropped me off to wait inside. Hopping out of the Jeep and walking up to the automatic doors, I could feel myself cower at the entrance. Knees weak and eyes welling with tears, I sat on a bench just inside the front doors, hugging Patches the dog, while Mom parked the car. Following Mom, I made my grand entrance into the pre-op office. Sitting in the chair in the waiting room while Mom filled out a bunch of paperwork, I looked down at my legs sticking straight out in front of me.

One day, these two feet of mine will rest on the floor.

"Kristen Dean-drah-day."

I couldn't help but giggle a little bit as the nurse butchered my last name. With what felt like stones in my stomach, I slid off my seat and followed her into the back while Mom finished the remaining paperwork. With the nurses help, I began the process of getting prepped and ready for the operating room. Climbing onto the hospital gurney, the nurse drew the curtain and handed me a folded gown with moon and stars all over it.

Sweet Jesus! This thing is ginormous. One size fits all, huh? I think not.

Handing me a bag for my belongings and a container for my earrings, my pre-op nurse was eyeing the chipped nail polish on my fingers and toes. "That'll have to go, dear," she said as she handed me a little towelette with nail polish remover on it. Apparently, I missed the memo of no nail polish or jewelry in the operating room. Next, she handed me a small plastic cup and pointed to the bathroom. "We need you to pee in the cup."

Seriously? Does she think I have the parts for this job?

There was no way. The look on her face told me that she didn't have time for messing around, so I took the cup and did my best. What a messy job. Boys would clearly have an easier time with this one. My cheeks flushed as I came out of the bathroom with the very warm specimen cup. Once I was all situated back up on the stretcher, another nurse came over, covered me in heated blankets, and went to get Mom in the waiting room.

Numerous people, all who seemed very important, dressed in scrubs with their hospital ID badges dangling from pockets or lanyards around their necks were pacing back and forth in front of my gurney. There was shuffling of paperwork and double-checking of my ID bands. As time wore on, the sense of urgency heightened. I assumed it was nearing time for me to take a ride to the operating room.

The anesthesiologist—whom I grew to love—Dr. Waxman, appeared and very quickly began to explain what was going to happen once I was taken back into the torture chamber. Before I was able to respond with a single word, he held my cheek in his hand. "How are we doing?" he asked.

Shrugging my shoulders, I didn't say a word. Tears were looming with a single thought of the anesthesia. All I could think about was the time that I had tubes put in my ears—the smell, the dizzying effect, and the overall feeling of helplessness did not excite me in the least, but it was nice to know I would be under the watchful eye of Dr. Waxman. I'd only known him for thirty-seven seconds, but I liked him. Picking up some of the paperwork, he said he would return shortly, tickling my feet as he disappeared behind the curtain, causing me to crack a smile.

Refusing an IV, I managed to bargain with one of the OR nurses and told them that I would rather go to sleep with the mask and they could stick me as many times as they wanted to once I was incoherent. After the anesthesia knocked me out, I did not care what was done to me. Believe it or not, needles scared the crap out of me. Ironic, I know, considering my legs were going to be plastered with pins twice the size of any needle by the time surgery was over. Oh, well, what can I say? My final moment of controlled wimpiness, I guess.

To make the experience a little sweeter, if you will, Dr. Waxman returned with the mask he would put me under with and a container of Lip Smackers Chapstick. Interesting, I thought to myself. Was he suggesting that my lips were severely chapped? He told me to pick a flavor. Whatever I chose, he would rub on the inside of the mask, and it would help make the anesthesia gas smell more pleasant. As I took the cap off and carefully sniffed each one, I made my selection: jelly bean.

Now the clock was really ticking. People in greenish-blue scrubs, little booties, and masks over their mouths and noses were in and out of my pod. It felt like a holding cell. A very tall woman with long blonde hair was my next visitor. I recognized her, by the kind smile that swept across her face, as the child life specialist, Marilyn. With hugs for both Mom and me, she handed me a lanyard full of key chains, clearly trying to keep me distracted.

Somehow, my twelve-year-old self felt confident with the team of people I had on my side, even though I didn't know any of them very well. I was also happily informed that Marilyn would be going back with me, which was very comforting. With final signatures to the last few forms, Mom signed her only daughter's life away. One of the operating room nurses released the brake on my gurney and told Mom to say goodbye. To say that neither of us were emotional would be a bold-faced lie. That's when my tears started—after a goodbye kiss and hug from Mom.

As I ride down the hall, still crying and holding Marilyn's hand, one of the nurses slaps a bouffant cap on my head and one on Patches's head. Oh, how great, a girl and her stuffed animal looking like they are ready to go join some meat-packers for a hard day's work. All of the hospital smells are melting together to make a sickening, sterile perfume and my stomach begins to lurch as a wave of nausea rolls over me.

Oh, please, not now.

We come to a rather abrupt stop outside the operating room doors and with permission, I jump down. Standing barefoot in the hall, stuffed doggy under my arm, I stare toward the cold, sterile room and take my last few steps as a little, little girl. As one of the nurses makes her way toward me, with a look that tells me to stop dilly-dallying, I put my hand up, signaling her to stop.

That's right. Who's making the rules now?

Longer legs would no longer—no pun intended—allow me to be a show-off the best way I know how: by sitting down and standing up without bending my knees. This is my last chance. So, I do it—right in the hallway outside of the OR. It just wouldn't be right to go down without raising some eyebrows and smiles. After my little stunt, the same nurse I halted, scoops me up, and places me back on the gurney. The doors swing open and I roll into the brightly lit, cold, sterile room. Draped tables are littered with saws, hammers, and all kinds of hardware. If that isn't intimidating, then I don't know what is.

My last moments being small and broken. Well, maybe not broken, yet. Dr. Paley will literally break me once I am asleep. With my eyes glued to the extensive spread comparable to Dad's workbenches in the basement, the operating room staff transfers me from the gurney onto a very hard, narrow table covered with a white sheet. Someone hands me a small marker and instructs me to mark an X on each leg and foot. I would hope that Dr. Paley doesn't forget what is happening today. Just to be sure he knows that I want both legs operated on, I do as I'm told. Laying back, my head rests on what looks like a brown plastic donut. Looking up into blinding lights, Dr. Waxman moves into view, gazing down at me. Even though his nose and mouth are covered by a mask, I can see in his brown eyes that he is smiling. He places small, round stickers on my chest. They are hooked up to a heart monitor, he explains. Then a small gadget resembling an alligator's mouth with a bright red light clamps onto my right index finger.

Marilyn secures a mask on Patches and snuggles him in next to me as she holds tightly to my left hand. I like that we're in this together.

Warm blankets cover me. More staff in their little hats and masks scurry about. Machines start to beep, and it sounds like someone is rummaging through Mom's cupboard of pots and pans. Scanning the room, my eyes fall upon more heavy machinery on the tables. The surrounding noise begins to drown out the voices. Suddenly I feel really nervous and begin to shake.

Marilyn squeezes my hand tighter.

Tears leave my eyes and roll down my cheeks, pooling in my ears.

She tells me to imagine us on the beach together.

Beep … toes in the cool, blue water, the warm sun on my face.

Beep … Dr. Waxman places the mask over my nose and mouth.

Taking a deep breath, I smell what reminds me of the stale jelly beans left over in my Easter basket from the previous year.

The faces of Marilyn and Dr. Waxman begin to spin.

Beep … I am walking in the uneven sand.

Beep … my entire body is tingling and feels weighted down.

Beep … I can barely keep my eyes open.

Beep … darkness. Out cold.

Meanwhile, in the waiting room, anxiously awaiting Dr. Paley's presence, Mom sat and waited.

After nine hours in the operating room, Dr. Paley was finished. He came out and told her that everything had gone extremely well. However, nothing could have prepared her for what was about to begin.

15

The very next thing I remember, or at least what I think I remember, is feeling extremely groggy. Not just groggy, queasy. And this time, I threw up, multiple times, in the recovery room. An exhausted, gross, disoriented feeling had taken over my body. You know those drunk goggles they have you wear when D.A.R.E. comes to visit your school? Well, I felt like I was wearing a pair of those, except I couldn't take them off. When I opened my mouth and tried to talk, no sound came out. My throat was burning from being intubated. Attempting to keep my eyes open took way too much effort. Hospital staff were talking, peeling blankets off, and then placing warmer ones back onto my body, hooking me up to monitors and IV fluids. My dreamlike state caused me not to care, until it hit me, and I remembered what had just happened: surgery. It was over. My entire body felt heavy with a very dull pain settling in my legs—the intense pain hadn't hit me yet. As I half-opened my eyes to get a peek, I was disappointed when I realized that my legs were hidden. A sudden urge to see my new erector sets had come over me. At that, I made the effort to speak. Still no words would come out. Noticing one of the nurses standing next to my bed, I motioned to get her attention and then pointed to my legs. She understood.

Slowly, she peeled back the blankets so I could catch a glimpse of Dr. Paley's handiwork. Out of nowhere, Mom popped up on the other side of my bed. A look of hurt and disbelief on her face told me that it was a painful masterpiece. Swears were not unfamiliar to me, thanks to driving, especially in Boston traffic with Dad, so I had quite the expansive, forbidden vocabulary. In gazing down at the frames on my legs, my first, audible, post-operative words were "Holy shit!" Both legs were surrounded by titanium erector sets. Small plastic blue caps covered the larger pins. Wires drilled all the way through my heel and ankle suspended my feet within the cages. Blood-soaked gauze was shoved in and around the Ilizarov rings. My legs felt really, very strange. Thanks to the morphine, I wasn't in an immense amount of agony. If anything, I was slightly uncomfortable and still hanging in a cloud of nausea.

Mom is standing over my legs with a horrified look on her face. She looks back over at me, and realizing I'm watching her, she smiles and walks toward the head of my bed. Placing a cool rag on my forehead, she asks what I need. Ice chips are all I want and really all I can tolerate. My throat hurts from being intubated. Even simply swallowing the melted ice feels like I am eating sand. Yummy. My stomach is unsettled, but this morphine? I see a true friendship blooming for the next few days—or as long as the hospital staff allows. Anytime I feel pain, I push the button on the little joystick they gave me. Just having that bit of control makes me feel loads better. Good thing I don't have total control over my morphine dosage since I push that button nearly twenty times a minute.

After an hour or so in recovery, to the point where I can force down some graham crackers and ginger ale with a smile on my face, I am moved to my very own room on the pediatric floor. While in transit, all I could do was stare at my covered legs, knowing all too well what rested beneath the blankets. What in the hell had I gotten myself into? Gazing down at my uncovered toes, my heart sank a little bit. It was sad that I no longer had free motion of either of my feet now that both were fixated in the frames. Wiggling my toes was all I could do; as if I wasn't restricted enough in my mobility. Then something else caught my attention; in addition to the blood all over the place, my legs were painted in a nasty yellowish-orange substance. Betadine, I later learned, was not easily removed from one's skin. From the waist down, I looked like a bottle of sunless tanning cream had exploded on me. Willy Wonka would have been proud.

My little room was much quieter without all the hustle and bustle from pre-op and recovery. My nurse, Akisha, handed me some fancy-looking remote that controlled my very own television. It also had a button on it that connected me to the nurses' station. She told me to page her if I needed anything. My heart leapt a little bit. So this meant that I had people at my every beck and call? Oh boy!

16

Two words: Pin care.

One word: Horrible.

My first experience with this new soon-to-be daily ritual was by far the worst. I can assure you that the previous statement does not contain one ounce of drama.

It's day two and barely 7:00 a.m. Dr. Paley and his rather large entourage come through the door to take a peek at my new hardware. Oh, you know, just chillin' in my bed wired for fun. Dr. P talks to his team as if I am simply a subject under examination and not a young girl sitting right in front of everyone listening to his every word.

Hey! Over here, big guy.

Inquiring as to how I am feeling, he reiterates how well the surgery went and tells me that I have a to-do list of things to accomplish today. This ought to be smashing fun: pin care, physical therapy, and lengthening. Now I'm on high alert. I have surprised myself with how well I'm doing . . . until now. Will someone please pass the Xanax?

Dr. Paley and company exit my room, and all of my energy is channeled into resuming a comfortable resting position in my hospital bed, which I am happy to find can be controlled via my universal remote.

After Mom and I pile pillows and fold blankets, I finally manage to find a position that is the epitome of cozy when two members of Paley's posse, nurses, who both go by Pam, are standing in the doorway, both with a "you're not going to like what we have to say" look on their faces. Cozy feeling—gone. Immediately I know that whatever is about to be thrown at me next is not going to be fun. The duo that stands before me have a way about them that makes me feel a little less uncomfortable with the unknown; their mannerisms, voices and overall presence are gentle. The Pams begin putting small pink bullets of saline solution, gauze, individually wrapped sterile Q-tips, and small circular sponges on the table beside my bed. Time to get down to business. I'm sure my excitement is palpable with the clear knowledge that it is time to clean up my bionic legs via pin care. Following my nurses' suggestion, I take an extra dose of oral pain meds. Before I can even access my pin sites, all the gauze stuck to the open wounds has to be removed. I imagine it'll be comparable to ripping off thirty Band-Aids. Excuse me while I curb my enthusiasm, this is going to be a blast, and much to Mom's disdain, she's got a front-row seat.

Giving another push of the button on the morphine pump should, I think, help take the edge off—on top of the oral meds my nurse just gave me. With my saddest puppy-dog eyes, I look up at the Pams and shrug. How does one proceed?

"You're all right honey," one of them whispers in a very loving tone. "There is nothing to be afraid of."

Oh really? I think to myself. We will see about that.

Before anyone does anything, I get the rundown. Pin care is to be done every day. For the first week or so, the sponges and gauze need to be replaced. Once the sites and incisions heal, I won't need them. Incisions? I have stitches too? Geez. The goal is to keep the sites clean and avoid infection at all cost. Reading the look on Mom's face, as she is ferociously scribbling down notes at the foot of my bed, I can see that it's not one of thrill.

No need to worry, Mom. The only person touching my legs will be me. You're off the hook on this one.

One of the Pams goes back to the clinic, and one stays with me. As she squeezes saline from the pink bullets into a medicine cup, the one Pam and I get further acquainted. We discover that we are birthday buddies. And I soon realize that, I know she is quite special. Her words are gentle; her dark eyes sparkle with compassion. Control. It makes everything better, so I ask Pam if I can do the pin care … all of it. Inflicting pain on myself is much easier than having someone else do it. She agrees.

Together, we soak all the gauze with saline so that it lifts a little more easily from the open sites on my legs. Gently peeling away the bloodstained gauze reveals the pin sites and incisions from where my tibia and fibula were cut. There is blood—lots of it—stitches, staples, and more of that nasty yellow body paint from the OR.

Mom maintains a safe distance in her chair next to the bed with her knitting.

After all the gauze and sponges are gone, Pam opens a package of two sterile Q-tips and places them in a cup that we fill with more saline solution from the little pink bullets. She explains that one swab should be used per pin site to prevent cross-contamination. Noted. Rolling the wooden stick between my fingers, I use the cotton swab to push the skin down away from one of the bigger pins and remove all the crusty stuff. Bleh. And then I realize, there are thirty of these things to be cleaned. Part of me wishes I was a little more prepared. Who can I convince to go snag me some chocolate milk, Dunkaroos, and a bag of Funions, please? It's going to be a while, and I need nourishment.

From what I hear, pin infections are no fun, so if this is the prevention, so be it. As mind-numbing and extremely uncomfortable as it is, I figure this will be the epitome of my excitement for the day. The little wires are more sensitive and cause me to wince with even the slightest touch. I don't remember who said, "What doesn't kill you makes you stronger," but something tells me I am going to be repeating that to myself on a more regular basis.

That day, I realized that expectations are not necessarily a good thing. Immediately following the completion of pin care, I was whooped. I thought I had a little bit of time to rest before item number two was ticked off my list of daily accomplishments. Wrong. That expectation was shattered when two physical therapists walked in the door as soon as my new bestie Pam exited.

My hospital room, a place that most associate with healing, was quickly becoming my own personal torture chamber. There is not much that I remember from my first physical therapy experience other than screaming and crying for a solid hour with the fear of God instilled in my bones. There are no words that could possibly describe the pain I felt. That pain, mixed with fear and complete loss of personal control over the situation, was just too overwhelming. Both women who came in to get me out of bed had failed to notice that the footplates had not been attached to the bottom of the Ilizarov fixators. So, with wires going through each of my feet, I was forced to stand on them. Without acknowledging my resistance or fear, they wrapped a pink "safety" belt around my waist and practically dragged me to the edge of the bed—legs, hardware, and all. Let me tell you, other children and parents on that floor probably thought they were in a psychiatric ward with the amount of screaming and struggling coming from my room. What I would have given to have my own personal Taser.

My white flag isn't waving just yet. I am determined to hold onto what little control I have left. Sorry, ladies, we are moving at my pace now. Slowly, I lift each leg frame and begin to wriggle myself toward the edge of the bed. My mobility now involves an intense upper body workout. Apparently, I'm not moving fast enough, and the women keep attempting to help me. Each time they reach for my legs to speed up the process, I scream, "No!" For fear of falling off the bed completely, I realize I do need their help to hold my legs over the edge of the bed while I scoot my butt to the edge. Delighted to play a role in this fiasco, I promise myself that their hands-on involvement will be short-lived.

The moment I get my bottom to the edge of the bed, they set my legs down with my feet hitting the floor. My world begins to spin. The pain is so intense that my blood begins to boil. I'm sweating, and all the air has suddenly escaped my lungs. I can't scream. Immediately, I sit back down and hoarsely yell for someone to get my legs. This is not going on any longer. Hyperventilating and struggling to take in a full breath, I cross my arms in front of my chest and refuse to move. Given the severity of my frustration, tears, and screaming, the physical therapists retreat, promising to return later this afternoon.

Pssh, try me, ladies. We will see if you succeed in that!

17

After shuffling of pillows, I was once again settled in bed, following my first physical therapy visit, more like total disaster, when there was another knock on the door. Just hearing that sound made me want to throw the sheets over my head and hide. With nowhere to go, I took a deep breath and watched Mom open the door.

I'm pretty sure we were both relieved to have the Pams walk back into my room turned torture chamber. Their smiles and overall demeanor proved they were there to help. And help they did—in a big way.

With hardware and wrenches, they had come to apply footplates to the bottom of my fixators. Due to the wires running through each heel and ankle, it was agonizing to bear weight directly on my feet. By screwing a separate plate onto the bottom of the Ilizarov, leaving my foot suspended within the frame, the weight was distributed throughout the frame and not directly onto my fragile feet, giving me the ability to stand and eventually walk without misery. It sounds complicated, I know. And when you are unfamiliar with the Ilizarov fixators, it can be, but I became comfortable with everything relatively quickly. Really, it's all simple mechanics. The footplate was made out of one ring segment from the Ilizarov with the bottom of a cast shoe screwed onto it. That entire piece was then attached to the bottom ring of my fixator.

Neither of the Pams were happy to hear that I had just gotten out of bed with physical therapy. As it turns out, the physical therapists should have waited until the footplates were in place before making me stand up. *Jerks.*

Dr. Paley would hear about it, and I no longer had to worry. After the hardware angels descended upon my room and worked their magic, my bionic legs were walkable. Physical therapy deserved another shot— tomorrow. This time, it would be outside my room, down in the PT clinic.

The Pams promised me success and said they would be back the following day with another big learning opportunity. When they left my room, I took a deep breath and felt like a whole new girl. Mom had some peace of mind too. Three days post-op, and things were finally starting to look up. Well, almost. If I was going to escape my room and walk, I needed to let go of the IV pain medications. No one likes to be leashed. However, I was willing to walk around tethered to the IV pole if it meant that the super juice was going to continue running through my veins. With that realization, I was hesitant to let go of my liquid flowing leash.

But why? Just one more day? Please?

The IV meds were so lovely and took effect ten times faster than oral meds. In the back of my mind, I knew walking with an IV pole would be a pain in the rear—and I certainly was not allowed to go home with an IV in my arm. To be honest, I don't think I would have been very happy with that either.

Okay. Fine.

My first stab at oral pain meds was an ultimate fail. No more than ten minutes after popping the little white pill that morning, my entire body began to itch. My tongue began to swell. Mom and I were panic-stricken. Furiously hitting the call button, we requested a nurse's presence immediately. Akisha was a doll, and she did everything in her power to make me as comfortable as possible while trying to resolve the allergic reactive mess I was in. Filling a big pink hospital bucket I was gifted upon arrival in my room with ice water and washcloths, Mom began rubbing my body down to help relieve the itching. Then came the IV Benadryl, followed by eventual relief.

Oral meds: 1 Kristen: 0

Attempt two wasn't any more successful than the first. The Tylenol with codeine caused me to vomit—violently.

Oral meds: 2 Kristen: 0

Welcome to my melodramatic life.

I am happy to report that the third time was a charm. We finally found a pain medicine that I wasn't allergic to so I no longer needed my PCA pump. That was my big win for the day, and after all the drama, I was done. It didn't take much to put me down for the count. Untethered from my IV pole, using my hands became much easier, but I was still tied down by the Foley catheter. Getting antsy, I made a gutsy move and told Akisha that I wanted to make an attempt at going to the bathroom on my own—sans Foley catheter. Quickly I realized that meant that someone was going to have to take it out. Talk about awkward. When you're in the hospital, your decency goes out the window. What better way to get acquainted with someone than have them ask you to spread your legs? Getting the Foley removed was just weird; I'll spare you the inappropriate details. After all was said and done, I felt a lot better.

One step closer to freedom!

The pressure was on. I had a few hours to pee on my own. Geez, these hospital people really have high demands. Settle down, folks. Girl doesn't work well under pressure. When I finally got the urge to go to the bathroom again, I made the trek all the way to one side of my bed, scooting my cute bum onto the commode and resting my caged legs on the bed. By the time I actually got myself seated on the commode, I was hurting and out of breath. I'd only shifted a total distance of about two feet in bed, and I hadn't even gone to the bathroom yet.

Enter: stage fright.

I sat on the commode, and everyone in my room was just staring at me: Mom, Akisha, the physical therapist, and the CNA. Kernan Hospital's latest production: Kristen's bathroom exploits. Uh, no. That was just not going to cut it. Everyone out. Mom and Akisha checked and double-checked to make sure that I didn't require any further assistance. I assured them that I would be just fine, and they left the room, turning on the water on their way out.

Is this what quiet sounds like? I almost forgot how beautiful it is.

With the call button close by I sat, and sat, and sat. The more I thought about it, the less I had to pee. So, I turned on the television. A *Full House* rerun? Yes!

Akisha poked her head in, and I told her that I needed more time. Minutes later, after I lost track of time and my task at hand, it happened. I actually peed—a lot!

The dam broke. Yahoo!

By now, I am sure it's obvious that the little things sparked big excitement. After my ethereal or shall I say urethral event, I received some applause and then made the long, slow slog back to the middle of my bed.

Why is it that as soon as I get settled back into a comfortable position, someone comes in demanding I expend energy? Rude, just rude.

It was the morning of day four and my first stop was physical therapy, take two. Surely they were not going to let me out of the room scantily clad. I needed to put some clothing on before I went anywhere. My oversized hospital gown revealing my heinie wasn't a fashion statement I was down with. The next time I showed my face in Kernan Hospital, I did not want to be known as the little exhibitionist. I was tired of that stupid, huge gown anyway. No more getting tangled up in bed between the gown and the sheets.

Good thing Mom came prepared. Being the crafty woman that she is, she came up with the idea to cut one side of my undies and fasten them back together with Velcro. Thinking about it now, they might as well have been a big girl cloth diaper. Mine, with little Keroppi frogs all over them. Desperate times call for desperate measures, and they worked. Some of my shorts were big enough to stretch over the birdcages, and we had to fashion others with Velcro or ties on one side. Oh, to have normal clothes on. What a wondrous thing. Rollin' in style down the halls to the therapy clinic was another big step. Finally, I had escaped my jail cell—er, hospital room.

A young man named Greg was my physical therapist. Having the events of my first encounter with physical therapy fresh in my mind, I was a little hesitant to try again. This guy looked like he was still in high school. He told me that I was in charge, and we were going to move at my pace. I liked him already.

Let's do this.

With brakes on the wheelchair and some assistance from my sweet new crutches, I mustered up the courage and stood on my own two legs for the first time. At first, it was very strange to stand on the frames; my feet were just dangling in midair without a whole lot of pain. Like a little Bambi trying to find her legs for the first time, I was quite wobbly. It took me a minute to figure out how to balance on my new hardware, but after standing with the crutches for a moment, I realized how comfortable I felt and began to shift my weight side to side.

Check it out, people! I'm upright and makin' moves!

And then there were steps. Feeling accomplished with the couple of baby steps I had just taken, my confidence grew even more when Greg had a look of total surprise on his face. His expression was a combination of excitement and shock. I don't think he expected me to walk as well as I did—or he had heard about the PT fiasco a day earlier and was expecting a horror show. Then there was Mom, with the camera snapping pictures and borderline in tears.

It feels so good to be wearing normal clothes—well, my new normal. In order to get underwear, shorts, or pants over the titanium cages, Mom had to get a little creative with her sewing machine. She cut one side of my underwear and sewed Velcro to the two ends. This way, I only have to stretch one side over the fixator; that alone is a chore. For the shorts and pants, it depends on how stretchy they are. Some have one side with ribbons or Velcro, and others have it on both sides. Call it a new fashion trend. Maybe I should put a call into Tommy Hilfiger and see what he thinks.

Anyways, I make myself look as presentable as possible. Just having underwear on instills that "Hey, Kristen, you're still human" feeling. No more tubes allows for an easier transfer out of bed and into my wheelchair. Just to be clear, I move at a sloth's pace. The words fast and quickly no longer exist in my vocabulary when it comes to movement. Mom wheels me down to physical therapy to take a second stab at standing and walking after surgery. When we roll in, the look on Greg's face leads me to believe that he had heard about the events of the day prior.

Cut me some slack, dude. Those ladies got me out of bed before my footplates had been attached to my fixators. You would have made a scene too—trust me.

"All right, missy," he says. "Let's do this." Handing me a set of strange-looking crutches, he sets the brakes on my wheelchair. Noticing the confusion on my face, he shows me how the odd-looking contraptions work. The cuff goes around my upper arm, and I grab a hold of the gray bar down below. Seems easy enough.

Unlatching the leg rests, Greg and Mom swing them out to the side while I hold my legs in midair before easing them to the ground. It's not so bad now that I'm not putting pressure directly on my poor feet.

Before I stand, Greg wraps a belt around my waist. "Just in case," he says with a wink. With a crutch on each arm, I scoot my bum to the edge of my seat. So far, so good. Holding onto the belt, Greg gently guides me forward to stand.

Those two women from yesterday should be here taking notes. Then they can look up the word gentle in the dictionary. Sheesh.

A weird snapping noise distracts my concentration, and I realize that it's Mom with her camera. No more paparazzi, please. All I need is to get blinded by the flash and face-plant. No need for more excitement—the feeling of being vertical is more than enough. My legs don't hurt, but they feel strangely heavy. It takes me a minute to get rid of the wobbles and gain the confidence to take a step forward. My motion is slow and rigid. I imagine the lower part of my body moving similar to Megazord from Power Rangers. Better yet, a transformer. That is what's happening after all: transformation. From my wheelchair, I muscle over to the therapy table and sit down. Feeling like I just walked half a mile, I look up to realize it's maybe eight small steps. Physical therapy is no joke.

After transferring back into my wheelchair and signing off with Greg, Mom and I make our way to occupational therapy. After sitting in my bed for the past couple of days with nothing to do, these are welcome field trips. Dr. Paley had said that I would need to have foot plates made so that I don't get drop foot. Whatever that means, I suppose I am about to find out. It's day four post-op, and I already feel like I am on my way to a medical degree.

Pulling brightly colored squares of plastic from a cabinet, the occupational therapist, Stacy, fans them out in front of me and asks which one I want. Much to my dismay, glitter is not an option. I choose the next best color: neon pink. Taking two squares of the hard, hot pink material, Stacy rolls me over to what looks like one of those big freezers that they keep ice cream in at the convenience stores. It is quite the opposite. When she opens the top, steam billows into the air. Hot water. Taking tongs, she dips the pink squares into the water to heat the plastic-like material, making it malleable. Allowing them to cool off and dry a little bit, she then holds one of them to the ball of my left foot until there is an imprint on it and repeats the process with the right foot. While the foot plates are still soft, Stacy trims them down so that they fit more comfortably within the bottom ring of my fixators. Once hardened, she glues white Velcro straps to the bottom of each foot piece. The long straps loop up and around the top ring on the Ilizarov frames to hold my feet in place. Stacy explains that I have to keep my feet pulled up to prevent nerve complications, especially while lengthening. The stern expression on her face tells me that she isn't kidding. I lock my feet into a comfortable position and feel pretty good about where each of them is resting. Stacy feels otherwise. She undoes the Velcro and cranks my feet right up there.

I let out a tiny yelp and grab tightly to the arms on my wheelchair.

Geez, woman!

18

High as a kite after my successful little field trips, I didn't think my day could get any better as I lay resting in my self-proclaimed chamber of torment.

Knock knock.

Part of me was frustrated to hear that noise. For once, I wanted to do nothing but lay there and rest. A girl can dream. The Pams poke their heads in. Cracking a tired smile, I can't even be upset about their presence. And from the look of the loot they hauled in, it seemed as though they had some fun activities planned. Mom took the opportunity to give herself a break and headed to the cafeteria.

Pam 1 arranged an array of nail polish colors on my bedside table. Time for a mani-pedi? Oh boy! Not exactly. Time to learn how to lengthen my legs? Yes! Pam 2 explained that they came in to decorate my fixators and show me my new, very important job. Hospital Art Class 101 courtesy of the Pams. Using nail polish, colors of my choice, of course, I helped them paint each of the four sides of the threaded screws on my fixators, a different color. Each color represented a time of day: breakfast, lunch, dinner, and bedtime. Using an ordinary wrench, I needed to make a quarter turn on each of the screws four times a day. Pretty colored pieces of tape with arrows indicated the direction I needed to turn. God forbid I turn those things the wrong way! The last thing I wanted to do was shrink. So many screws, so many colors, and only one right direction—this was definitely a multiple-person job. The actual lengthening part looked easy; if this was all I had to be concerned about, I would pass with flying colors. Alas, something told me I wasn't going to get away with anything so easy. My turn schedule was to start the following day. One of the Pams was going to give me a print out with a checklist so I could keep track. And I got excited about a list? Clearly, I am my mother's daughter.

Holding this wrench makes me feel so powerful. Knowing that I am in total control of changing my entire life. Holy cow. Where's my cape? And will someone please cue "Chariots of Fire"? I'm having a moment here.

By now, I was starting to feel like an animal at the zoo. Dr. Paley wanted to keep a watchful eye on his anaphylaxis-prone patient and make sure that the oral pain medicine was not going to suddenly send me into an unexpected reactive state. Bless him. Pain control wasn't the only thing that discharge was dependent upon. I needed to keep drinking lots of fluids, pee, and maintain a decent appetite.

If all goes well today, this little jailbird could break free tomorrow.

And the time came to make my first turns. Using my new best friend, a wrench, together we made magic happen. Following along with the printout I had been given, I made a quarter turn on each of the painted square nuts. Expecting to feel a twinge of something with each turn, it was rather anticlimactic when I didn't experience any sensation at all. Breakfast turns were done. Check!

The excitement continued. While Mom and I were hanging out in the room, there was another knock on the door. Part of be began to think that I was hearing phantom raps on the door. I appreciated everyone's politeness and it was getting really old. You remain in the hospital to heal and get well, yet people are in and out of your room twenty-four hours a day. Expecting another nurse or doctor to waltz into the room, I kept my focus on the television. It was a rare occasion that I could fully commandeer the television remote, and you bet I took full advantage of that while I could. Michelle Tanner and *Full House* reruns required every ounce of my attention.

Mom gasps a long and drawn-out "Oh my God!" as she opens the door, and I hear familiar laughter coming from the hallway. Someone has made a surprise visit. My attention is now drawn to the little alcove by my door.

"Missy-miss! How are you doing?"

It's Suzutte! One of Mom's sisters. Mom comes around the corner crying and following her is my aunt Barbie. Two surprise visitors, all the way from Maine and Colorado—in one day? I'm feeling the love, people.

With so much focus on my plan of care, I know it is a relief for Mom now that she doesn't have to be with me all twenty-four hours of the day. Under the watchful eye of my aunts, she goes back to the hotel to take a nap. The bed there is a capacious and comfy upgrade in comparison to the rollaway sleeper chair that the pediatric ward so graciously provides for their patients' caretakers. I know that any Paley patient parent can vouch for Mom on this one. In the meantime, I am happy to share all of my new medical knowledge with Barbie and Suze. I whip out my wrench and show them how I do my lunchtime turns. Looking at the complexity of the contraptions on my legs, they find it hard to believe that I am doing as well as I am.

Thankfully, my pain had become manageable by Roxicet, oral pain medicine, without any withdrawal from the morphine. With an audience of hospital staff who clearly wasn't going to put up with any of my anti-medicine-taking theatrics, I learned quickly how to buck up and just swallow the disgusting red liquid. The "spare" IV was taken out of my left hand. My appetite had almost returned to normal, and transferring to the commode got easier with each go. These little things were big wins and reasons to celebrate. Compared to my first day after surgery, I had made leaps and bounds. With those victories under my belt, Dr. Paley cleared me to break free and go home. Thank God. As much as I had come to adore my nurses, I needed *out*!

Mom, Suze, and Barbie packed everything up. We made sure that I had my walker, crutches, commode, pin care necessities, and meds before Mom put a final signature on the discharge paperwork. Leaving the parking lot of the James Lawrence Kernan Hospital was a huge relief, but at the same time, it was nerve-racking as hell. It was like I had two new babies to take care of and nurture. The responsibility weighed heavily, and for some reason, I could not help but feel a little sadness upon departure. Perhaps because I was leaving behind my hospital family; everyone who had been taking care of me knew what they were doing. Now my family and I were on our own. Yikes!

The ride home so far has been an interesting one. Despite having the entire back seat to myself, I cannot get comfortable. Whether my legs are propped up sky-high with pillows or not, the status of "happy camper" cannot be achieved. Twenty minutes down, and eight hours to go. Could time be going by any slower? Due to my constant discomfort, we are forced to stop every few hours so that I can reposition my legs. It isn't something I have mastered solo ... yet. I lift the frames while someone maneuvers pillows.

Sue and Barbie are following behind us, available as on-call emotional or physical support. Thank God none of our stops involve me having to go to the bathroom. I'm determined to hold it in the entire trip. There is no way I feel comfortable transferring to a public toilet from my wheelchair. No, thank you. I am telling myself that this whole "riding as a passenger" deal is going to get easier. It better. We will be making this trip every two weeks for x-rays, nerve testing, and to measure my progress. God, please let it get easier.

Flipping through my CD case, I open my Discman, pop a blind choice in, and hit play. B*Witched "Rollercoaster." How fitting—I feel like I'm on one right now.

19

Arriving home to High Street, with Sue and Barbie in tow, Mom and I were greeted by Dad, Derek, and Grammie. Judging by the looks on their faces, I don't think any words could have prepared them for us rolling up, my new erector sets and all. The first order of business was getting me into the house in one piece and a somewhat pain-free manner. My gut told me this might not be possible.

Dad has the wheelchair inside the front door awaiting my heinie's arrival. Slowly, I inch myself to the edge of the back seat. These fixators are magnets for anything they can grab ahold of: seatbelt buckles, cloth upholstery, and even each other. Maneuvering the titanium beasts within a small space is challenging.

No one told me that I should have dabbled in weight lifting prior to surgery to prepare myself for this transferring process. It's a tight squeeze out of the car, so it's just Dad and me on this one. I grab a hold of the second ring down on each of the frames on my legs.

Dad reaches his arms around under my arms and clasps his hands in front of my chest. "You ready?" he asks.

I can hear the hesitation in his voice. I nod and gulp. Picking me up ever so slowly, he steps backward, easing me out of the back seat. It was like a real-life game of Operation—minus the light-up red nose and being naked. Duh. If my legs hit anything, I can assure all within a mile radius that my cry will signal the alarm.

As he slowly lifts me off the seat, I immediately realize just how heavy my legs are. Maintaining my grip becomes a struggle. Once we are clear of the car door, Mom takes a hold of my legs for me. Baby steps all the way from the garage and into the house where my tush finds the wheelchair. The eagle has landed and immediately requests pain medicine. Mental note: medicating will come before any major movement from here on out.

For the first time in almost a week I am able to "bathe." I use that term very loosely. It is more along the lines of a sponge bath than anything else, but it is something. Only a couple more days until I can actually shower. It's mandatory for the sutures to heal prior to any major soaking. It sounds like a silly rule, and I know better than to argue with the professionals.

After my wipe down, I begin the tedious task of pin care since we didn't do it before leaving the hospital this morning. I carefully soak the foam pads and gauze around my stitches and pin sites with saline before carefully removing the debris, cleaning each pin site with a sterile Q-tip, and replacing the glaze and foam pads.

Because my makeshift bedroom is now downstairs, Mom and Dad agree to take turns sleeping on the couch. God forbid something happens, and no one is within earshot to hear their bionic daughter crying wolf.

My own bed. Lord, there is not anything like it. After a far-too-long, agonizing trip home, I was exhausted. Nothing could possibly feel any better than a nice, soft, cushy place to rest my titanium-impaled, aching body. A makeshift bedroom had been fashioned for me, sans privacy, in the sunroom on the first floor because climbing stairs was not an option and wouldn't be for quite some time.

Now out of the hospital setting, it officially sinks in that sleep and I are no longer friends. It is beyond frustrating for a girl who prefers to sleep on her stomach or in the fetal position to be robbed of that luxury. Any position other than on my back is virtually impossible at this point. So here I lay, flat on my back, legs propped up on pillows, eyes wide open. The initial excitement has worn off, and there are no more nurses to help out and no more excuses to be laying wide awake at three o'clock in the morning. When I hurt, I whimper. That's just what I do. Some people cry or punch things or sigh. I whimper. I'm not going to apologize. Sorry, I'm not sorry.

After a week home, my whole sleep schedule has reversed. I nap all day and am awake and in discomfort all night. There isn't much to do during the day besides watch TV, play Nintendo 64, read (yeah right), sleep, and eat when my appetite decides to be present. Transitioning from an active lifestyle to a sedentary one is far from easy. Getting in and out of the house remains quite the chore since my legs are still uber-sensitive and the wheelchair is a pain in the ass for Mom to fold up and transport in and out of the car. We are learning. This has to get easier.

Sending silent prayers to the bicep Gods, I gradually build my upper body strength and learn how to successfully transfer onto the toilet in the bathroom by myself from my wheelchair. Eventually I can wheel myself in, angle my chariot into the precise position, and transfer on and off, no problem, but if I want privacy, someone has to follow me in to close the door behind me and then open it once I'm finished. I never take going to the bathroom by myself for granted. Ever again.

Some people enjoy being waited on hand and foot, but after a week or so, it's gotten old. I need help with everything. Ev-er-y-thing.

Independence is gone.

The adjustment to flying solo at home was an interesting one. Hospitals are quite wheelchair accessible. My parents' house? Not so much. Throughout the course of the day, I could roll from the living room, to the dining room, to the kitchen, to the sunroom if the doors were open and to the bathroom. Can you sense the excitement? Perhaps the biggest challenge was getting over all of Mom's beautifully braided rugs with my hot wheels. Those things were like sand traps, and getting stuck on one caused an eruption of frustration.

Losing my independence was the hardest part for sure. As soon as I began to hold a sense of pride with all that I was able to do by myself, it was gone. Asking for help was difficult before surgery, but it became harder than ever after the fact. There was a little bit of guilt surrounding needing so much attention all the time. Literally, someone had to be at my every beck and call: maintaining privacy in the loo, getting dressed, making meals, brushing my teeth, showering. You get the picture. Assistance was required in all areas of my life. We made do, and I learned to accept the fact that I was going to need a lot of help for a while; it wasn't permanent.

One girly plus to the whole situation was commandeering the downstairs bathroom. A few months before I went under the knife, Dad had it remodeled, complete with a new shower, including a seat and handrails. With the help of a handheld showerhead and a stool for my legs, I remastered the art of showering, with a plethora of intoxicatingly sweet scents, thanks to my favorite spot at the Independence Mall: Bath and Body Works. That first official shower, post-op ... a fly on the wall would have thought they were witnessing the filming of an Herbal Essences commercial. "Ooh! Ah! Yes!" It was that good. Showering was beneficial to myself and those around me. And it was also a little bit of proof that things were gradually getting easier and I was adapting to some of the little bumps in the road.

Breakfast, lunch, dinner, and bedtime became more than just meals and attempted sleep. They were little moments of independent "me" time.

My little wrench resides on a smiley-face lanyard that Marilyn gave me before I was discharged from the hospital. You hear of most kids having an imaginary best friend—mine isn't fictitious. She's tangible, shiny, and a solid figure in my life. Paired with the spreadsheet that I use to mark off all of my turns, my little wrench and I accomplish big things. Initially, I anticipated the turns hurting, but I haven't felt anything yet. One quarter turn isn't that much, really, but four times a day over the course of a week, and then a month, and it all adds up.

20

Trips to Baltimore were now a thing, every two weeks, for routine clinic appointments and nerve testing. I didn't mind at all. In fact, I always looked forward to making the eight-hour trek. Granted, I was not driving, Mom and Dad rotated as my personal chauffeur. Check-ups had become an opportunity to nourish my social butterfly tendencies, meet new people, and simply be in the presence of those who understood me and everything I was going through. Clinic days at Kernan Hospital were crazy! No, crazy is an understatement: they were insane. Dr. Paley and Dr. Herzenberg were pioneers in their field, and it showed in patient attendance on clinic days. My parents' attempts to leave the hospital at a reasonable hour involved arriving at the clinic no later than eight o'clock in the morning—no matter what time our appointment was scheduled. Sometimes that technique was successful, and other times, it backfired miserably, resulting in another night stay in Baltimore.

X-rays were always first on the agenda. Every radiologist in the hospital was knowledgeable and knew exactly what they were dealing with when it came to patients wearing external fixators. The pictures had to be precise so that the new bone growth was visible between the frame and forest of pins and wires.

Amy, my favorite x-ray tech, tells me that I should write a book. A memoir. Every time I see her, we talk about it. Maybe, just maybe ...

After x-rays, we went back into the waiting room and sat. This was fine by me. Marilyn was there with gimp, sand art, beads, and coloring supplies—every arts and crafts addict's dream. At twelve years old, I was surely becoming my mother's daughter. Maybe an hour or so of creating later, I was called in for nerve testing—not my favorite. There was always an underlying hesitation. What if something was wrong?

Anil was the head physical therapist at Kernan Hospital, and he administered the test. Everything was done via the computer. A profile was created for the patient, and all records were kept to ensure there were no indications of nerve damage or further complication. A pressure-specified sensory device with two prongs was used to touch certain areas of my foot ever so lightly. As soon as I felt the device touch my foot, I pushed a button. A computer recorded it. I also had to report whether or not I was feeling one or two prongs. The computer then advised whether or not the patient's nerves are in trouble. Fortunately, I never suffered from any nerve damage throughout any of my operations. To this day, I consider myself very lucky. In the event of nerve aggravation, the patient may need to slow down the rate of distraction, stretching the bone apart, or require a nerve decompression. This is a surgical procedure in which the tissues around the affected nerve are cut to open up a place for the nerve to continue growing. Early detection and immediate treatment are key. Hence the nerve testing at every single clinic visit.

After nerve testing, it was back to the waiting room. After another hour, two, or maybe three—depending on how crazy it was that day—one of the Pams came out to check the struts on my frames. If any were getting close to the end of the threads, we went back into the adjustment room. All the way down the hall, past the examination rooms, it was the last room on the left. Out came the toolboxes and wrenches. Extra bars were inserted into the frame before the original lengthening rods were replaced. The additional rods made sure that the two ends of the bone remained apart and the tension didn't break within the frame. Once the new struts were in place, the new four-sided screws were painted with nail polish and the tape with the little arrow was replaced. Being one-on-one in a room with caring souls who "got it" when it came to my questions, concerns, and little wins was everything to me. Sometimes I wanted those moments in the adjustment room to last for hours. These were my people who made my heart happy.

Ah, yes, you guessed it—back into the waiting room once again. Neither Mom nor Dad were too keen on waiting for hours on end in the clinic. Especially Dad. He was a man of speed and efficiency. If we were still in the clinic around noon, his blood pressure would begin to rise, and his patience level would slowly drop.

I, however, loved when the appointments were long and drawn out. If I could, I would stay all day and socialize with the other kids and parents. An invisible, mutual, compassionate understanding hung in the air at the clinic, and breathing it in gave me a feeling of inclusion that words can hardly touch on. Friendships formed quickly without judgment of any kind. Patients from all over the world were there for different diagnoses seeking the same dose of empathy and expertise from the team at the Maryland Center for Limb Lengthening and Reconstruction. To this day, I remember many of the patients, their parents, and the simple gestures and advice that have held a lasting effect on my heart: Laura, Elliot, Cindy, Holly, Maria, Griffin, Emily, Maddie, Jamal, and Mariela. Whether it was in the hospital, the clinic waiting room, Ronald McDonald House, or physical therapy, I had found a new, ever-growing family of those who understood me in the rawest form. Social play time was cut short as soon as my name was called to be taken back into the exam room to see the big man himself.

Always accompanied by an extravagant entourage of fellows and visiting surgeons, Dr. Paley got right down to business explaining what he saw upon examining the x-rays. Looking at the films on the huge lit display boards was a fascinating part of the visit. Technology is amazing. Even though no real length was visible during my first visit, those were my legs and they were getting longer and straighter by the day. Once I was cleared with a good report and any necessary adjustments were made, I was free to go. After hugs and a few "see you laters" to my favorite nurses and office staff, it was back in the car for eight hours to get back home to Massachusetts.

21

Contractures, spasms, drop foot, achiness, pain, permanent nerve damage—all of these became words I knew I wanted to avoid. As I continued to turn the struts on the Ilizarov frames and the new bone began to grow, the tissue, muscles, and nerves in my legs began to stretch as well. This is where the majority of the discomfort stemmed from, not the lengthening of the bone itself. The only way to prevent pain, tightening of the muscles, and other possible complications was to stay on top of my physical therapy. My very first time attempting this torturous ritual was, well, torture. Since transferring in and out of the car was still a work in progress and getting the wheelchair in and out of the car was quite the ordeal, my physical therapy took place at home on the living room floor with the help of a visiting nurse.

Physical therapy, exercise, infliction of pain—whatever you want to call it—cannot be stressed enough during this lengthening process. Donna, the visiting nurse, came over to the house today to help me with my exercises. I have to do heel slides and straight leg raises to strengthen my muscles so that I won't get any muscle contractures. She is sitting next to me on the floor as I lay on the poop-brown-colored camping mat that Mom got from God knows where in the basement. Holding one hand a good twelve inches above my left foot, she indicates her disapproval of my effort to lift my birdcage to meet her hand.

Ma'am, I don't know if you're aware, but these cages aren't weightless— and you just strap a two-pound weight on top of it all. Your expectations are a wee bit high, don't you think? As I say this to myself, the only thing coming out of my nose and mouth is hot air. My right leg isn't any easier. I'm over it. Someone, get me out of this house. Please.

All of my physical therapy is being done at home because it is too difficult to get in and out of the car right now. It takes me an eternity to maneuver these erector sets. This will change—you have my word. Until that glorious day comes, here I lay, on the poop mat, eyes rolling and attitude raging, watching television, legs out straight with two-pound weights on top of my knees to force them flat. I can't say that I'm a huge fan of this method, but the last thing I want is some sort of complication thrown into this craziness. So, I agree to the cruelty with the utmost sass, which is easily read from the twisted expression on my face. My legs are really sore, especially the skin around the pin sites. With each turn I make during the day to lengthen, the soft tissues and muscles are getting tight. It is very uncomfortable. Hmm, no. It's more than uncomfortable. It's vindictive.

Much to my dismay, I was given a list of exercises during my first consult with the home health nurse. Not even two weeks after surgery, and I already had homework. *Yuck. Newsflash, people. School is out for this little lady.* The exercises had to be done daily to keep the muscles and surrounding tissues in my legs loose and limber. When I was just sitting around the house, cruising in my hot wheels, I had to refrain from keeping my knees bent and force them out straight. That sounds easier than it really was. Keeping my knees in extension was extremely difficult. Those little hot pink footplates had to be kept tight, putting my foot at a ninety-degree angle so that I didn't develop "drop foot." Half of the terminology constantly being thrown around hardly made sense to me, but I knew the good words from the bad and did what I could to stay on top of things.

My first major appearance out of the house after my operation, aside from my first follow-up appointment, was sixth grade promotion night. Skeptical about whether or not I was going to make it through the entire ceremony, I decided I would just have to put my best foot forward—well, wheels actually. It was my special night, and I planned on riding in style, via wheelchair, of course. Sitting among all of my peers as we made the giant step from elementary to middle school was kind of awesome. It was also a mini reunion since I hadn't seen any of my classmates and teachers in nearly a month.

Looking back, I'm not really sure how I even managed to make it there in one piece. Parked alongside the stage, when my name was called, I rolled into the middle of the floor in our cafeteria to receive my "diploma" and yearbook from Mrs. Valeri, and that was it. I was no longer an elementary student.

As excited as I was to move on to bigger and better things, it was also very sad and a little bit scary. Sixth grade had been a pivotal time in my life. I found myself among a great group of friends, I made leaps and bounds academically, and I discovered more about myself than I had ever known: the bright, sassy, loving little spitfire spirit that resided in me. Truthfully, I can attribute most of that to Mrs. Valeri; an extraordinary individual, she never accepted anything but the best from me. All the more reason why I found the strength to be there on promotion night in a wheelchair with a big smile on my face. If anyone could do it, I could—and I wasn't about to let a few extra pounds of titanium hold me back.

After the ceremony, we started talking to Brenda, the mom of one of my classmates who also happened to be the director of physical therapy at a small clinic in the next town over from us, Duxbury. Hearing the possibility of making a daily escape out of the house for a few hours during the week gave me the motivation to ace being able to transfer in and out of the car. Since Dad wasn't there during the day to lift me in and out of the car like he had been doing, it was all up to me. There was one teensy problem: since Dad had been carrying the wheelchair from the car into the house and then doing the same with me, we needed a way to get me and the wheelchair in or out with as little effort as possible. Closing my eyes, I had this horrific vision of my wheels and I rolling not so gracefully down the stairs and landing in a tangled heap at the bottom of the steps. No, thank you.

Being the handyman that he is, Dad hopped to it and built a ramp in the garage. A bit steep, as he only had so much room to work with, it made me shake in my britches the first few times I was wheeled up and down that thing. Just in case the person at the helm lost control and let go of me, I kept my hands on the brakes at all times. Precious cargo shall take no chances.

Eventually, Mom and I felt comfortable enough with our dry runs of ascending and descending the ramp and transferring in and out of the car to schedule my evaluation appointment with Brenda at New England Sports and Orthopedic Therapy. I was ready to have more of an agenda; I had places to go and people to see. And no more exercises on the poop brown mat!

22

Another two weeks passed, and we went back to Baltimore to monitor progress and make sure I was continuing down the right path without any speed bumps in sight. My itinerary was the usual: x-rays, nerve testing, and appointment with Dr. Paley. While in the exam room at Kernan, Dr. Paley asked about my pain levels as he put my x-rays on one of the lit display boards. So far, my pain tolerance was great during the day: I was taking pain medicine on an as-needed basis, and most of the time, I opted out of taking any at all. Unless the medicine tasted like chocolate or bubblegum, I didn't want anything to do with it. Horse pills were also out of the question. Achiness was something I could handle. Consuming anything I deemed inedible was not, and still isn't, my thing. If I can avoid it at all costs, then I will. That seemed fine by him. Sleep was still difficult to come by. He suggested I take something before bed to help me catch a few more Zs at night.

Looking at my scans, he took a pencil and made a small mark where the gaps of new bone growth were in my lower legs. Since each leg was a double-level lengthening, I had two gaps of new growth in each the right and the left. It had been a month, and I could see the length I had already gained. One inch. One of the fellows, George, took a pen and marked out those same gaps on my legs. This put everything in perspective. Wow. No words at that moment could have possibly described the rush of emotions I felt. All the speed bumps I had hit in my life no longer mattered. It was truly amazing. When you make the commitment to go through such a drastic procedure, it is comforting to see results so early. Right then, I began to live in the moment, to live for every inch and ounce of straight bone that was forming. Though my progress at this point was barely visible, that small margin of length and improvement was a defining moment for me.

Holy cow. I'm growing. Not only that, if you look really, really closely, you can see that my legs are even a little bit straighter. I never even noticed until Dr. Paley measured the gap of new bone on my x-rays in the clinic today. He told me an inch a month, and the man wasn't lying. For the first time since surgery I feel like all the sacrifice and boredom are actually paying off. It's better than awesome.

Speaking of boredom, desperate times called for desperate measures in that department. One afternoon, while sitting at home doing my usual bit of nothing, painting my nails seemed like a great way to pass the time. Looking at my hefty supply of nail polish and then at the Ilizarov frames on my legs, I had a sudden spark of creativity. Tired of the same old ugly black titanium frames and blue pin caps day after day, I decided that could change. Right then. So, with a little nail polish—correction, with a lot of nail polish—and a channeling of my inner creator, I turned my caged legs into works of art. Picasso and Van Gogh would have been so proud. Glitter, flowers, stripes, swirls, animals, and polka dots in every color you could possibly imagine. Every titanium ring, pin cap, and even my pink footplates—no surface went untouched. My legs looked much girlier after I was through with them. Thanks to my artistic flair, my legs began to attract attention for more than just the gore factor.

23

The ever-so-familiar word *complication* hit home about two months into the lengthening process. One evening after my more-than-lengthy shower, without warning, I discovered what *pre-consolidation* was.

Dad always threatens to make the water bill my responsibility with the amount of time I spend in the shower. Listen, if you had to meticulously care for bionic legs, you'd be taking your sweet-ass time too. Once I finish making my nightly contribution to the monthly H_2O payment, and manage to get my pajamas on, I am ready to be carried into my bedroom to do pin care. Same as always, Dad comes in and picks me up under my arms to transfer me into my room. In transition, as I hold my legs, I begin to feel an intense pressure building up in my left leg. With each passing second, it becomes more and more aggressive. I start to whine hesitantly. Something is happening, and it's too fast for me to figure out how to react. It feels like my left leg is in a vise grip, and the pressure is reaching a point I can no longer bear. As Dad pivots in the doorway, the pressure seems to subside for a millisecond; then, there is a loud pop. Thinking he had hit my leg against the doorframe, Dad yells, "Sorry! Sorry! Sorry!"

Accompanied by my hysterical screaming, the pop causes an immediate and powerful surge of agonizing pain. Two of the pins by my left knee start to bleed. Crying to the point of being speechless, I am too hysterical to even force out the words to tell Mom and Dad anything. They still think I hit my leg on the doorframe. All three of us are panicking. Catching my breath, I explain that my leg didn't hit anything—and the horrific noise came from my bone. Mom immediately calls the hospital. After conferring with Dr. Paley, the doctor on call says that it is most likely pre-consolidation.

What in the hell is that?

It turned out that pre-consolidation occurs when the new bone grows faster than expected, and the two ends actually fuse together. By lengthening, the bone is rebroken. That certainly sounded like what had just happened.

I broke ... my own ... leg. How wonderful!

We literally had just returned from an appointment in Baltimore, and Mom and I were back in the car again the next morning. Dr. Paley said it was imperative that we come for a consult to make sure everything was all right after the break. Also, in order to relieve the pain I was having, the struts on the Ilizarov frame had to be turned backward to help reduce tension. Needless to say, pain medicine was riding shotgun with me on that emergency trip to Maryland.

Per the usual at clinic appointments, I am in for x-rays first thing, but this time, there is a sense of urgency—and everything goes a tad quicker. The pictures confirm that I had indeed rebroken my left leg by lengthening and, shockingly, I have pre-consolidation in my right leg, too. How fantastic. Just the news I was hoping to receive. Not!

Three choices are what I am given. One: I can stay in Baltimore until the right leg breaks from me resuming my usual lengthening schedule, then come in to clinic and have the fixator turned backward and the tension relieved. Two: I go home and break the bone, and then turn the frame back myself the way I had been shown. Three: I have the bone surgically broken.

Surgery is a definite no-no. Anesthesia and that whole mess? Totally out of the question. Since I am no veteran, and don't trust myself to correctly turn back the frame and no one aside from a trained medical professional will be laying a finger on my legs, I opt to go back to the Ronald McDonald House in downtown Baltimore, home away from home, and return to the hospital after my leg breaks. Just in case something goes terribly wrong, we want to be close by. Knowing that my favorite nurse, Pam, is only a phone call away takes the fear factor down a wee bit.

I am sitting on the bed in the house just waiting for the other shoe to drop ... er ... leg to break. What the hell am I thinking? Is this what they refer to as bad karma? Pain is inevitable. Been there, done that already, but I have no idea when the break is going to happen, which is the most daunting thing. This suspense might actually kill me.

A guardian angel was certainly watching over Mom and me that night. While in the community kitchen in the Ronald McDonald House, we met another patient of Dr. Paley's, Elliot, and his mom, Cindy, who happened to be a nurse. After explaining our predicament, Cindy offered to help in any way she could. Oddly enough, she and Elliot were in the room next door.

At three o'clock in the morning, I startled awake to a loud pop and sleep-severing pain. My right leg was broken. Was it a nightmare? Nope. Real life. Considerately, my big mouth probably woke up the whole hallway because Cindy immediately knocked on our door. Pain pills already popped, she came in to help make sure that everything was as tolerable as it could be and situate me so Mom and I could go back to bed. Bless her heart.

First thing the following morning, back to James Lawrence Kernan Hospital to have the slack taken up in the frame and ease the discomfort unsolved by Roxicet. X-rays again confirmed what we already knew. However, there was a new wrench in the situation. It looked as if my left leg was only partially broken.

I'm sorry. What? Partially broken, as in it's going to happen again? No, no. Not possible.

Two complications under my belt, and now I was facing a third. Was the universe trying to send me some sort of message? Turn back? No, I don't play that way. Second thoughts about the whole decision to go through with the lengthening tried creeping their way into my mind, and I fought mercilessly to keep them at bay. Nearing my teenage years, I surely thought I'd qualify for entry into the Guinness Book of World Records as the youngest girl to have gray hair.

The plus side to the whole pre-consolidation disaster was our super-extended stay in Maryland. Since we were going to be there longer than expected and I required physical therapy at least five days a week, they squeezed me into the schedule to work with the talented therapists at the Kennedy Krieger Institute. And they had a pool.

There is a God.

Other kids with external fixators in wheelchairs my age are here at Kennedy Krieger going through similar pain and setbacks. We all yelp out in discomfort as the e-stim machines electrocute our muscles awake and hold hands as we lay on our stomachs for knee bends.

Never in a million years would I admit in the moment to loving the torture, but a little piece of me did. It's safe to say it now. The attention was welcome, and the therapists there were stellar. They worked with limb lengthening and reconstruction patients every day and knew the proper techniques and exercises appropriate for each individual. In my mind, I was convinced that it was suitable for me to become a permanent fixture there. Between land and water sessions, I ate lunch with my friends. We were able to act like kids, forgetting about the fact that we were dragging around ten extra pounds of titanium and hardware.

The cherry on top of it all was most definitely the pool. Therapy or not, in the water, I was weightless. My family would always tease me about how I practically lived in the water, calling me a little fish, though I prefer a mermaid, so it's obvious that the pool would be best thing for me. The only issue that stood before me was the fact that I did not bring a bathing suit with me to Baltimore. We had some trouble finding one that would fit over the ginormous cages encasing my lower legs. That was until we came across bikini bottoms that tied. Genius. Thank you, Old Navy. Bathing suit issue solved.

But how on earth am I going to get into the pool? I'll get into a tangled mess of hardware if I attempt a ladder. I don't think both legs will even fit through the bars. Jumping in will result into more of a belly flop turned 911 call to the Baltimore EMS for a patient who has sunk to the deep end of the pool. Stairs seem like the obvious choice, but I haven't tackled one stair on land yet. No need to worry, Kennedy Krieger has it all figured out. I show up in my sweet little glitter bikini number and they have a cute little chair that takes me from the side of the pool into the shallow end. A patient forklift of sorts. And a free ride at that! My therapist straps a floatation belt on me, and I scoot off the chair. The water is so warm, and I have a complete aha moment. I don't sink. I float effortlessly in the water. I feel weightless. After sitting on my tushie, day in and day out, for the past couple of months, it feels so good to be vertical. My tailbone is more than delighted. Being weightless in the water allows me to move around without the ache of weight bearing.

My aqua glory was short-lived. After both legs had fully broken from pre-consolidation and I was granted permission to resume my lengthening schedule, it was time to drive north to Massachusetts. Now my little adolescent heart was broken. Everyone at MCLLR and Kennedy Krieger had become more like family than anything else over the course of five short days. There were friendships made that, until then, I had been unfamiliar with. They were friends who understood my ups and downs, down to every last inanimate detail, and now I was forced to leave them behind. As we drove out of the city, on the ever-familiar I-95, I began the countdown to our next two-week checkup.

24

You would think a girl could catch a break after a crazy stint with, not one, not two, but three instances of pre-consolidation. Yeah, not so much. Not long after we returned home from the bone-breaking debacle in Baltimore, I started to feel downright yucky. My skin was clammy, and I moved between fever and chills. There I was, face-to-face with another round of complications: pin infections. Go. Me. I can truthfully say that I took excellent care of my pin sites starting on day one. Every night, Mom or Dad would make saline solution in a little pot on the stove. Using sterile Q-tips, I cleaned each individual pin site. You can imagine how long that took, with a total of thirty pins and wires. Time-consuming and tedious at best, I knew I had to do it to avoid infection. Unfortunately, that ritual only lasted a few months, and then I started to get pin infections left and right. The infected site hurt like a "mother-trucker," if you know what I mean. Redness, swelling, tenderness, and drainage accompanied by 24/7 ickiness. A culture at the local medical center confirmed infection. Then came my favorite part: antibiotics.

As if the infection itself wasn't enough, the antibiotics were a whole other story. Those tiny little pills made me feel even more like shit. A ten-day course of antibiotics made me feel like I was suffering from the flu for the entire ten days. Don't get me wrong, I am thankful that I had them to help fight the infection, but the whole experience was just miserable.

It doesn't make any sense. I do pin care every freakin' night before bed. One sterile Q-tip with saline for each individual pin. This is in addition to showering! So how on earth do I get three—yes three—pin infections at once? And right after we get back from Baltimore, no less. Keflex is the antibiotic they prescribe, and it is gross. Every time I take that little red and gray pill, I swear it makes me feel worse. Swallowing pills isn't my forte either. We know this by now. It takes me five or six tries before I can actually get the pill down. Even then, it feels like the damn thing is lodged in my airway and not even my esophagus. Twice a day for ten days, I have to pop these antibiotics and be vigilant about keeping my pin sites clean.

Oh, hey. Me again. And now I'm on my sixth (?) infection. It has gotten to the point where I feel like I have been on antibiotics for months straight. I might as well make them a food group. Is it something I am doing wrong? Am I a failure?

Frustrated and upset, I racked my brain for the next best option. Stage a rebellion? Sounded like a plan to me. Rather than swallow the antibiotics with my meals like a good girl, I begin hiding them. One of my favorite spots is in Mom's potted plants. Don't worry, I have already patted myself on the back for this one. Stealthily, I wheel by one of Mom's forty-seven house plants and push the little pill right into the soil. It's important to keep a mental log of which plants have already been medicated so I don't cause a botanical overdose. You have to admit, it's a borderline genius idea, right? (Sorry, Mom.) For the days where I prefer a lack of effort, I simply wrap the pills up in my dirty napkin at meal time and make sure they go in the trash still hidden.

Three months into the lengthening, and I am internally pleading with my body to cooperate.

I am in position on the recliner, which is already showing signs of wear and tear from the birdcages, when Mom comes into the living room with a huge plastic storage bin and drops it on the floor in front of where I was sitting.

I am confused. Have I been that much of a pain in the ass that she wants to pack me away and throw me up in the attic? Ha. Not yet.

Since pin care with saline solution clearly wasn't working, we were going to try something a little different. I put one of my titanium-impaled legs into the bin and began pouring pitchers of warm water mixed with Victoria's Secret "Love Spell" body wash all over them. Yes, Victoria's Secret and not some antibacterial soap. I know what you're thinking, but it was all we had at the time—and it seemed better than our homemade saline. After one leg had a fragrant cleansing bath, I repeated the process with the other. After a few weeks of this strange regimen, done every night before bed, my pin infections completely disappeared. We made an executive decision and scrapped the saline solution altogether.

Most women praise Victoria's Secret for their extravagant lingerie, push-up bras, and sexy little nightgowns. Not me. Their body wash was a blessing. Not only was I infection free, but every night I went to bed smelling like I had just gone tumbling through a field of wildflowers. Finally, a winning moment, and I don't think we even let Dr. Paley in on it.

Our little secret—and Victoria's too.

25

By mid-August, I found myself antsy and hardly able to enjoy the last of the summer weather. Taking up space on the couch, playing *Banjo-Kazooie* on N64 while indulging in a BLT and some Ovaltine was of no interest to me anymore. Staring at the computer screen for hours on end playing solitaire started giving me dizzy spells.

Thank goodness we did have the pool in the backyard. Although swimming was quite the project altogether. Someone had to wheel me onto the back porch and get me onto a chaise lounge, which I would scoot off of to the edge of the pool. Then someone needed to be in the pool to hold my legs while I lowered myself into the water. I should probably mention that swimmies or some sort of inflatable were a necessity since I would otherwise sink to the bottom of the pool like a ton of bricks—and the water was over my head. We weren't equipped with the floatation belts like Kennedy Krieger in Maryland. Regardless, it was good exercise, a healthy dose of vitamin D, and a way to spend some time with friends.

Still, sitting around the house in Massachusetts continued to drive me crazy. If I didn't have ants in my pants before, I certainly did now. With the stipulation that I remained vigilant with my physical therapy, it was time for a road trip, so off to "Camp" we went; our cabin up on Little Sebago lake in Raymond, Maine. Mom and Dad bought it when I was six years old from Mr. and Mrs. Rogers, an elderly couple. After meeting Derek and me, they decided we were the perfect family to call the little one-story box on the lake home.

Despite my very limited mobility, the change of scenery was perfect and exactly what my mind and heart had been craving. We had family and friends who planned on coming up to visit, too. Nothing and no person was going to stop me from swimming, making s'mores, fishing, and going for a cruise in the boat, with some lifting assistance, of course.

Mmmm. Lob-stah and Italian sandwiches! My belly can hardly wait! There is something about crossing over the Piscatiqua River Bridge, into the state of Maine, that just gives me goosebumps. Maine is a special place to visit and has been ever since I was a baby. Mimi, Grampie Dick, and Suzutte live here. This trip is a big deal. Aside from our weekly trips to Baltimore, it is my first big excursion since my surgery. As soon as we cross into Maine, a newfound feeling of accomplishment settles in my chest, and it grows a little broader with pride. Mom's affinity for Maine is rubbing off on me. She swears that the air is sweeter and the drivers are more courteous up here. Dad begs to differ. Rolling down the window after we cross the bridge, I stick my head out as we pass the big blue sign: Welcome to Maine: The Way Life Should Be.

You know it!

When we get to Camp, the whole fam is here, and we run into our first major problem: how in the world am I going to actually get in the house? We don't have a ramp for the wheelchair, and there are stairs all around. An ATV would be very helpful. Good thing there are strong men in my family willing to haul my ass all over the place. Getting inside turns out to be easier than I expect. With the teamwork of Dad and Uncle Tom, they carry me up the front steps while I remain sitting in the wheelchair. Once inside, we all look at each other with questionable expressions. The confines of the small house make it pretty pointless to even have the wheelchair inside. I transfer onto the couch and Dad eases my chair down the three big stairs, out the slider, and onto the big covered porch.

My heart sinks a little. So badly, I want to jump up and make a beeline for the lake. I imagine my feet thumping on the soft grass down the hill and pulling my body into an underdog as I hit the shallow water. Not this year, but next summer, I'll be taking off down that same hill on longer legs. For now, I settle with slowly rolling down to the lake in my black chariot.

Once dockside, Uncle Tom lifts me out of my chair and into the bow of our Bayliner. As the engine rumbles to a start, so does my stomach. Maine in the summer means lob-stah and steamers. Tonight, we feast! Auntie Barbie is here and she is a very talented cook and baker. I'm sure she's creating something deliciously sweet for dessert.

Taking off down the lake, the wind in my hair, the smile is impossible to take from my face. This is what I look forward to every summer. Derek is bringing up the rear in the tube, towed ruthlessly in circles and over waves behind the boat. That tube wouldn't stand a chance against me and the legs. It'd be deflated before I could say go!

Everyone is working really hard to help me have as much fun as possible. When we stop off at Spider Island, I am amazed at how carefree I feel. Probably because I am doing things that I love when I think of the summertime. And for those moments that I forget being weighed down by the fixators, they can remain forgotten. Swimming in fresh water with open pin sites is not advised, but that is the last of my worries. With the help of a few noodles, I carelessly float alongside the boat off of the sandbar. I have to be very careful swimming though. Knowing how pin infections are not fun and a very common occurrence for me, an immediate rinse off is mandatory for my legs. Bacteria is more common in fresh water than the ocean. Sitting on the platform off the back of the boat, Mom whips out a juice jug full of clean water. Always prepared, she is. I give each of my legs a quick rinse, knowing that the Tupperware bins and Vicki's body wash await me at the house.

Careful not to get too tight while on vacation, we enlist the help of a visiting nurse who comes to Camp to help me with my physical therapy. I am skeptical. Her name is Barbara. She is an older lady with gray hair and glasses. Quickly I learn that looks are very deceiving and I like her a lot more than the other woman who came to the house in Pembroke. On one of her hands, she is missing her pinkie. It doesn't even faze her. I think it's kind of cool; we all have a story to tell. Today she even got me up on crutches and walking. The most exciting part is that my whole family is in the living room watching me do it. The distance is short, and I am pretty wobbly. No more wheelchair in the house, period. That is the new rule. I'm okay with it.

Despite my exciting moments of freedom on the lake, my spirits were strained. One evening in particular, the frustration was palpable. The advice from family—focus on the positive, be grateful for what you have—it wasn't helpful. I'd hit a low point, a very, very low point. Not being able to just get up and walk down to the beach, jumping off the dock to swim, or get towed behind the boat waterskiing was overly maddening. For some reason, no one else seemed to understand why I was having such a hard time grasping my inabilities. My outer shell enveloping the hurt, disappointment, and sadness was cracked. My emotions were seeping through and became too much to ignore. I had no choice but to feel, fully.

Call it what you will, a twelve-year-old temper tantrum of sorts. No hug or statement of, "everything is going to be okay," was going to help. I didn't want to talk about it. What I needed was a release. Everything negative had been building up—the negative outweighing the positive—and so, the emotions began erupting out of my being. All I could do was act out. I wanted to cry, to let go of the unconscious, unrecognized pain that had been building up inside of me.

Sitting on the bottom bunk, slightly hunched, as the top of my head grazes the boards above me, I request the door to the bedroom be closed. Reaching through the erector sets drilled into each of my legs, I grasp each calf in my hands and give a gentle squeeze. The tears on my cheeks are hot, and I bow my head to rest on the top rings, warm tears falling from my eyes onto my legs. My mind is whirring, and I can't quiet it down. I blindly feel around behind me for my pillow. Meeting Hello Kitty eye to eye, I place my face on hers and scream. My lungs expand with every breath I take in and twang in my chest when I have nothing left.

I'm angry, and for a moment, I begin to spiral out of control. I don't want this anymore. Taking the wrench, my best friend for the past three months, the tool that has lengthened my legs three inches already, I fit it to one of the top bolts and tug, trying to unscrew and take apart my fixator. I'm done.

Hysterical, my strength is minimal (thank God), and I fail to loosen the hardware or inflict any damage. Laying in a helpless pile on the bottom bunk bed, my tank on empty, the noise in my head lessens. Am I acting like a baby? I decide no. I'm human, and I have every right to feel my feelings.

Now it's up to me to change my thoughts. There is a light at the end of the tunnel. Currently flickering in the distance, but I know it's there. Never in my life have I been a quitter, and now certainly is not the time to give in.

That night, I defined life on my own terms. This was my decision. It was not going to be easy, and this was just the beginning. My longing to prove my free-spirited ferocity was not about to stop there.

🐍 26 🐍

Departing for yet another trip down to see Dr. Paley before school started, and I swear I could have gotten us there with my eyes closed. Mom and Dad switched off with travel duties because someone needed to stay home with Derek. Once in Baltimore, it was the same familiar routine: x-rays, nerve testing, and waiting.

In the examination room, Dr. Paley said that he wasn't happy with the angle of my feet. He explained that the muscles were beginning to weaken, and my nerves showed signs of irritation. What I wanted to shy away from was drop foot. Drop foot? That sounded like the name of a large primate. What in Pete's sake was he talking about? He clarified that if I was not careful about keeping my foot splints on, he would have to go in and surgically release my Achilles tendon and potentially do a nerve decompression. One mention of surgery, and my ears perked up. There was no way I was going back into that operating room unless it was for removal of these silly apparatuses.

Crank up the foot splints! Something told me that more rigorous physical therapy awaited me with that report from the doc. And now with surgery as a threat, hanging over my head, I was going to do everything in my power to avoid going back under anesthesia.

Nothing about keeping my muscles loose and stretched out was easy. Dr. Paley wanted my knees to bend, but he also wanted to make sure they did not stay bent constantly for fear of a contracture. It was confusing to me because it hurt to keep them so straight all the time. All they wanted to do was bend. Go too far, though, and that hurt too. Looking back, staying loose was one of the hardest things I had to deal with. The more length I gained, the tighter my muscles and ligaments became.

This whole therapy out of the house thing—I like it. No, I love it. I have an agenda. After my last appointment with Dr. Paley, I'm slightly nervous about possibly having to go in for a decompression or tendon release. He gave me a sheet to give to Brenda and the girls at therapy. The looks on their faces read something along the lines of "game on." Yikes?

If I am going to pull through all of this and more rigorous physical therapy is what I need, something tells me that I am in the right place. The Ilizarov frames are new territory for the ladies of New England Sports and Orthopedic Therapy, and they welcome me with open arms. Since I have only really had an evaluation and one or two visits before we left for Maine, these girls are just getting started.

Adam Sandler would be proud of the can of "whoop-ass" they open on me.

Each visit starts with electrical stimulation and heat on my quads, front and back. Sounds like an easy, relaxing start to the visit, right? You know when your leg falls asleep and you get pins and needles? Imagine that, times a thousand, so intense that it elicits a contraction in your muscle, and despite that, your therapist continues to turn up the intensity until you begin to shriek. Every. Time. Not so relaxing.

Then my exercises begin: heel slides, straight leg raises, quad sets, knee bends, and more. If left alone for too long, my attention wanders. My counting begins 1 ... 2 ... 3 ... 4 ... oh, look at the birds out the window ... 8 ... 9 ... new friends to talk to ... 19 ... 20. Done! Fool them once, and I get away with it. Fool them five times, and it becomes two sets of twenty—not one.

My behavior and ability to follow simple rules on a particular day seemed to determine the level of gentleness bestowed upon me by my torturer. I mean, who doesn't love some heated lotion and massage? That was my favorite part of therapy. And then the not-so-fun part: scooting to the edge of the table until my legs were totally off of the blue leather surface with a therapist holding both fixators suspended in midair, I turned my upper body around, grabbed the edges of the table and twisted my lower body around to follow and drag myself back up onto the table as someone juggled my erector sets. Now positioned on my belly, finding a comfortable position was a bit more challenging. The Ilizarov rings and pins were awkward. Placing towel rolls under my hips and knees helped alleviate some of the discomfort.

With one leg straight out on the table, Brenda picks up my other fixator, bending my knee to ninety degrees—not so bad. As she pushes further, my death grip on the table strengthens, causing my knuckles to turn white. Burying my face into the white paper pillowcase, I let out a muffled scream. This is the worst part of therapy.

A lot of the time, I leave feeling like a new person, but everyone has their days. Sometimes, after being pushed really hard, I find myself in tears. Everyone here at PT goes beyond their duty as therapist or aide—they are friends. Actually, they are family. They understand my bad days and the frustration of everything involved with the surgery. Let me tell you, being accepted for all that you are, no matter what that looks like, is one of the greatest feelings in the world.

Physical therapy and I had what you could call a love-hate relationship. Those guys pushed me to my limits with stretching and exercises up the wazoo, partly to keep me out of trouble. And yet each and every person took their time with me during each appointment to address any pain I was having, whether it was physical or emotional. They even tolerated my antics. When you tie one end of a Theraband to each fixator, sit in a straddle, put your socks in a ball, place them in the middle of the Theraband, carefully choose your target, pull back, and then release, you have your very own slingshot. I found that the more resistance on the Theraband the farther my ammo would go. Black Therabands proved to be the most effective.

27

Before summer was officially over, Mom and I decided to make one last fun trip. No, not to Baltimore. This time, we were headed to New York to see the Taddeos, the family that we met back in Maryland when Monica and I were patients of Dr. Kopits. Recently, Gerri and Mom had been in touch. Monica was considering having the lengthening surgery done, and they all had many questions and concerns regarding the surgery. Lucky them, they were about to witness firsthand what the process entailed.

The drive was a mere four hours, through western Massachusetts and up to New York; it was a piece of cake compared to the eight-hour haul to Baltimore. It'd been years since we had seen them, yet it felt like just yesterday. Despite being in a wheelchair, getting into the house wasn't an issue. Using a piece of plywood as a makeshift ramp Frank made it look easy. Now that I was walking around a little bit, my crutches came in handy. I was able to get up and hobble around the house. The whole gang marveled at the contraptions on my legs and at how much longer and straighter my legs already appeared. While Mom chatted with Frank and Gerri, Monica, Adrienne, Joey, and I spent some quality "kid" time together.

An in-ground pool fuels a whole lot of fun for four kids. Getting in and out of the pool is a piece of cake now that I am a seasoned veteran, but a pool with a shallow end? I die. I can walk unassisted for the first time ever since surgery. Of course, while in the pool, Mom urges me to squeeze in some physical therapy at the same time. Cue the eyes rolling. Okay, okay, Ma.

For dinner, we cook burgers and hot dogs on the grill. Us kids, we just laugh—a whole lot. It could have been the Ace Ventura reenactment courtesy of Joey or the endless bathroom humor at the dinner table. Sometimes I wonder if the Ilizarovs are wired for immaturity.

After dinner, we all pile into their white minivan and go out for ice cream, convincing the parental units that we need to rent a movie too. Every girl's obsession: Spice World. Poor Joey. He does not "wannabe" part of this movie night. (See what I did there?) He is outnumbered by us gals, fair and square. Mom and I bunk up on the pull-out couch, and for the first time in a long time, I actually get some sleep.

This morning, Frank treats us to doughnuts for breakfast—because that's exactly what we kids need first thing. Now that we are frosted, sprinkled, and filled with sugar, what do girls do best? Shop. Limited Too is so in right now. And you know what they have lots of? Glitter. I come out of there looking like a little diva who has been shaken up in a sparkly snow globe. We won't even start on the conglomeration of fragrances I sprayed and slathered on.

On our way back to the Tad's Rad Pad, we stop at a farm stand to get some New York peaches. Yum! We visit for most of the afternoon, getting a little bit more serious about Monica's decision to pursue longer, straighter legs. She seems pretty dead set on going through with the procedures, and now I will have a buddy to continue the high road with. The scary frames, pins, and all didn't even faze her. She is just as determined as I had been in considering the operation. Their next step is getting a consult with Dr. Paley. We give them all the information to contact his center at Kernan Hospital.

Saying goodbye is sad, but we promise to keep in touch and plan another visit in the near future. Maybe a Baltimore reunion? Mom and I pack up our things and head out. My heart sinks as I realize that school starts up in a few days. Ugh. As we begin our drive back toward the interstate, I pop the Spice Girls into my discman and turn up the volume, attempting to drown out my anxious thoughts of middle school. We haven't made it more than five miles down the road when the car phone rings. Yes, I said car phone, one of those old built-in ones that is a permanent fixture in the vehicle. It's Gerri calling. We left the walker and my pain medicine at their house. Go figure, but not to worry, she is coming meet us where we have pulled to the side of the road.

Five or so minutes pass, and I know it will be a little while before they get here. Scanning through my book of CDs, deciding on my next musical selection, I glance at the side-view mirror of Mom's Jeep and see Gerri and the girls flying—and I mean flying, like bats out of hell—down the road in their white minivan. Gerri comes to a screeching halt behind us, resulting in a huge cloud of dust. Wide-eyed in disbelief and brimming with hysterical laughter, I roll my window down and pivot slightly in my seat to see Monica and Adrienne opening the sliding door of the van, doubled over with laughter. I explode as they walk up to the passenger window recounting their recent brush with the New York edition of the Daytona 500. Gerri and Mom are laughing too. I'm downright impressed. We make the quick exchange of priceless goods. With the walker and pain meds now safely in our possession, we say our goodbyes for the second time and officially part ways.

Shortly after our visit with Monica and her family, Gerri called Mom to announce that they had scheduled surgery for Monica's first phase of limb lengthening. How exciting! Now Monica and I would each have each other to confide in, and our families would have one another for support. The thought of coordinating clinic visits with them made me feel giddy all over.

28

It seemed that soon after I was operated on, the subject of limb lengthening caught fire throughout the media. One night while watching television, Dad and I caught glimpse of a preview for an updated *20/20* documentary on the Maryland Center for Limb Lengthening and Reconstruction. Immediately, I recognized people from Kernan Hospital in the preview. We made sure to catch it.

Based off of the earlier segment that I watched before undergoing surgery, Dr. Timothy Johnson checked back in with a few patients and introduced a couple new ones. One of them was a young boy around my age in the second phase of the lengthening on his arms. In awe, I stared at the television. The boy was riding a bicycle. Yes, riding his bike! He was just as active after his first lengthening as he was prior to any surgery. Presently shown with the fixators on his arms, he had no pain complaints and had much more freedom. Heck, I was ready to bounce ahead a year and go right into the arm lengthening; it looked that easy! He and his mother talked about all the positive aspects of his first lengthening surgery. Since his lower legs had been lengthened, the young boy was no longer falling. He was more independent, and he had decreased levels of pain. That was exactly what I anticipated as a result.

Nothing, however, could have prepared me for what I saw next. The segment took a dramatic turn when they began to focus on the views of the LPA, the Little People of America. An older woman, born with dwarfism, sat on the interview couch with Dr. Timothy Johnson and laid her views on the line for him. Obviously set in her ways with her view on limb lengthening, she said things like, "It is a purely cosmetic procedure," and "They just want to blend in." She was entitled to her opinion, but how dare she use such an admonishing tone.

Hold it right there: blending in will never be an option for me! Sitting in the recliner in the living room, I find my body begin to tense in a state of defense. Even though I am only twelve years old, I understand judgment on a profound level, deeper than many may think. Twelve years ago, I was born a dwarf, and there was—is—nothing I can do to change that. For the rest of my life, I will live having short stature, dwarfism, as a little person; however you want to put it. Personally, I don't think anyone ever really blends in. How can we? Try as we might, we were made to stand out. Everyone is different and unique in their own way, and that is what makes living fun. Just imagine a world where every single person looks the same. Lame and boring. Regardless, my intention from the very beginning has never been just to become taller or blend in with society. My future is what matters most to me. As much as listening to this woman angers me, I refuse to let one person from LPA bring me down. Hell to the no. We are all entitled to make our own decisions, right? It has never crossed my mind or my heart to sit and chastise members of the LPA community for turning down the surgery. There is no right or wrong way to approach the obstacles you face as a little person. As long as you stand up to them with a willing heart and an open mind. Any surgery is an extremely personal decision. Mine has nothing to do with another person or society as a whole. It only concerns me. End of story.

After the show aired, I caught wind that there were some people, prospective patients, calling MCLLR to inquire about the limb-lengthening surgery purely for cosmetic reasons. On one occasion, an individual explained that she simply wanted to be the same height as her spouse. Yes, an average-height person wanted to stand eye to eye with her significant other. Fine, that is her personal decision, and that, I will gladly point out, is cosmetic. This surgery, and the cosmetic accusations, were not something I took lightly. Limb lengthening and all that it implied, physical therapy and rehabilitation, was not a walk in the park. Why on earth would someone make the commitment for just a couple of inches? I wasn't sure, and I couldn't be too quick to judge. It made me feel a little sad that those choosing to undergo the procedures for cosmetic reasons had no deformity or medical issue to be corrected. The motivation was purely cosmetic. There was a tiny part of me that felt violated, like someone had just stomped all over me. Is that how the LPA viewed my decision? Surely not. Surgery was inevitable from the beginning and these ginormous cages on my legs were a promise of uninhibited independence. I decided right then that I did not belong in the superficial category.

Deep down, something began to nag at my psyche. I questioned whether I really made the right choice. Why did other people, strangers, care so much? Then I remembered Gillian and her success story. That could be me. It was going to be me—regardless of what others thought.

29

Middle school is a huge step in life. In addition to the move to a new school, I was going to be with a bigger group of kids because our middle school was regional. Pubescent kids from six different elementary schools merged together. Yikes.

Tomorrow is the first day of school. Am I excited? I'm not sure. Navigating a new school in a wheelchair seems a bit daunting. I know that Kate, Meaghan, and Lianna are pumped about leaving class early to help me. At Silver Lake Junior High, there will be kids from three other towns. I have never met most of them. What will they think of me? My legs? The apprehension is overwhelming. Something tells me sleep definitely won't come easy tonight.

'Twas the night before seventh grade when Dad came in to say good night before going into the living room to watch the news. Mom followed behind him. Every night since I was really little, Mom and Dad came in, sat on my bed, leaned over, and kissed and hugged me good night. Just like any other time, Mom came and sat in her usual spot. This particular time, she nearly sat directly on my legs.

I wince, trying to roll my legs to one side of the pillow to make a little bit more room. (It would have hurt her more than it hurt me if she caught part of the hardware.)

"Kristen, your legs," she says.

"What?" I reply.

"I always sit in the same spot to say good night, but your legs ... they are so long. I almost sat on them!"

Whoa, baby! Mom is right. For the first time since surgery, I see a very noticeable difference. I actually have goosebumps, and tears come to my eyes. Something so small had lit a huge fire in my heart. I knew then, at that very moment, that I was doing the right thing. Although the end seemed so far away, I was making progress and knew deep down that everything was going to work out.

Just a few weeks into my transition from elementary to middle school, I struggled to find a group of friends I felt completely immersed in and comfortable around. Girls I had been great friends with began to drift father and father away joining cliques as middle schoolers do. Many seemed to be growing up, just a little bit faster than what I was prepared for: makeup, bras, boys. Where was I supposed to begin? My plate was already full with medical hoopla and schoolwork. Now this? Gah!

It didn't bother me much in the beginning; transition was claiming all of our lives in one way or another. As I slowly began to fall behind the social standards of the typical twelve-year-old, I eventually began to feel alienated from friends I'd known since first grade. It was confusing and hard not to feel like I was doing something wrong. The emotional wounds gradually got deeper and deeper. Puberty in general is a tough phase in life. That on top of my already dramatic adolescence was just nuts. I realized I had to be thankful for the friends who chose to stand by me and take things one step at a time.

Every morning, a handicapped van picked me up to take me to school. Being picked up in a vehicle other than the big yellow school bus with my neighborhood friends irked me a little bit. In the back of my mind, I reminded myself that it wasn't forever. At the front entrance of the school, I was met by an aide who helped me to homeroom. From there, my friends decided they were up for the challenge of getting me from class to class, helping me with in-class assignments, retrieving books and getting my lunch for me on days I insisted buying. Who wouldn't use me as an excuse to leave class ten minutes early? I would be lying if I said we never went tear-assing through the halls that we had all to ourselves before the bell rang.

Since gym class was completely out of the question, I sat in the nurse's office for a study hall. This one was tough. I loved gym class. There was a little bit of jealousy toward everyone who got to keep a change of clothes in their gym lockers and participate in class, run around, and expend their energy. Little bits of inclusivity that I was missing out on. It may have been a study hall for me, but minimal studying was done. Positioning my wheelchair in the doorway of the nurse's office, I could see into the gymnasium and watched my classmates physically exert their able bodies. It was hard not to feel left out.

Sitting in my seventh grade math class, I see American Eagle, Pac Sun and Abercrombie & Fitch stickers on my friends' binders. Too embarrassed to ask what an Abercrombie & Fitch is, I continue to remain severely uninformed. What could the obsession be all about? Come to find out, the stickers and super cool, paper bags covering textbooks are stores in the mall where all the cool kids were shopping. I had no idea.

Some days, I feel like my outfits make me look like I am stuck in the eighties, with a little bit of Amish flair tossed in. Cotton athletic shorts work well to bang around in. Mom cut the sides and sewed in Velcro so I put them on in a diaper-like fashion, but I don't want to wear them to school. The only other appropriate "bottoms" that fit comfortably and over the cages are long skirts that Mom sews for me. They aren't exactly a fashion highlight in the latest issue of Teen People. My options are limited, and I keep my mouth shut. I get it, Mom is doing the best she can.

Today at the store, I find the cutest dress for class pictures. I am really tired of wearing the same thing over and over again. A new addition to my wardrobe that is not a homemade skirt or athletic shorts is a necessity. Obviously, I have a valid excuse for the lack of fashion sense, but it is just getting old and mildly embarrassing. At this point, I am not afraid to say that the day I can finally wear long pants again—jeans!—will be the happiest day of my life.

30

Dad dropped an envelope on the kitchen table in front of me one night at dinner. It was from Dr. Paley's secretary, Katherine, regarding a bone deformity course that was held by the Maryland Center for Limb Lengthening and Reconstruction annually. They were requesting my attendance for the patient demonstration day. How special that made me feel! Doctors from all over the world traveled to Baltimore to see the work of Dr. Paley and Dr. Herzenberg directly. Over the course of a week, the attendees participated in courses and hands-on workshops that revealed the different lengthening and reconstruction techniques used at MCLLR. During the patient demonstrations, several of Dr. Paley and Dr. Herzenberg's patients, all with different diagnoses, were brought on stage in the auditorium, and their cases were explained to the doctors in the audience. People asked questions regarding the techniques used for each case, their time frame, and pain management. Details of the patients' procedures, pictures, and x-rays were displayed by PowerPoint while the doctors looked on. This was also an opportunity for the patient to describe, in their own words, their medical journey. Conveniently, the course coincided with one of our biweekly trips to Maryland. Sign me up!

As Dr. Paley begins his segment on stature lengthening, I sit on a set of stairs next to him in the Kernan Hospital conference room as his "before" model. Gillian stands on his other side as his "after" model. Gillian is the same girl from the People article in my green folder with all the limb-lengthening information. She was Dr. Paley's very first limb-lengthening patient, and clearly everything she went through was a huge success. Hello, living proof!

In front of us is a very large group of attentive doctors from all over the world; close to one hundred. Maybe more. They are here to listen to me tell my story. Incredible. My x-rays are displayed on portable, illuminated screens.

Gesturing at my fixators, Dr. Paley begins to explain the method of lengthening I am undergoing. Then he hands me the microphone.

"Why did you decide to go through with this surgery?" he asks.

Wow. My orthopedic surgeon just put me on the spot, but I don't hesitate. I quickly explain to my audience of medical experts that it is not just the height that matters to me. My lower legs are—were—severely bowed. I suffer from kyphosis, flexion deformities affect both of my elbows and hips, and I want to be more proportionate. My reasoning is not to just "be taller," and I will always stand by that explanation. Height is simply a number.

Looking at Gillian and seeing how happy she is as she explains that she has no regrets and the lengthening was the best decision that she has ever made, I have hope. Even though I am still lengthening, I am a little more than halfway through my first procedure. If she can do it, then so can I. For the first time in my life, I have a role model, standing before me, who proves that this dream of mine is a true miracle. As Dr. Paley, Gillian, and I stand—well actually I'm sitting—in front of all these doctors, I cannot help but have a huge smile on my face.

As our segment comes to a close, Dr. Paley looks at me again. "Can you show everyone how you walk?" he whispers, holding the mic away from his mouth.

I freeze with a more than surprised look on my face. Uh, I don't have my crutches with me. Geez. In the hot seat again? In case you haven't noticed, I have very heavy bird cages drilled into my legs so walking isn't exactly my forte.

Dr. Paley motions for one of the staff members to bring over my wheelchair.

"Here. Walk pushing this," he says as he turns the chair around so the handles were facing me.

Unable to say no and 100 percent up for the challenge, I scoot down the few stairs I am sitting on. All eyes on me, my heart in my throat and beating so fast that I fear people can hear my pulse, I stand on my two bionic legs—bone, flesh, and metal. With white knuckles on my wheelchair, I take the tiniest of steps, walking down the center aisle. I hear the shutter of several cameras taking photographs. So this is what it's like to come face to face with the paparazzi? Standing over the wheelchair, pushing it, I feel taller. I'm looking over the chair, no longer just eye level with it.

After I walked out of the conference, my legs holding a dull throbbing feeling, Mom helped me back into my chair. Doctors who didn't speak good English came up and pointed to my legs and then their cameras. I nodded, and they begann taking pictures from every angle. How could I possibly say no to all the publicity? For one, I felt special, and deep down, I knew that I was helping the surgeons to learn a technique that they would in turn use to help their patients. I basked in all my glory, sure to soak up every second. Every medical professional I talked to expressed their gratitude to all the patients and their families for sharing their stories. I was more than happy to do it.

After the presentation, Mom and I caught Gillian in the clinic. She was the first success story we ever read about and the first patient of Dr. Paley's, a little person who had completed all the operations. I had never met anyone else like her. We may have scared her a little bit with all the hugs, questions, and pictures.

That afternoon I left Baltimore with a solid understanding of acceptance. I felt it in the depth of my bones. Being surrounded by those people and sharing my heart, I was home.

31

A soon-to-be teenager, two weeks had come and gone and I found myself back in Baltimore at The Ronald McDonald House. The following day, my checkup, was also my thirteenth birthday. Little did I know, Dr. Paley had something extra fun in store for me. After we arrived at Kernan Hospital and I had my x-rays completed, they told me to wait in the "adjustment" room. To my knowledge, I wasn't due for any strut changes. I wondered what was going on. While we waited for Dr. Paley and his entourage, Pam, my favorite nurse, walked in. We shared the same birthday, and she said she had a surprise for me after we were finished, but first things first.

With an unusually concerned look in her dark brown eyes, Pam asks gently, "Did Dr. Paley explain what is being done today?"

I rack my brain, but I am unaware of anything out of the ordinary on today's agenda. Then I remember, a while back, Dr. Paley explaining that a top pin, I have one in each leg—referred to as a half-pin—would have to be removed at some point. Those half-pins, one large pin with a smaller wire in the middle, which ran through my tibia and fibula, were set to be taken out today.

Today? Clearly, that valuable little piece of information had slipped my mind until now.

Pam confirms that my fears are true.

I look at her, knowing her honesty, and ask, "Is this going to hurt?"

With a hint of sadness in her eyes, she nods.

I know she is telling me the truth. I immediately request pain medicine and pop a pill.

From my wheelchair, I watch as Pam begins to lay some supplies out on the table next to me. I swallow hard, trying not to freak out. The anticipation slowly gnawing away at my nerves.

Dr. Herzenberg walks in and announces that Dr. Paley is out of the country—and he is here to do the dirty work. Wait. What? This is a little too convenient. Wasting no time, Dr. Herzenberg begins rifling through one of the many toolboxes until he finds a very large set of pliers. Let me place emphasis on the words very and large. These things look like something Dad keeps in the garage. My heart is in my throat. Next thing I know, things are happening really, really fast. Too fast.

Pam puts the brakes on my wheelchair and sits next to me.

I hold my hands in my lap. And then Pam's hands are holding mine.

Dad steps out.

The anticipation is going to kill me.

Hot tears begin to sting my eyes, and I fail to blink them away as one rolls down my cheek. My hands are squeezing Pam's with intent.

In a few swift motions, Dr. Herzenberg removes the blue plastic cap from the top half-pin in my left leg, grips the wire that was sticking through the middle on the half-pin with the pliers, and without a countdown, yanks. Hard.

Holy. Hell.

My mouth is dry, and with what air I have left in my lungs, I let out a murderous, blood curdling scream. The pain is indescribable and overwhelming. Quickly, I wriggle free from Pam's grasp and wrap myself around my right leg so Dr. Herzenberg can't gain access to the other wire. Three against one in the room, I'm going down.

Whispering in my ear that everything will be okay and let's just get it over with, Pam grabs of my arms and holds me against the back of my wheelchair.

I squeeze my eyes closed and feel Dr. Herzenberg grasp my right fixator. Audibly sobbing, I begin to count in my head. Before I get to three, intense pain rips through my right leg. The last wire is out. Happy birthday to me.

My face is white, my eyes are red, and my voice is hoarse from endlessly screaming. This goes down in the books as one of the worst experiences of my life, right up there with the physical therapists dragging me out of bed. When the pain finally begins to subside, my body returns from a state of hyperventilation.

Pam rolls me out of the adjustment room and down to the waiting room where Dad sits to avoid the torture that had just unfolded. Rounding the corner into the waiting area, a group breaks out into a rendition of "Happy Birthday," and Marilyn presents Pam and me with a beautiful—and delicious—cake made by her husband who is a professional pastry chef at the White House.

Call it a pleasant ending to a hellish day.

Clinic appointments always seemed to make for quite the adventure, especially when company was along for the ride. On another particular trip, one of my best friends from school, Lianna, and her mom, Betty, joined us. Lianna and I kept each other busy in the back seat with games of "Punch Buggy" and lots of teen magazines. Betty rode shotgun and helped Mom out with some of the driving. Usually on the lengthy excursion, I was able to hold the urge to go to the bathroom until we reached our halfway point in New Jersey. The thought of having to get out of the car, into the wheelchair, and then transfer to a public toilet made my stomach churn. There were trips where I tried to avoid it altogether; that's right, bladder of steel. This trip, I had no choice. Due to laughing so hard with Lianna— about what I don't remember—I had to get out and go. Once we saw the golden arches of the McDonald's rest stop, we pulled off in Connecticut.

I haven't laughed this hard in a long time. I think Mom and Betty might be getting a tad on the annoyed side with our girlish antics. All laughter aside, the longer my legs get, the harder transferring in and out of the car becomes. After finagling myself out of the tight squeeze that is the back seat and into the wheelchair, we venture into McDonald's in search of the bathroom.

Lianna's only job is to hold the handicapped stall door closed because it didn't lock. Mom and Betty are each holding a leg while I pee. I don't think I have ever had so many friends accompany me in the loo. Luckily, we are the only ones in here. I'm not sure where Lianna is or why she keeps wandering away from her position as door holder, but it's making the act of going even harder. Each time the door swings open, we yell, "Lianna! The door!"

Between the laughter and confusion, we somehow make it out of McDonald's alive, in one piece, and our bladders emptied. With all the excitement and movement, my legs are now throbbing. I have nothing to take my pain medication with. Mom refuses to go back in, so we hit the drive-through instead. Big mistake.

All I want is a root beer; that isn't too much to ask, right? As a staple to a soda consumer's diet, it is expected that most fast-food places carry it. We approach the menu—which lists root beer as one of their beverages—with the little intercom and attempt to order.

"Just a small root beer please," Mom says into the speaker.

The man on the other end replies in a sentence we find inaudible, and snickers rise from Lianna and me in the back seat.

Mom tries again, "One small root beer, please."

The man, clearly having a foreign accent, once again forms a string of garbled words that we all find difficult to understand. "Sh ... thing ... en rutbier ... yesh?"

Lianna and I are howling with laughter. My pain is getting worse. This go-around continues for at least another two minutes. There is a very long line forming behind us, and someone is honking their horn.

Finally, all four of us girls yell simultaneously out the windows, "We just want a root beer!"

A different voice comes on the intercom, the manager. "Ma'am, we don't have root beer."

Are you kidding? All this time, and their menu had misled us into believing they had root beer. How rude. And the guy did a terrible job of trying to tell us that they didn't have root beer. The language barrier was a little over the top. My stomach hurts from laughing so hard, and I settle for a Sprite.

As we pull away from the drive-through, Lianna sticks her head out the window toward the cars in line behind us and screams, "Don't bother asking for root beer ... 'cause they don't have any!"

Laughter makes the hurt a little more tolerable, and thanks to the Sprite, I finally get the pain medicine into me.

32

After I made the video based on the short story *Thinking Big* in third grade, teachers continued to invite me back to their classrooms years later as a guest speaker after their classes read the story about the little girl named Jamie. After the kids watched my video, I got up in front of the class and spoke. I answered any questions, and then I went into detail about the surgery I was going through. For my health class in middle school, we were required to do a major project on a specific medical condition. Well, duh. I obviously researched dwarfism in great detail and included the extended limb-lengthening procedures as part of my findings. It was an attention grabber for the entire class—especially my instructor—and I aced the whole assignment with flying colors.

Surgery was no longer just an event in my life. I began to find comfort in it and used the act of educating others as a coping mechanism. Rather than channeling some of my pain into tears or anger, I began to journal and started a large binder of articles and information I'd found along with my ever growing number of projects and reports.

Sitting on my tush at the computer, day in and day out, I became very familiar with the world wide web. AIM was every young teenager's obsession back then, was it not? Eventually I came across several Yahoo listservs regarding dwarfism, achondroplasia, and limb lengthening. I thought, *Well, what the heck? There's no reason not to join.*

At first, scanning through the posts from other members on the dwarfism listserv, I realized that there were other people who were looking for advice or information on "living little." Adapting to school, hemming clothes, and dealing with the public's ignorance were all popular topics. Many of the individuals posting these inquiries were parents of average height who had a child with short stature—my very same situation. I responded to many of them, and all were very grateful for any advice.

My first time in the limb lengthening chat room was drastically different. Think of it as an online war zone of sorts. The posts would begin with a simple, curious question about the procedures, and the responses were either adamantly for or against the surgery.

Oh boy.

Now this was my kind of party. After watching a few television specials, reading early articles on limb lengthening, and now actively going through it, I was well versed, even at thirteen years old, and the Little People of America's view of lengthening limbs was not going to fall silently on me. Why would they join a limb lengthening listserv if they completely disagreed with the procedures? Apparently, they wanted to make their views well known. Well, so did I. Rather than cause trouble for myself and making a universal post speaking my mind about those individuals, and them perhaps toning their thoughts down, I responded directly to people who were inquiring about having the surgery. It was shocking to find that many of the people asking questions were actually kids my age with parents of average height. Knowing that I was being somewhat of a mentor to them made me feel good about myself. When I first looked into the lengthening procedures, there wasn't anyone for me to talk to. That is how I knew my experience was very valuable to some of these individuals.

For years, we researched extended limb lengthening, seeking out any and all resources. When this journey began, I never imagined that I would be sought out as a source of guidance. Yesterday I received an email from a woman a few towns over from us in Massachusetts. Her son has achondroplasia and is expressing interest in the procedures. Now she is turning to me for the inside story. Me?

Holy crap. I never imagined acting almost as an advocate for others considering the limb lengthening. Is this what purpose feels like? If so, I like it. No, I love it.

The whole family is coming over to visit with us and see firsthand what could be in store for them if they choose to walk this path.

33

Clinic visits at Kernan Hospital never failed to provide some kind of excitement, wanted or not. It was already November, and I had gained around five inches in length. My legs were unbelievably straight. I never thought I would see the day. Dad had to extend the footrests on my wheelchair because my legs were so long I couldn't straighten my knees. Too long! All of the new bone growth led my muscles to be very unhappy with me.

Today is another routine clinic visit. Waiting to be called into an exam room, my legs feel twitchy and more uncomfortable than usual. While I'm working on my sand art at the craft table, I feel intense pressure building in my calf muscle. My leg begins to shake uncontrollably, and it hurts like hell. I don't know what is happening.

"Mom!" I yell as my hands reach through the back of my fixator to massage my leg. The throbbing sensation is increasing exponentially. "MOM!"

Another parent in the waiting room suggests that it's probably a muscle spasm. It seems like a no-brainer to whip out the muscle relaxers and pop one down the hatch, right? Well, we try, but here's the catch: nowhere in the clinic area can we find a water bottle or cup for me to drink from. Being in a wheelchair, I can't simply hoist myself up to the water bubbler. There's no vending machine, and the cafeteria is not close by.

Maybe it is because Mom is in such a rush to find some sort of cup and all I can do is remain seated in my panic-stricken state, but we don't seem to be getting anywhere. You would think there would be a little paper cup hanging around here somewhere. Nope, nothing. My discomfort level is far from manageable. I feel lost in the pain, swimming in a pool of heightened anxiety without an escape. My rising emotions are due to spill over in the form of tears any second. This pill isn't quite small enough to where I can choke it down dry without something to drink. Why is this happening?

Mom comes running back into the waiting room, grabs my chair, and runs me over to the water fountain. I've been holding onto this little white pill so tightly that it's practically disintegrated in my hand. Gross. Mom produces an empty film canister and begins to fill it with water. Yes, correct, an itty-bitty film canister. I am washing down my now powdery muscle relaxer with sips of water from a film canister. One of the mothers in the waiting room was nice enough to lend a hand and provide us with the very puny but useful container. What I would give for a firehose right about now.

Moral of today's story: always carry a receptacle for drinking on your person.

The excitement at that particular appointment seemed endless. Dr. Paley showed concern that I was losing valuable flexion and extension in my knees and decided that the top rings of my fixators were preventing me from achieving maximum range of motion with my knee bends. An "easy" procedure, they said, will fix that problem. Yeah, right.

Yet again, I find myself in the beloved adjustment—more like the punishment—room, for this so-called easy fix to my plaguing range-of-motion issue. Residual trepidation from my most recent visit to this room is clouding my mind and causing my heart to race. Dr. Paley walks in with what he calls a "jiggly saw." I'm sorry, jigga what? A saw? Like, the kind you cut wood with? But there isn't a tree in sight. He is going to saw the back half of the top ring off each of my fixators. My jaw drops, and after hearing the news, I just stare at him with disbelief. What I would give for legs that can run right now.

No sedation is necessary? Ha! I've heard that one before. Funny, I am the one wearing the fixators, so just how would anyone else know whether or not I should be medicated? Good thing I have a solid head resting on my shoulders and know to premedicate before rolling into the room of death. Sometimes it's amazing how accurate my thirteen-year-old intuition can be.

I transfer from my wheelchair up onto the paper-covered exam table. Left side first. Oh, joy. My favorite girl Pam holds onto the bottom of the frame, some fellow or intern has the audacity to just jump right in and join the party holding the middle ring. I quickly shoot him a searing gaze of fire. As much as I want to lecture him on how it is a privilege to stake claim on such an invaluable piece of real estate, I let it go and hold firmly to the top of the frame. Dr. Paley maneuvers what looks like a long piece of barbed wire with a handle on each end, around one side of the top ring.

"Ready?" he asks.

Ha. Am I ready? No, of course I'm not. My answer comes in the form of an "I hate you but still love you because you're a magical man" facial expression with a slight pouty lip curl and overly furrowed brow. I know this is going to hurt like a mother-trucker. His first tug on the saw sends a jagged earthquake of discomfort through my body and throws me off to one side of the table. Cool—so that barely put a dent in the titanium ring. Dad steps in behind me to brace my shoulders. Now I am surrounded on all sides. There is no escape.

Dr. Paley begins again. Each tug on the saw jars my leg and jostles my body from side to side. Trying to be strong, I let out muffled yelps. Little beads of sweat began forming on the master of torture's forehead. This is not a quick process, and it's nice to see I'm not the only one struggling. After about ten minutes, half of the back ring is sawed off of the left frame.

We still have to saw off the right side.

Seriously? I am shaking in my big-girl panties and praying this side goes just a little bit faster. Closing my eyes and clenching my teeth, I nod and give the okay to proceed through the gridlock of arms surrounding me. After what seems like forever and without a tear, the back half ring comes off of the right side.

Since the edges where the ring was cut are extremely jagged, we cover them with moleskin. As I bend my knees up, well past ninety degrees, for the first time, I give a huge sigh of relief. The trauma was worth this wonderful feeling of having full range of motion, but man, I never "saw" that coming.

In addition to the hack job on the top rings, I had another little surprise. Thankfully, no hurt was involved with this one though. Dr. Paley decided that he wanted to release two of the pins, on each leg, from the fixators, simply by unscrewing the cube that held each pin in place against the ring. The whole idea of these pins just hanging out in my leg irked me a little bit. They just didn't seem like they would be stable enough floating around. What if I bumped them somehow?

Dr. Paley assured me that they would be just fine. The only way they would actually move was with some kind of wrench or other tool.

I promised to stay clear of Dad's tool belt.

34

The lengthening of my legs was more than visible now. They were so long and straight. In fact, come December, I had reached my goal of six inches. Three pre-consolidations and a gazillion pin infections later, the time had finally come to stop lengthening and begin the consolidation phase.

From here on out, I was told that things would become easier as muscles and nerves no longer had to stretch and accommodate new length. According to Dr. Paley, I had more reasons to celebrate: I had achieved my desired length, six inches in six months, and I did so without the need for any nerve decompression or muscle releases. I knew that I had the ladies at physical therapy to thank for that. Their care and expertise combined with my hard work and determination made my first lengthening so successful, but the work didn't stop there. We still had to make sure I maintained range of motion in my knees and walked with my walker as much as possible to help my bones consolidate. Easy enough in my mind because I was one step closer to the end of phase one.

My parents were happy to hear that since the lengthening phase was over, our biweekly trips to Baltimore were now deemed unnecessary. Instead, we ventured a mere ten minutes down the road to the local medical center for x-rays and then sent them to Dr. Paley. Obviously I felt a little differently about the lack of Baltimore excursions. Those trips were my escape from reality.

A month or so after I stopped lengthening, I was pleasantly surprised when Dr. Paley beckoned us down to Kernan Hospital. My legs weren't completely healed quite yet, but he wanted to remove the wires keeping my ankles suspended in the birdcages so that I could start working on range of motion and continue walking. Fine by me. The wires also prevented me from being able to wear socks and shoes. My hardware-laden feet and the chilly New England temps were not getting along too well. I was constantly cold due to all the hardware going directly into my bones. I couldn't wait to wear shoes and socks. Pants obviously weren't too much of an option with the contraptions. Even though this procedure wasn't going to take the frames off completely, the load of hardware I had been lugging around was going to be lightened significantly.

So, off we went down I-95, arriving at the Ronald McDonald House to the ever so friendly friends turned family. People I like to call framily. The day before surgery, Mom and I had to go in for the beloved pre-op appointment and discuss the risks of anesthesia. Yadda, yadda, yadda. Old news. All I wanted to do was get the whole thing over with.

It's dark and early as we arrive at the main entrance of Kernan Hospital. Per usual, I am a nervous wreck. After I am all suited up in my spiffy hospital gown, pee in a cup, and get poked and prodded for an IV, I wait and wait and wait with happy meds freely flowing aplenty through my bloodstream.

After two hours or so, the calming effects of the Valium begin to wear off—unacceptable. Before a full-blown panic attack sets in, the nurse notices my growing restlessness and gives me more—bless her heart—and she says that there is a complication with the case ahead of me. How convenient. I will have to wait a while longer. As long as they keep the good stuff running through my veins, I assure her that I won't pitch too big of a fit.

Marilyn popped her head around the curtain that provided me what little privacy one is granted in the pre-op waiting area to say hello. She sat with me for a bit to catch up on life, and Mom took a well deserved break to grab a coffee. I was happy to report my latest success with finding the Princess Diana Beanie Baby since the last time I had seen her. After all, Marilyn was the one who introduced me to the plush little critters that I hoped would one day turn me into junior moneybags, especially since I now possessed a few of the rarities.

Mom returned, and after promising to go back into the operating room with me, Marilyn moved on to comfort and visit with the Paley patient playing the waiting game in the bay beside me. To see a familiar face among all the masked strangers in the operating room was heartening for me at thirteen years old. I can only imagine how the littler kids felt.

After waiting a total of four hours, it was finally my turn to go back. Amidst a tornado of nurses, anesthesia staff, paperwork, bouffant caps, and blankets, I was ready to go. It was a teary goodbye between Mom and me, which was nothing new; my emotions always getting the best of me. Marilyn, with sections of her long blonde hair falling out from the blue cap, held tight to my hand as she and some of the nurses rolled me back into the OR.

My transfer onto the operating table is a quick one. Looking down at my legs, I realize that I barely fit; the frames each hanging a few inches off the side of the table. I pull my legs together until I feel the jarring friction of frame on frame. Noticing my entangled appendages, the nurse assures me that I won't lose a leg. I lay back and place my head in the little, brown, doughnut-looking headrest.

Marilyn's gentle eyes are peering down at me over her mask. "Where are we going today?" she asks, taking my hand and squeezing it as the nurses start placing monitors on my chest.

"Somewhere warm," I mumble, already beginning to feel light-headed. I hear a faint beeping in the background, and someone places a mask over my nose and mouth. I am fighting to keep my eyes open and can barely understand the voices conversing around me.

Marilyn gives my hand a big squeeze, but before I can return it, I'm out.

Goodbye, hot pink footplates—and hello, new shoesies!

The wires were out, and my feet were free. And holy shit was I stiff. Still groggy from the anesthesia, I pick one of my legs up off of the gurney. It felt so much lighter. The (partial) removal was done as an outpatient procedure, and I didn't have to stay a night in the hospital.

The recovery nurse brought me ginger ale and graham crackers to cure my now ravenous appetite.

As I shoved my face full of crackers, she warned me to take it easy, assuring me that there was more if I wanted it, but my stomach may not like the ferocity of my current eating habit.

Overall, it took me an hour or so to fully wake up out of my postsurgical stupor.

After getting dressed and back into my wheelchair, Mom and I were free to go. We opted to stay the night in Baltimore and head home to Massachusetts the following day. On our way back to the Ronald McDonald House, I insisted on making a small pit stop at the mall on Security Boulevard. I had not been so excited about shoes in my entire life, and I'm sure that is why Mom couldn't deny me the trip to Payless. They didn't look like anything special—plain white girl's Keds—but they were to me. Being able to put socks and shoes on for the first time in seven months was extraordinary. That day I promised myself never to take the simple pleasure of feeling the ground beneath my feet for granted.

After that stellar purchase, I couldn't wait to give my new shoesies a good ol' stompin' to break them in. Standing for the first time without the wires in my ankles, I was a bit wobbly and sore, but I was also very proud. I remember sitting down in the playroom at the Ronald McDonald House with my walker determined to walk back up to the room instead of using my wheelchair. My heart was overflowing with determination in addition to the tears in my eyes from the discomfort, and I had a huge smile on my face. I knew I was that much closer to the end. Step left, step right, move the walker forward. Heel to toe. All the way back to the room.

Despite waiting a day to return home to Massachusetts, we still managed to hit a rather large, obnoxious issue during our travels.

This morning, my head feels funny, like it's full of cotton balls, and there is a massive headache nagging away at my eyeballs. Mom is busy packing up the car, and I know she wants to get home. I transfer from the bed into my wheelchair as she comes up for the last load of stuff. Something is not right. Surgery, no matter how minor, is a big deal. Now that the excitement has subsided, my body might simply be adjusting to less hardware. I don't know.

A few hours outside of Baltimore, I begin feeling worse. I'm hot, I'm cold, and my head is pounding. It feels like an ice pick is being driven into my skull. Mom, trying to keep her eyes on I-95, notices the drastic shift in my condition and calls the hospital from our ancient car phone. Handing me the receiver, I hear Pam's voice on the other end.

"Sweetie, what is wrong?" she asks in the gentlest voice you can imagine.

"Pam, I don't know. Something isn't right. My head is pounding. I'm sweating, but I'm cold—and my hands won't stop trembling," I whisper between sobs.

Handing the phone back to Mom, I close my eyes and rest my head in the slack of the seatbelt over my right shoulder as she continues to nod and say okay to Pam until I hear her click the phone back into place. Sound pains my ears, and light makes my eyes burn. What is happening? While driving, Mom folds up some paper towels, douses them with water, holds them out the car window to make them cold, and slaps them on my forehead. This pattern continues until we pull into a TGIFriday's parking lot. The hospital suspects that I am having a morphine withdrawal. But it was only given to me once right before I woke up from the surgery and I'm certainly not a drug addict. How does this make any sense?

Mom runs in to get me some soup, bread and water. How delightful, a prisoner's lunch for the little druggie riding shotgun. The hospital stresses that I need to stay hydrated. Nauseous beyond words, eating and drinking are the last thing I want to do. After she climbs back into the car with some chicken noodle soup and a few bonus breadsticks, we make one more stop at the gas station for some Gatorade. Choking down what I can, I would most prefer a large fast-forward button to press and get me out of this hellish situation.

After that road trip from hell, it took a couple days to return to my norm.

Morphine and I broke up after that encounter.

35

Having the wires removed from the fixators made physical therapy ten times more difficult. With the focal point now being on my ankles and "un-stiffening" them, in addition to my knees and overall strengthening, my plate felt very full. After nearly seven months of both ankles being restricted of any movement, you can try to imagine how noncompliant they were to a fluid heel-to-toe motion, but the ladies at physical therapy pushed me; they pushed hard. Within a week of getting those wires out, I was scootin' around everywhere with my little walker.

And then, it happened. I paid my price for my newfound life as a free-range bionic girl.

This freedom on new, longer, straighter, and more mobile legs is quite wonderful and exhausting. Roaming around the house with my walker makes day-to-day tasks so much easier. And the physical exertion causes me to be one tired girl at the end of the day. It's no longer necessary for me to transfer from the wheelchair onto the toilet. Yup! Now I waltz right into the bathroom with my granny walker and sit on the john like a normal teenager. And then, here I am, standing at the kitchen counter, six inches taller, without a kitchen chair beneath my feet and able to reach everything. Talk about a defining moment. I remember standing on the stool, looking down and dreaming about the day I would no longer need its assistance. This, right here, is one of the best feelings in the world. Move over, Mama, there's a new chef in town!

Life is getting better even with the birdcages still on, a scenario once clouded by complications and discomfort, I am now living and am one step closer to the frames coming off altogether. Dr. Paley says that weight bearing promotes bone growth, so I walk all over the house. What can possibly go wrong?

Let me tell you. While walking out of my bedroom, the end of one of my wires gets hooked on a braided rug that Mom made. Beautiful as they are, these things are like land mines. I know what you're thinking: "Kristen, stop exaggerating."

And I swear to you that I am doing no such thing. One wrong move on or around those deceiving, woven masterpieces and boom! Wire gets hooked, and down I go—walker and all—face first onto the hardwood floor. Holy mother of God does it hurt. At first, all I can do is stay there and curse all the rugs in the house and their apparent mutiny toward my walking. Then, I scream. Loud—unaware that the calamity from my fall already has Dad standing over me carefully attempting to peel me up off the floor. More frightened than anything from the jarring impact, I continue to swear at every rug in the house. I am my father's daughter, especially when it comes to my extended expletive vocabulary.

Upon close inspection of my legs, I notice two of the pins are bleeding on my right leg. Cue hysterics and body trembling in fear. I seriously hope that nothing detrimental has happened to the bone. Mom puts the phone up to my ear.

Pam assures me that nothing could have possibly moved on the frame. Those pins are not going anywhere, so the bone isn't either. Everything is okay.

I feel much better talking to Pam, and just in case, she instructs me to keep an eye on the pins. In the meantime, clear paths are paved downstairs for the bionic babe and her clunky legs.

At such a young age, resilience certainly was one of my best qualities. Surprisingly, after every mishap thrown into the mix, I managed to bounce back quite quickly. After my most recent tumble, I made sure to be extra careful and watch where I was moving around, hesitant that I would become entangled in something and take another digger. In school, my wheelchair was only used for transport between classes, and I was sitting at an actual desk during class. My ability to transfer was a beautiful thing. My adolescent life seemed to be reaching a level of normalcy I'd hoped for. My legs just needed to consolidate.

With the monthly X-rays, a knot in my stomach formed at every visit to the medical center. The anticipation of hearing whether or not the bone was healed nearly sent me into convulsions. For any lengthening patient, the typical rule of thumb was one month of healing for every inch of length. Whoa, baby. Right? Another six months in the frames was not anything I was particularly looking forward to. Although, the hard part of lengthening was over.

After hearing that news of my potential timeline, my goal in life became defying the odds. Could I do it? There was no doubt in my mind. I did everything in my power to hurry along the healing process: calcium, vitamin D, and lots of weight bearing. Sitting on my high horse with the mentality that I was special and a healing fiend probably helped a little too. Healing thoughts abound.

Sure enough, my February x-rays showed that both legs had almost healed, and we scheduled the removal of my Ilizarov frames for late March.

Hallelujah!

36

A month later—on March 22, 1999—I was sitting on the increasingly familiar gurney in the pre-op holding area. My IV was in, and rather than a feeling of fear instilled in me, I was excited. Let's get this party started! This was it. The fixators were finally coming off—no games. Before I signed my life away to the anesthesiologist, Rick, the cast man, came over and gave me a choice of cast colors. Slightly disappointed that glitter was not an option, I openly decided that one color just wasn't going to cut it. So, following my unicorn instincts, I opted for the ever-so-glorious rainbow.

Next thing I knew, I was awake and groggily feasting my eyes upon two very long, colorful legs. Due to a slight difference in healing, my left leg had a cast that went above my knee, and the right cast fell a little below, and in the moment, I didn't care about anything other than the fact that those cumbersome metal bird cages were history. Gone, gone, gone! No more pain. No more muscle spasms. No more pin infections.

My excitement overshadows the fact that the casts are heavy, hot, and very, very restricting. And don't even get me started with trying to shower. I have to tape garbage bags around my legs so the casts don't get wet. I have decided that I would rather be cold than hot. There's no escaping my over heating, especially at night because I have to have covers on me. Dr. Paley's orders: casts stay on for six weeks, at least. Blah. I slowly transition from celebratory happy dance to disgruntled, rainbow painted teenager; one hell of a hot mess. These casts are a nightmare. Every itch is literally impossible to scratch. I try all the hacks: hair dryer, chopsticks, baby powder. I am about to unwind a metal hanger as an option which is probably not a good idea considering I have puncture wounds that are trying to heal. I can see it now: teenage girl contracts tetanus in an attempt to scratch an itch. This is yet another small bump in the road: one very big step closer to the end.

Less than a week after I returned home from getting the fixators removed, another issue arose. This time, it just involved my right leg. The cast was digging into the back of my knee and causing serious discomfort. The rubbing was making my skin raw. Before taking any action, we put a call into Dr. Paley. He gave me permission to go down to the local medical center and have the cast adjusted. The key word there is "adjusted." It seemed foolproof. Little did I know that I was about to have a very traumatizing experience with an orthopedic doctor who would haunt my dreams for years.

Mom calls South Shore Medical Center to make an appointment with an orthopedist, Dr. Mayo, who, we are told, is the one who can solve my present cast issue. I have a smile on my face, like always. Mom wheels me into the doctor's office, and we sit in the waiting room. My biggest concern is making sure that he does not cut away any part of the cast that one of my friends has already signed. I have quite the collection of signatures and congratulatory messages on my legs.

A nurse calls my name, and we follow her back into the casting room. I transfer out of my wheelchair and onto the exam table. Something doesn't feel quite right, but I can't be sure why. This is a good thing, I tell myself, but the minute this doctor, with short white hair, glasses and a demoralizing look on his face, walks in, I can tell that my gut is right. He and I aren't friends.

In a very short exchange of words we have, I explain that I simply need a small adjustment on the back of my right cast so it will stop rubbing my leg raw.

With a look that makes me feel minuscule and unworthy, the words rolling off his tongue belittle me below existence. He scoffs at all I have gone through, saying that limb lengthening is foolish. "Why would you ever do such a thing? You should be ashamed."

You can hear a pin drop. Mom and I are stunned. The nurse says nothing. I close my eyes and think, be strong. Don't cry. Put up a brick wall.

Without warning or saying a single word to me, Dr. Mayo instructs the nurse to hold my toes, suspending my right leg in midair. That man picks up the cast saw, not an ounce of hesitation in his movements, and makes a cut down the entire side of my cast. Keep in mind that the fixator has just recently been removed and my bone is still very soft.

"What are you doing?" Mom screams.

My wall crumbles, and I begin to wail, tears streaming down my face. I am hysterical. Voice shaking and overwhelmed with fear, and I howl, "No!"

Who is this man? He calls himself a doctor? Is he unaware that doctors are compassionate human beings responsible for the healing and well-being of their patients? What the hell?

Uncontrollably, I am shuddering under this man's depravity as he peels the entire cast off my right lower leg. Mom is beside herself, trying to explain that this cannot be happening: my bone is fragile, and all we need is the back of the cast trimmed. Her words fall on deaf ears.

The nurse looks indifferent to the situation, but looking deeply into her eyes, I think I catch a glimpse of horror. Dr. Mayo—the devil—ignores Mom, continuing to go about his business as he throws the fragments of old cast to the floor and begins wrapping my leg in gauze. What I believe are my first true sentiments of hatred toward another human being begin to form.

The emotion I feel in this very moment is indescribable. Somewhere between the anger and fear, I become lost. I don't even know how to react other than to lay on the table, completely still, weep silently, and accept my complete helplessness. Moving rather quickly, the menace continues the steps to reapply a cast, adding more padding and then ending with an ugly white fiberglass layer. In doing so, and without my present knowledge, he changes the position of my ankle and wraps the cast tighter at the distal end of my tibia and fibula, making it even more uncomfortable than before. A hack job compared to my lovingly applied rainbow cast.

Without looking him in the eye or saying a word, I get back into my wheelchair, and we leave. Looking at the disgusting white cast on my leg, I am overwhelmed with sadness. All I can do is cry. It was not put on with caution or care; in fact, it looked like a very careless job had been done. How can anyone calling themselves a doctor do such a horrible thing?

Once we arrived home, Mom immediately got on the phone with the hospital and informed Dr. Paley and staff about what had just happened. She asked if I wanted to explain what happened to Pam, but I couldn't.

Curled in a ball on my bed, minus my left leg jutting out, I lay there sobbing, not wanting to talk to anyone.

Dr. Paley assured my parents that everything was fine. To confirm this, he wanted a set of x-rays. Like hell we were going back to that medical center. We opted to get the scans done at a different office. Everything checked out all right at the time.

Unfortunately, six weeks later, following x-rays in Baltimore, we saw some horrifying proof that Dr. Mayo truly was a terrible excuse for a doctor. His repositioning of my foot, and the misapplication of the cast caused my right fibula to bow inward, and my ankle to become supinated. With my bones permanently healed, the deformity became indefinite. If I had it my way, Dr. Mayo would have been sued. I was—and still am—devastated that people of this nature actually exist.

❧ 37 ❧

Living life in one beautiful, eye catching cast and one that was a harsh reminder of how cruel some people can be was interesting, to say the least. Constantly having to tape trash bags to my legs in an effort to create a watertight seal to shower was still no quick and easy feat. Who knew that tie wraps from the garage would come in handy, offering a quicker solution? That's right. The tiny plastic tourniquets prevented my casts from getting sopping wet. God forbid the medical world create casts that were waterproof! Using a stool to rest my legs on in the shower, I did my best to keep those stupid things dry. Walking in them was extraordinarily difficult, considering the left cast came well above my knee, so hanging out in the wheelchair for the time being was inevitable.

After about a month of healing in the restricting fiberglass jailhouses, we returned to Baltimore. On April 29, 1999, the real removal happened by the people I trusted most. Freedom. As in, nothing wrapped around, encasing, or causing curtailment to my new legs. After examining the standard set of x-rays, Dr. Paley gave me the good news: my right leg had completely healed, and the cast was able to come off altogether. Rick, the cast man, worked his beautiful magic with that terrifying cast saw.

It is like something out of a horror movie, I tell ya. The blade resembles that of a table saw, and the noise after it turns on sends a shiver down my spine. Is he sure this thing is safe to use on humans? Noticing the sudden look of horror on my face, Rick takes the saw, power on, and allows it to graze his skin. No blood, and he didn't even flinch. Then he touches the saw to my hand. Point proven. No pain, just vibration to the point that it actually tickles. As the whirring saw sinks into the fiberglass, all I feel is vibration, like my wheelchair is being pushed down a cobblestone street at 126mph. And yes, I am that annoying patient, mouth open saying, "Ah," as the feeling reverberates off my vocal cords. White powder is everywhere, and I begin to sneeze rather uncontrollably, which makes me giggle. Rick makes cuts down both sides of my cast, knee to toes. I learn this is called "bivalving" the cast. My medical vocabulary is expanding quite rapidly.

With the cast cut, Rick lifts off the top portion of my cast. Eyes wide, I gaze down at my skinny chicken leg. My first thought is one of disbelief. How is this leg, sans cast, supposed to hold me up and take me places? Without all the hardware, my leg looks even longer. Like, abnormally long. Long and beautiful. It's mine, and I will take it.

For the first time in nine months, I have one of my very own legs back to normal. As for my left leg, the long rainbow cast is cut off. Oh, to bend my knee! It feels borderline euphoric. However, my left tibia is not fully consolidated quite yet. Rather than risk a break, I get a bright purple cast that Rick bivalves to make it removable so it is more like a brace and I am able to shower without getting tangled in a mess of tie wraps. Now it's only two pieces of fiberglass and cotton sandwiching my left leg that stands between me and complete and total freedom.

Looking down at my legs, I relish in the fact that they are so long and straight! But it is socially unacceptable to go walking around with legs looking like they belong to a prehistoric cavewoman. Apparently, the pins in my legs caused an increase in blood flow for healing purposes. Well, this led to two very hairy legs. Gorilla-esque would be a fair description. Yikes.

My newfound "freedom" meant one very important thing: a shower. As in a real, big-girl, no-tie-wraps-or-trash-bags, unencumbered shower. Something my legs were desperately in need of. Both appendages were actually pretty gnarly looking between the hair, the dried blood, the betadine, and the scars that were still healing, which resembled little bullet holes. Simply put, those little legs of mine required some serious tender loving care. Let me tell you, that first really real shower was utterly glorious.

I have never shaved my legs before. I am not sure that using a razor is the smartest move. In fact, I know that it isn't. What on earth is going to hack through the forest growing on my legs? I opt for Nair. It takes two bottles, I kid you not. It is a little tedious and a test of patience, having to wait for the strong, cucumber scented lotion to work its magic. Paired with aggressive scrubbing from a washcloth, the result: two very shiny, soft, and hairless long legs. No more gorilla legs—thank goodness.

By the end of May, the removable cast on my left leg was no longer necessary. It became official: I was free of any and all baggage, but I was not completely out of the woods. Physical therapy, or the fun, as my therapists put it, was just beginning. After growing six inches, I had to relearn how to walk with a longer gait and regain my strength. The muscles in my core and lower extremities were exceptionally weak, and my walk was more like a waddle. Even walking the shortest distances—like between classes—was exhausting. With continuing persistence from my therapists, I gradually came to find my stride. Walking on sunshine—I was in heaven.

By the end of seventh grade, I was walking unassisted around school and was finally able to participate in gym. No more hanging out in the nurse's office—and no more handicapped van. Riding on a big yellow school bus had never felt so good. No more friends struggling to haul my ass up and down the ramps in the wheelchair either.

Despite all the obstacles throughout my first year of middle school, I maintained high honors every grading period. Looking back, attending school in my wheelchair, coupled with a tutor at home, for the majority of the year was the right decision. For me, the whole process of being homeschooled was just downright difficult. Being immersed in the classroom setting made it much easier to pay attention, learn, and understand the material. Honestly, I think I was more concerned about keeping my social life afloat than anything, and being physically present for the inside jokes and hoopla that came with going to school kept me a part of the inner circle.

My freedom extended to more social interaction with my friends. I was able to walk the length of the Independence Mall thirty-two times on a Friday night, go to the movies, and navigate friends' houses without having to worry about how I was going to do it in a wheelchair.

And clothes. With clear knowledge about Abercrombie & Fitch and American Eagle, I could wear pants that only needed minimal hemming. Shopping had become fun rather than a pain in my ass and more of a financial burden on mom's wallet. I'd like to think it was a welcome one.

38

After phase one of lengthening was all said and done, I was soaring. Life was everything I had hoped it would be, well, almost. At the immature, young age of thirteen years old, my life had changed drastically. Despite my physical transformation, I still struggled emotionally with a lot of different feelings and assumptions about myself. Many kids at that age don't make life-changing decisions like the one I had chosen. After my first surgery was complete, I had a difficult time finding someone I could identify with. Someone who would understand what being different felt like. Maybe I was six inches taller and walking straighter, but I was also still a teenage girl living with dwarfism.

Aside from Monica and her family who lived in New York, I didn't have anyone I was really close with who could truly understand what I was going through. The teasing and staring, I knew, were always going to be inevitable, especially out in public. Despite knowing that, the words and glares still hurt. Each time that I experienced others' ignorance, I found myself digging deeper and deeper to find that happy place. Music, art, and talking about it only went so far as coping strategies. Stress began to take its toll; my efforts to keep that smile on my face only covered my outward sadness, and everything building up on the inside caused me to spiral downward.

People can be so cruel. *Ignorance* became a word I quickly familiarized myself with. In fact, the greatest disability that plagues our society is ignorance. For some, it can be bliss. In my book, it became an excuse, one that I was using, not for myself, but for others. It didn't seem fair though. Why was I finding it necessary to justify other people's actions and words that they had complete control over? Even as a child, I was taught early on that it wasn't nice to point and stare, judge, or make fun of anyone, especially people I wasn't acquainted with. You never know what a person's situation might be. An overly skinny person might be struggling with a health issue. Someone dressed differently may not have the money to afford nicer clothes. You get the picture. So, what made my situation any different? Why couldn't everyone look past what was on the outside and see me for the bright, bubbly girl I really was?

Not until after my first lengthening procedure did I realize how truly tiring it was to constantly be worrying about how others perceived me and regularly making excuses for those who were rude. Before the surgery, none of the ridicule really bothered me, but I realized that it wasn't the limb lengthening that opened my eyes and broke my innocence: it was me growing up. No longer was I the totally carefree little girl running around without giving a shit about what other people thought of me.

Rather than continue to cower in the shadow of others' actions and words and my own assumptions, I made my best attempt to reverse my thoughts. My mind was telling me one thing: every time I walked by a person who was looking at me, they immediately saw me as a dwarf, casting me in a negative light and discounting me for my height. I realized I couldn't read people's minds; therefore I didn't really know what they were thinking.

Little Kristen was a brave, happy, and carefree young girl. The new, little-bit-older Kristen could be the same way. It was just going to take a little more effort on my part.

School was out for the summer and I did anything and everything that I possibly could with my new legs. Absolutely nothing stood in my way. Family vacation in Maine this time around was go, go, go! Swimming, waterskiing, kayaking, and running up and down the beach, no strings attached. Not to mention my developing resemblance to a chocolate brownie thanks to good ol' Mr. Sun. The return of my ever-so-familar independence was embraced not only by me but by my family too. It was a relief for everyone knowing I was back to being self-sufficient and no longer in so much discomfort. Walking was getting easier and easier, and I gradually found my longer stride. Before I knew it, I finally settled into my life on longer legs.

My happiness proved that the first phase of the lengthening was totally worth it. All of the pain and frustration was miniscule compared to the enormous amount of positive energy that began to fill my life. I was visibly taller, and I began to notice little things that sparked pure excitement within.

After all those years of dragging a kitchen chair over to the counter to throw in some of my own culinary expertise, the chair was no longer necessary. The light switches throughout the house were now within reach, along with the freezer door and some of our taller cupboards. Getting in and out of any vehicle was now done with a lot more grace and finesse. Brushing my teeth at the bathroom sink was done without a stool, and getting into bed at night didn't require a stool or a running start. All of the positives made getting over the occasional bout of ignorance or self-doubt that much easier.

Pants! You guys! Finally—and longer pants at that! After months with nothing but hardware physically touching my legs because of the frames (no, the casts do not count), I am able to adorn my long-lost pants at last and with autumn at our heels. Jeans, sweatpants, dressy pants, pajama pants—give me all the pants. One problem: all the pants I currently own are now too short. This, of course, is a great problem to have, in my eyes. An update to my wardrobe is immediately necessary. This time, when Mom hems my jeans, she doesn't need to cut as much length off of the pant legs. Something so small has never made my heart sing so loudly.

Freedom had never felt so good. Yet, as the summer wore on, my mind continually focused on phase two of surgery. Though I knew very little about the humeral lengthening, one thing was for sure: it had to be a piece of cake compared to what I had just endured with my legs. No need for a wheelchair must mean more mobility.

Sign me up!

It was time to move on and get some longer, straighter arms. Not only was this procedure going to make my arms longer, Dr. Paley also said that it would make the "growing pains" in my elbows go away and decrease the severe flexion deformity that I suffered from. Most people can extend their arms to be perfectly straight. My arms, held straight, looked like I was trying to flex my muscles. Not the consistent effect I was going for. It was also another big step toward proportion. After discussing it with Dr. Paley and my family, we decided it would be best to wait until after I was through with most of eighth grade. Convinced I would be able to bounce back much quicker in round two, we scheduled surgery for the following spring during April vacation.

Normalcy had been elusive for so long aside from the little taste I had gotten at the end of seventh grade. The excitement of taking the bus at the start of a new school year, with all the neighborhood kids, using my locker, and participating in gym made the experience a little more inclusive. No longer was I the one always asking for help in class or at lunch. What a relief that I could reach across and grab a spicy chicken sandwich or choose my toppings from the salad bar at lunch without any assistance.

Yet now, even without a wheelchair, I quickly learned that junior high was not all milk and cookies. My knowledge of proper middle school etiquette had fallen to the wayside during seventh grade due to my immense focus on all things medical. The Abercrombie & Fitch secret I'd been let in on, but in terms of fashion and makeup, I was lost. My secret attempt at self-teaching how to put on an eighth grade face via *Teen Magazine* and online tutorials severely backfired as can be seen in my school picture. Blue backdrop, blue sweater, blue eyeshadow, and sheer purple lip gloss. What I should have done was send that photo in along with an application to be a member of the Blue Man Group. I think they would have been delighted. Mom was a little on the old-fashioned side, and I definitely didn't think she was the one to get pointers from. I was too embarrassed to ask my close friends. These are things you are supposed to know. No one hands you a manual at the beginning of middle school on how to be a teenage girl.

In elementary school, you could be friends with anyone. There weren't any guidelines stipulating who you should spend time with and why. Now there certainly seemed to be. Classmates split off into cliques of friends, and the criteria for acceptance had become totally unclear to me. I never fell into one group, and I didn't want to. There were so many things already defined in my life. Why did that have to go for who I associated with, too? Middle school was hard. The awkward boundaries set among my peers didn't stop me from staying on top of my academics. My high honors status warranted me a spot in the National Honor Society. It was exciting and an honor to have Mrs. Valeri present for my induction ceremony considering she had been a huge catalyst for change and achievement in my life.

Those nine months off were a big step in my surgical trilogy, giving me plenty of time to catch up on life and continue being a teenager without having to worry about biweekly doctor's appointments, tutoring, physical therapy, and the constant nagging pain of surgery. Through it all, I stayed on top of my schoolwork and made my eighth grade experience as worthwhile as possible.

39

Let's do this.

April vacation had arrived, and it was time. Mom and I ventured back down to Baltimore for the first time in quite a while. And I have to admit, it felt really good to be back. A little piece of my heart was—is— permanently tethered to that city and the people there.

Just as before, Mom and I checked into the Ronald McDonald House downtown, our home away from home. Going into it the second time around did not bring nearly as much stress. The presurgical jitters were still there, but there was a huge relief in knowing that the fixators on my arms were not going to knock me off my feet—pun completely intended. My ability to walk was not going to be compromised and the word *freedom* would play a bigger role during this second phase.

The preoperative appointment was still a little harrowing. What got me every time? The anesthesia consent forms. It was—and still is—a very scary thing to think about. No big deal, just signing my life away to a team of doctors, you know. Following our appointment with anesthesia, Mom and I moseyed on down to clinic and right into the usual sea of waiting patients and chaos. I didn't even care. Seeing everyone made me so incredibly happy, and I was home away from home for sure.

To defuse my growing nervousness, the day before surgery, Mom and I headed down to the Inner Harbor. Despite the fact that I had been to the Baltimore Aquarium more times than I could count on two hands, it never got old—and that is exactly where we began our afternoon. Somewhere between the hundreds of fish, dolphins, and rainforest creatures, the weight of what was to come had lifted off my shoulders. It's hard to say, but I think my favorite part of the day was spending Mom's money at the strip mall in the harbor. What girl doesn't enjoy indulging out of her mama's wallet?

Back at the Ronald McDonald House, Mom made dinner in the community kitchen, and we called it an early night. Tomorrow was a big day. The alarm went off at eleven thirty, and I ate my last ceremonial meal of Cheerios and some cantaloupe. Come midnight I was NPO (nothing by mouth) in preparation for surgery that morning.

Up early before the sun, I had butterflies in my stomach. Mom and I gathered our things, headed out, and pulled up to the front of Kernan Hospital at six thirty. Jumping out of the car, I sat on the bench outside the main entrance while Mom parked.

A man in spandex shorts, a cycling jersey, and a bike helmet sauntered toward me. *What an odd outfit to wear into the hospital.*

"Hi, Kristen," says the familiar voice.

Dr. Paley reaches out his arms and takes me into a big hug.

Wow. So relaxed. A far cry from how rushed he usually is in clinic.

"Are you ready?" he asks, his hands on my shoulders as he looks down at me.

"Sure am," I say, surprising myself with the level of concrete confidence in my voice.

"That a girl. I'll see you soon." With a gentle squeeze of my shoulders, he moves past me and in through the main entrance of Kernan.

So that's what doctors do to prepare themselves for a big day of surgeries?

Mom walked up, and we knew exactly where to go, taking a seat in the preoperative waiting area. Once the admitting paperwork was completed and I had my hospital bracelet on, I followed the nurse back to where all the pre-op patients were corralled, got into my oversized gown, and hopped up onto the gurney.

Before my little panic-stricken self tried to make a quick escape out of presurgical jail, my nurse came over with what she called a little "happy juice" drink. It resembled the cold medicine "Dimetapp," which I despised with a fiery passion. Anything artificially grape or orange flavored was pure yuck and gag reflex inducing in my book. Assuring me that it didn't taste bad, I tossed back the purple liquid. What it was exactly, I'm not sure, but I liked it. A lot. Knowing that I was somewhat breaking the rule of drinking something before surgery made the whole process that much more exciting. My inner rebel tapping her fingers together and mischievously mumbling, "Muahahahaha!"

As I tried to bargain with my nurse to put my IV in after I was under anesthesia, she convinced me that it wouldn't be that bad. Crazy, I know. After all the pins and pokes from the first surgery and what I was about to have done, needles still scared the shit out of me. Everyone has a weakness or two, and that happened to be mine—whether or not it made any sense at all. Yet, that sweet little cocktail must have had a dose of fearlessness in it because I agreed to play the role of human pincushion.

Surgery was scheduled for eight in the morning, but they weren't ready for me in the operating room until ten. Good thing the magic purple elixir had calmed my nerves. The wait didn't seem to faze me, but Mom felt a little differently; any parent would at that point.

Marilyn showed up in her scrubs with Dr. Waxman and one of the OR nurses in tow. I said goodbye to Mom, clutched onto my puppy partner in crime, Patches, for dear life, and was rolled back.

Here we go again.

Waking up from surgery was not nearly as traumatizing since I was now a veteran. My nausea from the first procedure was dually noted during pre-op, and before I woke up, they made sure to give me something for it. Grogginess? Yes. Blowing chunks? Not this time, baby!

Once I had completely come to, I realized that the pain really wasn't that bad. However, at the same time, I was very happy to see that I had my PCA pump button beside me. My upper arms were wrapped heavily in gauze and felt strange. Looking down, I noticed that my hands were bare and that the IV had been placed in my foot. I can't say that I was a huge fan of that, but I was going to choose my battles wisely. Even with the aches and pains following the surgery, I couldn't help but smile. I had made it through the actual procedure and was ready for the second part of my journey.

Wait for it.

Yep, that glorious feeling was so short-lived. Next thing I know, I am surrounded by a whole bunch of different people and a phlebotomist begins wrapping a tourniquet around my forearm.

Um, hello? Can you not see that I just had surgery on both of my arms, you numbskull? It isn't like I can just take my arm out of her grip either. I use my vocals as a warning that she better back off and tell me what the hell is going on before she dare touch me again. "*In case you aren't aware, I just had pins drilled into my arms,*" *I hiss.*

The wide-eyed woman in maroon scrubs steps back.

Yeah that's right—don't mess.

Mom isn't even back in the recovery room yet, and that is probably for the best.

Marilyn steps in before anyone else dare lay a hand on me.

It turned out that one of the OR nurses had gotten cut in the operating room with a bloody instrument, and they needed to draw blood from me to make sure I didn't have any serious diseases. Judging by my reaction to the situation, they ought to have tested me for rabies while they were at it. All I needed was an Alka-Seltzer tablet to get the foaming mouth effect, and it'd be a party. Despite their very good explanation, I refused to cooperate and let them stick me.

Nope. I will not allow it. They can draw blood from my IV line before they try to put a needle in my arm.

Next thing I know, I am staring face-to-face with Dr. Paley, and he does not look happy. He says, "You don't have a choice. Stop being a baby—and get it over with."

"Yes, sir."

The last thing I wanted was for my orthopedic surgeon to think I was a big sissy, so I took a deep breath and consented to let them draw blood. Since all the trauma from surgery had occurred in my arms, Dr. Paley told the woman that she needed to draw from my foot. Oh, goody. After all was said and done, the phlebotomist knew what she was doing, got the blood on her first stick and it wasn't overly horrible. You wouldn't know it from holding my hand though. My palms were pouring sweat, and the bed railings were clattering from the reverberation of my trembling body. All in my head.

After that most embarrassing scene, I was cleared to roll up to my own personal hospital room, away from all the chaos. Then I got the visit that I was waiting for. Pam, my favorite nurse and birthday buddy, popped her head in to check on me. A hug from that woman could make the most chaotic, and bad days, easy. After a short visit, she promised that she would be back to help me with lengthening and pin care.

Psssh. Pin care? Piece of cake. Only four pins in each arm to keep meticulously clean compared to the fifteen I had in each leg? A total cinch. My real plan is to ditch pin care altogether just as we did halfway through my leg lengthening. For now, though, that is going to stay on the downlow.

Both Mom and I were resting comfortably in the room. I was in control of the television, and Mom was knitting. There was such a sense of relief with four pins now residing in each of my arms accompanied by an Orthofix titanium bar. The fixators looked like futuristic swimmies, minus the floating capability. My pain levels were manageable, and I no longer needed my IV since I was drinking liquids like a champ. A Foley catheter wasn't even necessary because I had full use of my legs.

Getting out of bed for the first time was a little iffy. When you feel like you're about to take a tumble, your first instinct is to put your arms out to catch you. Well, not this girl. My arms were unusually heavy, and I felt like a peewee football linebacker with robotic shoulder pads on. My steps were tiny to avoid tripping and falling and I was followed very closely by Sandy, the physical therapist. Getting my undies down and then up again required some assistance, but other than that, first trip to the bathroom accomplished.

The final task before I was discharged from the hospital was learning the ways of humeral lengthening with my best girl, Pam. The process was a tad different with the arm contraptions. My tool was a cute little Allen wrench, and I only had two screws to turn. Easy peazy, lemon squeezy. With first turns made and clean pins, I was ready to blow that popsicle stand.

Physical therapy came by one more time to make sure I had basic ambulation down pat and showed me some exercises to do until I could get my PT evaluation with the ladies at Plymouth Bay when I returned home. They said that the soreness would eventually go away and that my strength would return. Getting dressed took me a little longer with the arm bling, and I needed a little assistance getting my sleeves over the hardware. With that, I was a free bird.

Mom and I headed back to the Ronald McDonald House. Staying one night before heading home was important—just to be sure all was well after discharge. My only restrictions were to take it easy in regard to physical activity and absolutely no heavy lifting: five pounds max.

40

Once home, it was almost as if no major surgery had ever taken place. Yes, I had these robotic titanium bars on my arms and pins sticking into my bone, but my pain was minimal. Adjusting to life with the humeral fixators on was the cat's pajamas compared to the Ilizarov frames that once resided on my tibias. Within a week or so, I had become accustomed to the extra weight on each arm and regained most of my mobility.

Another major convenience was the clothing situation. Tank tops and T-shirts did not cause any obstacles since they were easily put on over the orthofix bars. Long sleeves posed more of a problem. Luckily, I was also able to find some small little zip-up sweatshirts with sleeves that stretched and were wide enough to cover my arms—fixators and all.

Minor adjustments had to be made in school. Since I was limited in the amount of weight I could carry around, I was gifted two sets of books (please hold your jealousy): one for the classroom and one for home. Teachers allowed me to leave class five minutes early so I wasn't clobbered in the hallways by perfume and cologne-soaked pubescent teenagers. Although, I'm sure that if anyone bumped me, it would have hurt them more than me.

My early dismissal meant a few things: prime location in the lunch line, complete with priority seating, an excuse to roam the hallways with a friend in tow, and an automatic guarantee that I got to my next class on time. I didn't have to worry about catching the bus on the way home because my friend Meaghan and I somehow convinced her mom that we were worthy of a ride home in the green bus (her mom's ginormous suburban) every day.

Before the end of eighth grade, Silver Lake Regional Junior High School threw a semiformal dance. It was an opportunity for teenage bodies to fill the gymnasium and bump and grind to loud music. I wasn't sure I wanted to be a participant, especially with my fixators on, not to mention the fact that I wasn't "going out" with anyone. Flying solo to social events wasn't the end of the world, and since some of my dateless friends banded together, I agreed to join in.

Macy's has provided me with the perfect pink dress that falls right below my knees (God forbid I break any of the dress code rules.) Shoes are the major issue. I simply have to wear heels. You just don't show up to a school dance in flats. My size 2 feet don't exactly warrant a nice pair of wedges. The smallest women's size that Mom and I can find in a wedge is a women's size 5. Finally, I settle on a pair of white wedges that my feet are strapped into—good thing because they are a little on the big side in terms of heel height and size. I probably have a solid half inch of extra shoe behind my heel. Hey, sometimes sacrifices are necessary. Mom fashions a little cardigan, the same color pink as my dress, with sleeves wide enough to fit over my arms.

It wasn't exactly how I pictured it would be, but it was pretty darn close. Our cafeteria had been transformed into a seizure-inducing room full of flashing lights and loud music. Crowds of kids gathered in the center of the dance floor by the DJ, thrashing their bodies wildly about. Others stood in small groups along the perimeter. Chaperones were keeping a close eye on the untamed teenage absurdity that was unfolding.

The boys soon decided that their ties served better purpose tied around their heads, and I acknowledged that my dance moves were executed better without my shoes on. As I migrated from one friend group to another, we all danced. We were shaking it like Polaroid pictures all night long. Despite some of the annoying aspects of my first dance, like not being asked to dance by any boys, I went—and I had fun. It was one giant step for my little legs toward achieving a sense of normalcy that my big heart craved.

Although many times, I found myself frustrated with the implications of the lengthening surgeries, I also found many ways to bask in all of my bionic glory. My way of doing so was a little different, but that didn't change the all-encompassing experience.

The summer that bridged the gap between middle and high school, was a welcome respite from the consistent dedication to my studies. Per the usual, I made it a point to make the most of those summer months. During our family vacation time in Maine I swam nonstop. Even with pins in my arms, I manhandled a kayak paddle like you wouldn't believe. Mom and Dad did have to draw the line when I insisted I would be fine to waterski. That would have to wait. Derek and I were thrilled to find out that Monica, who had just finished the first phase of the surgery on her tibias, was coming up to Camp with her family for a visit.

There is something special that resides in a friendship between two people who have been through so much together. Monica and I have an understanding and appreciation for life that not many people possess. It's fair to say that our siblings, Derek, Adrienne, and Joey, are troopers for being dragged along in this journey. Maybe that is why we all have so much fun together.

Tonight, we are pitching the tent in the front yard by the beach and camping out. With lights out and the loons singing on the lake, everything is going smoothly until Derek and Joey decide that lullabies composed of fart noises are a superb idea. It's hilarious ... for the first two minutes—and then it gets old. Really, really fast. So they move on to Ace Ventura impressions.

"Hi. I'm looking for Ray Finkle ... and a clean pair of shorts."

By Derek's fourth attempt of talking to me via his butt cheeks, and Joey doubled over laughing, Monica, Adrienne, and I are over it. Boys will be boys. We pick up our pillows and sleeping bags and make our way inside to set up camp on the pull-out couch mattress in the middle of the living room floor.

The boys won't admit to being scared, but we all know that is why they followed us inside a short while later. We banish them to the bunk beds where they can continue their bathroom-humor skits behind a closed door. And now sleep.

I groggily wake to pitch-black, and the girls still next to me. There is a noise that I can't quite place. Sitting up, I realize it is coming from directly in front of me. It sounds like something repetitiously landing on the floor. What the—?

I lean over and shake Monica awake. She hears it too. Soon all three of us girls are awake and uneasy about the situation on hand. Holding onto the couch, I stand and click on the light. Simultaneously, all three of us scream and huddle in a big ball in the middle of the living room floor.

We discover that the noise is the sound of our cat, Montana, jumping into the air and then landing on the floor because there is a bat circling overhead—in the house!

The girls and I continue to scream from our human ball of safety on the floor.

When the boys wake up, open their door, and see what is happening, they scream like little girls and slam their door closed.

Gee, thanks, guys. You're a big help.

At last, the commotion wakes my parents. Mom is no help aside from her constant begging Dad not to harm the bat. Dad grabs a broom, and with us girls screaming and laughing in our huddle, the cat running and jumping about the room, and Derek and Joey screaming while continuously opening and closing their bedroom door, he manages to intercept the bat. It is now clinging to the broom. Derek runs out of the bedroom and opens the slider, and Dad throws out the bat and broom.

Game over, Mr. Bat. Game over. This Taddeo/DeAndrade family vacation is one for the books.

Thankfully, the frequent visits to Baltimore for my arms were a little less dramatic and eventful than those we had with my lower legs. My progress was on point. As I continued my turns, there was a noticeable difference in my arms. The visible length put meaning into each and every adjustment I was making with my Allen wrench. Even though I no longer needed a stool for most of the things up on the kitchen counter, periodically I would have to jump thrust my upper body onto the counter for that extra bit of reach. Now, when I went to reach for a cup beside the sink, I realized that my little bit of extra hop-off effort was no longer necessary. My reach across the counter was now effortless. My hands could almost fit entirely into the pockets of my shorts, and straightening my arms meant my arms were almost all the way straight. Not only that, I could reach into some of the top cupboards and into the back of the freezer.

Right before high school began, we set off for one final summer trip to the beach, down by the Cape, with Lianna and her family. The waves were huge. Decked out in my oversized T-shirt to protect the newly forming scar tissue and open pin sites from the sun, I didn't hesitate to hop on a boogie board and conquer the swell with everyone else.

Dr. Paley probably wouldn't have advised it, but in the moment, the little devil on my shoulder was whispering, "Cowabunga!"

41

Beginning my freshman year of high school was intimidating in itself. High school? Uh, yikes. From the get-go, I was beyond nervous, but in my heart, I knew that physically being there was going to make my academic experience easier and would have a profound impact on my social interactions.

At that point in my life, I continued to secretly struggle with some major social issues. Despite my outward confidence about not letting others' opinions of me cut through my fragile skin, it was a little bit of lie that I was telling myself on the days where life just seemed hard. I began a longtime habit of swallowing my negative emotions and allowing them to pile up. They weren't anything anyone ever talked about. If you did, it was with a shrink. And if you needed therapy, you were most definitely not cool.

As children, we are taught that crying is a sign of weakness, and we are shushed by our loved ones. I'm not saying that it's a bad thing, it's simply habitual. With that instilled in my brain, I began to wear a mask. It showed everyone that Kristen was fine, but within myself and behind closed doors, I felt judged—constantly—by my peers and the public. When I was out with friends and family, people would stare. I immediately had to act like it was nothing. To improve my mask, I would just act goofy or laugh at the situation. Eventually, I became so good at my new defense mechanism that it became second nature to me.

Silver Lake Regional High School is an entity in and of itself. It is ginormous in comparison to the middle school, and my position was at the bottom of the totem pole as a little freshman. The rumors about the 112 hallway and how it can swallow you up if you aren't careful are true.

As soon as the bell rings at the end of class, an avalanche of students spills into the hallway. Courtesy is thrown out the window and replaced with gum snapping, running, pushing, groping against lockers, swearing, and fragrance-abusing chaos as everyone makes their way to their next class or the woods. Yes, the woods. Apparently that's the place to go to smoke—or the girls' bathroom.

My only reason to go outside is for Spanish class in the old portables, which smell like must and mildew, behind the school. There are so many kids that the brick walls are busting at the seams. The new portables, on the other end, can be accessed from inside. Not wanting to draw any more attention to myself by leaving class early, I opt to navigate the crowds to and from class. I assure you that many rib cages and arms fall victim to my hardware-laden arms when I push through the sea of students.

The first notice we receive in homeroom about a "bomb threat" is rather unsettling. By the fourth notice, it is old news. Just another day at the Lake. Pajamas and sweatpants are part of the school dress code. Except during spirit week, then tutus, boas, knee-high socks, and glitter are the norm—even for the guys. Classes are manageable, a little more difficult, but I also find more enjoyment in those that interest me. Particularly, English and Biology. Physically being present in school does make the entire experience easier when it comes to the learning process and it is highly entertaining.

We continued to track my growth progress and ensure that my nerves and muscles were accommodating to the new length of my arms as expected with trips to Kernan Hospital for a clinic appointment. Sitting comfortably in the car made the trip that much easier, and the time passed by a lot faster—or maybe that was just when I drove with Dad? He always meant business when it came to traveling: no unnecessary pit stops. We gassed up the car, went to the bathroom, and grabbed lunch at the first stop on the New Jersey Turnpike. That was it.

Whenever Dad and I make the trip to Baltimore, we are there and back in a flash. One of my biggest achievements to this day—a bladder of steel—is attributed to the time crunch and rush of the trip. True northerners for you, eh? In addition to my ability of "holding it," I have come to develop some stellar and exquisite highway vocabulary.

A "zippah head" refers to the bozo in the car in front of us, very much in our way, going entirely too slow. Zippah heads do not belong in the passing lane.

"Death behind the wheel" refers to senior citizens who should probably just give up driving altogether.

An "asshole" is usually a fellow driver who either refuses to use their turn signal, cuts people off, tailgates, passes on the right, or lacks any courtesy.

Then we have the classic exclamations.

"Sack!" is the Bostonian version of "suck," perfect for any moment of disapproval or disgust when it comes to generalized traffic or missing an exit.

"Are you shitting me?" usually occurs while listening to either the Red Sox or the Patriots on the radio. If something grave goes down, the phrase is tailored to, "Are you fucking shitting me?"

And, an all-time favorite, having a full-blown conversation with the person in the other car, who has officially ruined the next five minutes of life due to their lack of driving skill—as if they can hear what is being directed at them, let alone whether or not they care.

Over the course of our various road trips up and down I-95, I have come to learn many other hard, useful facts.

Officer Friendly, at least in New Jersey, likes to hide back behind overpasses, AAA will take their sweet time no matter how pressing the issue is, a can of Fix-a-Flat should always be kept in your car, a lot of drivers don't know how to use their turn signals, some travelers use their time to multitask and put on makeup, shave, or engage in sexual acts while driving, gas is always cheaper in New Jersey, and in the Garden State, they do the dirty work at the gas pumps.

As my father's daughter, I mastered the rules of the road. Needless to say, I can thank Dad for the constant expansion of my vocabulary with all the necessary expletives and teaching me how to drive with aggressive intention.

Physical therapy continued throughout my arm lengthening every afternoon after school. This time around, it was less rigorous. Don't get me wrong, the ladies at New England Sports and Orthopedic Therapy kicked my ass with all kinds of exercises and the beloved Stairmaster. I just didn't experience the pain and discomfort that came with rehab during my first phase of lengthening. Brenda, Chris, Cyndi, Flo, Jayne and all of the staff went above and beyond their therapeutic call of duty. Many times, I found myself sprawled out on the table with my homework. In addition to scholarly assistance, they were emotionally supportive during the really shitty days.

And then, just when I began to brag about my complication-free lengthening, disaster struck. Well, not disaster—tendonitis. As minor as it sounds, compared to all the impediments I was forced to overcome during the tibial lengthening, it was extremely limiting and agonizing. And it was on my right side—yes, my dominant side. The littlest things like writing proved to be difficult. I was put into a modified sling that fit over my titanium wings, and I could only use my left arm. Ambidextrous took on an entirely new meaning.

The week before my fourteenth birthday, I was gifted some good news: I was done lengthening my full four inches. With my elbows completely bent, my thumbs touched the front of my shoulders, a sign, according to Dr. Paley, that the lengthening was indeed complete. Aside from my one little bout with tendonitis, the arm lengthening had been a breeze. The hard part was now over, and all I had to do was heal. Since Mondays were clinic days with Dr. Paley, it was a full day of school that I missed and had to make up work for. I was glad that these were no longer necessary as the make-up work on top of everything else was getting to be a lot.

42

Merry Christmas, Kristen. Merry Christmas, indeed: both of my humeri had consolidated completely and the orthofix bars were coming off! As wonderful as the news was, I hesitated. It seemed too good to be true. It was the same news I had heard time and time again with the birdcages on my lower legs. Only to have casts and then removable casts and a horrific experience with that whole process. Who wasn't to say that I could be faked out this time too? We scheduled the removal date for the end of December, right after Christmas. Let me tell you, those few weeks leading up to the removal date were killer. Were they really going to come off? First time is a charm? So much anticipation, I could barely stand it.

Back to Baltimore we went, a little bit hesitant and a whole lot excited. The pre-op appointment was almost too easy. The removal was going to be done on that Monday, a clinic day. Removals are "quick and easy." Nothing compared to the application of the fixator, at least that's how I imagined it. Nuts and bolts unscrewed, titanium hardware comes off, Dr. Paley grabs a large pair of surgical pliers, one swift move with each pin (times eight) and presto!

On the morning of surgery, we arrived while it was still dark, once again, at the James Lawrence Kernan Hospital. Marilyn met us back in the holding area, and they began prepping me for surgery. I wore the loveliest of terribly oversized gowns, which, if I wasn't careful, would cause me to moon the hospital staff. That day marked the end of phase two of my lengthening procedures. I was two-thirds of the way there.

I opened my eyes in recovery, barely able to remember the events of the morning. One minute I'm in the OR, and the next minute, it's completely over with. Whoa. Then it registered: I was out of surgery, but were the fixators gone? My brain was working, but my body mechanics weren't so coordinated. With a deep breath and heart full of hope, I lifted my head and turned to the left and then to the right. No fixators. My arms were free of any and all paraphernalia. Time to spread my wings. The excitement was so strong I almost didn't know what to do with myself.

The second leg—or should I say arm—of my journey is over. Two procedures down and only one to go. Holy Santa Claus shit. The feeling of not having anything drilled into my bones is becoming almost unnatural. My arms are featherlight, covered in bloody gauze, and still very fragile.

My recovery nurse scolds me for flopping about on my gurney while I'm trying to work part of the gauze down so I can see my bullet hole-resembling wounds. The braces for my arms have not been made yet, and she warns me that I need to use caution when moving around to avoid fracturing anything. All righty then. I sit and wait as patiently as possible for instructions on what to do—or not to do—next.

An hour passes, I get a few packages of graham crackers, peanut butter, and some ginger ale down, and my nurse deems me worthy of being disconnected from my IV. They know the rule by now, no one touches my IV, I am the only one who is allowed to remove the tape and take it out. I would rather inflict pain on myself than have someone else do it. Standing with close supervision, I get into a wheelchair go down to occupational therapy to have the braces for my arms made. Similar to the hot pink foot plates that were made for my feet, the OT has to heat up the bracing material in hot water and then carefully mold it to my arms. I am in total shock and beyond disappointed to discover that the only color they have is tan. Tan? Really? Not my first choice on the color spectrum. Yuck. Looks like another opportunity to get fancy and take decorative matters into my own hands once I get home. The braces simply wrap around my upper arm to provide extra support and are secured with Velcro. To have something wrapped around my arm, making contact with my skin feels so, so good. The braces fit perfectly under my long-sleeved shirts and make me look mighty muscular. This removal is so simple that they do it as an outpatient procedure and now I can go home away from home to the Ronald McDonald House.

Dr. Paley wished for me to be seen in clinic before we got the final consent to head out. It was an informal meeting with my favorite person, Pam, just to go over precautions and post-op rules. In the final few weeks of the healing phase, sans fixators, I am instructed to take it easy. My arms are still fragile, especially where the pins were taken out. I cannot lift anything over a pound or two. No backpack, no groceries, no laundry basket. Sorry, parentals, Derek might need to pick up my slack on this one. Everything else looked good. I said my good-byes and Mom and I headed out.

Perhaps one of the most exciting, immediate benefits of the removal was being able to wear longer sleeves. There is something about clothing's physical contact with one's body that, when denied for a long period of time, is magical when it returns. Even more wonderful was the fact that a lot of my long-sleeved shirts no longer needed to be hemmed. What most people take for granted was now seen as a total luxury and physical evidence of my growth. That transition from surgical phase back to normality brought a huge surge in confidence and happiness. It was hard to believe that I only had one phase left. So close to the end.

The few months of my freshman year enjoyed in complete freedom gave me the opportunity to reconnect with my teachers, schoolwork, and friends. Meeting the demands of school was a lot easier with my arms. Throughout the entire procedure, my pain was minimal. My mobility was not overly compromised, aside from being unable to carry a backpack, but with so much focus on my physical well-being, my emotional ease seemed to take a hit. Not a drastic beatdown. More like a consistent whittling away at my teenage psyche.

Despite knowing most of the kids I entered high school with since elementary school, the pressures of adolescence rang true when it came to cliques and the well-known popularity struggles. Rather than be accepted for who I was on the inside, most of my peers took one look at what I was facing and decided that I was no longer the person—or child—I used to be. Friends I frequently hung out with in elementary school and junior high no longer were my "friends," just friendly towards me. Big difference. And it hurt—a lot.

When I began to notice the changes in how I was being viewed by my "friends," initially I thought it was me. Had I done something wrong to make them more distant? My focus became the people who were ignoring me and how I could win their attention rather than giving attention to those who continued to stand by me. At the time, I did not realize it, but the pressures of feeling like I had to change to be accepted were slowly taking a toll on me.

Acceptance. It's such a simple word, really, but the act of accepting can be downright difficult. I often found myself avoiding acceptance—and not just self-acceptance. The friends I used to talk to every day on the phone or spend hours over each other's houses with now hardly had time to flash a smile in the hallway. That was difficult to accept. Regardless of the internal battle, I pushed the struggle aside and kept a smile on my face.

By early spring, my arms were fully healed, and I no longer needed to wear my splints. Knowing that the last procedure was going to require a bigger time commitment and some homeschooling, I decided that it was time for round three. My teachers knew what I was up against. Feeling solid in my studies and having those I needed on my team, it was now or never. The thought of possibly dragging the process into my junior year did not sit well. I wanted to get it over with as soon as possible.

My femurs, from what I'd heard, were sure to be the most difficult surgery. There was comfort in knowing what I had already been through and how far I had come, and it caused that light at the end of the tunnel to shine even brighter. With an afflatus driven by that bright light, my focus was set on the next nine months or so.

Bring it.

43

There were days I questioned my own sanity. The goal with the next round was five inches of length and every last little adjustment possible, in Dr. Paley's bag o' tricks, which would allow me to stand and walk straighter. As old pros, we were prepared: wheelchair, walker, ramp in the garage, handicapped-accessible shower, game faces—you get the picture. As prepared as I told myself I was for the femur lengthening, I also left a small reservoir in my heart for disappointment and upset. All of the independence I had known was going out the window. Really, there is nothing that can completely prepare you for that. The positive attitude, paired with the expectation that the easy wouldn't last, certainly helped.

Stairs would be out of the question, so I reclaimed my downstairs bedroom. The lack of privacy was not favorable but being right next to the kitchen made for easy access to a possible midnight snack. Preparation this time around also involved a massive sewing party. Old Navy pajama pants were so in. Mom, being the crafty woman she is, bought a slew of the pajama pants—in all different colors and patterns—and matching ribbon. We cut each of the pant legs up the side, so that they resembled a long-legged diaper of sorts, and then sewed in the ribbon so that the pants tied closed.

Once again, Mom and I set up shop at the Ronald McDonald House. Between the house and the hospital, the most comforting part of the experience is always the familiar faces and new friends to be made. Our stay this time would be a little bit longer than our past few visits since this was major surgery. After unloading all the loot from the car, we drove to the hospital for my preoperative appointment.

Pre-op was the same as usual: long and strenuous on the emotions, causing them to run high. The paperwork listing the risks of anesthesia just made the tears start to flow. For people who are unfamiliar with surgery, it happens to be a big deal. No matter how many times you go through it. Once you are put under, your life is literally in the hands of others. The older I got, the scarier it became simply because I understood everything. As a young child, they tell you that you're going to breathe cherry air and fall fast asleep. The IV and blood draws were done while I was under during my first surgery, so everything was all cotton candy and rainbows the day of. With the second surgery, since I was a little older, I began to understand the risks, and it was scarier. And with the third one, everything made sense: the logistics, the process, and all the risks. And that made it scary as hell.

In clinic, I had x-rays, squeezed my best buds, and then went back into an exam room to talk with the medical magician. It always amazed me how calm, cool, collected—yet also in a rush—Dr. Paley was every time we met with him. By now, we had a system. All questions needed to be in written form on a visible piece of paper. The index of concerns sometimes consisted of many small sticky notes and miscellaneous jottings paper-clipped together. After he entered the room, I took a seat on one of the rolling stools and positioned myself in front of the closed door as a road block. Once all questions and concerns had been voiced and answered and I felt good about the appointment, I rolled myself out of the doorway to allow Dr. Paley's passing, but not before a hug. "Hugs over handshakes," was and forever will be my motto.

To keep my mind off of the looming surgery, roaming around the Inner Harbor always seemed to help. It was going to be the last time walking on my own two legs for a while, and with each step I took, I tried to imagine what my new stride would be like. Longer. Taller. Straighter. As many times as I had been to the National Aquarium, I knew that place like the back of my hand. While the sea lion show was a personal favorite, I had been a chosen receiver of a kiss from Ty in years past, I treasured the tropical rain forest exhibit all the way at the top of the massive building.

Riding the escalator up into the lush, muggy rain forest environment, tree frogs and birds are audible. I am beyond excited. I can hardly stand it. I have comrades up here. Sloths! With an innately friendly nature, they are always smiling, adorable, and slower than an asthmatic herd of turtles. We have so much in common. They are great at hide-and-seek, love to sleep, have bladders

159

of steel—they only have to go to the bathroom once a week—and are, believe it or not, graceful in the water. My furry, tree-dwelling friends are up here in the trees. I could care less about any of the birds. I mean, yes, they are beautiful, but they don't get it, life. Of all the times I have been to the aquarium, I have only seen a sloth up close and personal once. Most of the time, they can only be seen as a furry blur clinging to a tree branch among the leaves, but there was one time when a sloth was on the ground in the exhibit. It took every ounce of self-restraint not to jump the rock wall and embrace the two-toed creature.

And now I'm back. Please, God, National Aquarium, let one of my friends come down to play with me. As Mom and I make our way off the escalator, I notice a small crowd of people gathering around one of the volunteers. And then I see it. A friend, a few feet off the ground, wrapped around the trunk of a tree. Rapunzel is her name, and in this moment I have found my soulmate.

Psychologically built to "hang in there," I think I was a sloth in my past life. After standing in the same place, wistfully gazing at my two-toed spirit animal for what seemed like not long enough, Mom was over it. We were both hungry. To go along with my spicy attitude, I was craving buffalo wings. Everyone knows that there is only one place to get the best buffalo wings. Hooters, duh. That's right. Mom and I waltzed right on in to that place. It wasn't our first rodeo, and I promise that neither of us were there for the boobs—only the wings.

That night, as always, I enjoyed my ritual bowl of Cheerios at eleven thirty before my midnight cutoff for food and drink. Thereafter, I found very little sleep. *This is it—the last hurrah—and I am one big ball of anxiety.* I know what you're thinking, but back then, there wasn't an app for that.

At five in the morning, I was up and at 'em. I took a good long shower; it would be my last one for a little while. The whole time, my heart was racing. If I made an attempt to talk, I would erupt into tears. This happened the morning of every surgery; it was my body's visceral reaction. All I wanted to do was fast-forward to waking up in recovery. Alas, that was not possible.

Mom and I arrived at Kernan at six thirty. After more paperwork, I was taken back into the pre-op holding area. I got my fun oversized gown and allowed the nurse to go ahead with the IV. You would think a little IV would be a piece of cake after all the pins and wires that had already been drilled into my arms and legs. Nope. It still wasn't easy, but I braved the needle, got my IV placed before anesthesia, and stayed on the gurney. Big things for Little Miss Kristen.

Marilyn came by to say hello as she made her rounds to all of us waiting to be sedated and unconscious. Her presence was always welcome, yet nothing would have prepared me for the news she was about to deliver: Dr. Paley had an emergency surgery. What did that mean for me? Initially I was second in line, but now I was third. Time frame? There wasn't one.

Oh, spectacular.

Now what? We waited and waited. More than ever, I wanted a magical fast-forward button.

Well, folks, that was the day I met Versed. Easily equivalent to drinking six tequilas, that shit will have you slurring your words, seeing flying teal ponies and asking medical personnel out on dates only thirteen seconds after entering your bloodstream. It was love at first push of the syringe for me and an immediate conscious sedation.

Geez, I thought Valium was nice, but it has nothing on my new comrade, Versed. Within seconds of the anesthesiologist delivering the medicine into my bloodstream, I feel like I could fly. Nothing matters, and everything is funny—even the screaming child in the bay next to me. Here I am people, eyes half open, incessantly giggling to myself. Nervous? Who, me? Nah, dude. You've got the wrong girl. This feeling—can I hold onto it as long as possible please? Mom keeps telling me that she doesn't understand what I am trying to say. I only know one language and what I hear myself saying makes perfect sense, I don't know what she means. Is this what drinking a Manhattan feels like? No wonder Grammie loves them so much.

By noon the child who was the case ahead of me, the same one who earlier sounded like a wailing siren capable of making eardrums bleed, was finally rolled into the OR. At last, progress. One more dose of Versed, and I was good to go, floating again. Before I knew it, the OR crew was standing at my bedside, ready to take me back. A big goodbye hug to Mom, and off we went into the cold, sterile operating room. Floating into the unknown, feeling like I had just put the IV in sedative with a little sprinkle of fear. See what I did there?

No amount of loopy juice can mask the fact that I am in a flippin' torture chamber—or maybe the drugs are really messing with my mind. My eyes fix on the saws, hammers, trays of pins and wires, and a pair of huge-ass cutters similar to those that Dad uses to trim the huge pine tree in our yard. What exactly are those going to be used for on me? My eyes continue to wander across the endless, barbaric tools as I transfer onto the very narrow operating table and put my head on the little doughnut-looking pillow. My army of medical people, in charge of my life, are busy moving about the room, tending to the beeping machines, and completely unfazed by the tables of torment that have my psyche in a conniption.

Marilyn is standing by my side in her OR garb. My hand is in hers as a few of the staff begin placing monitors on my chest and covering me with warm blankets. "Everything is going to go beautifully," she whispers.

Wow. The meds have really taken effect now because I can't even seem to find the words to answer her. The next thing I know, the mask is over my face and I am counting backward from ten. Ten ... seven ... two ... (go back to elementary school and learn how to count, Kristen) out—or so I thought.

I'm hearing beeps and the clatter of metal on metal. My eyes open a little bit, and everything is blurry. It's hard. It feels like there are weights on my eyelids. I try to swallow, but I can't. Something is wrong. A tube is down my throat. I panic and begin to gag. What is happening? My eyes are wide-open, and I start to thrash, calling immediate attention to myself.

"More sedation!" someone screams.

Several eyes are peering down at me over masks, telling me to hold still. My body begins to tingle, my eyes get heavy, and the sounds begin to echo. I am out again.

Scariest moment of my life.

The next time I woke up, it was expected. The six-hour surgery was over, and everything had gone as planned.

That was until my tongue began to swell.

An allergic reaction. How wonderful—because the day hadn't been exciting enough. I was in pain, and I was afraid that my breathing was going to become compromised by my tongue, which felt like it had doubled in size. Fortunately, the nurses gave me some magical elixir that reversed the reaction. There was so much happening at once that it took more than an hour in recovery to actually take a deep breath and process the fact that I now had reentered the world of external fixation. The orthofix bars on my femurs looked much less scary than the big old Ilizarov frames that were on my tibias during my first lengthening. One thing that remained the same? Pain. It hurt. Two broken legs are a pretty good excuse for a trusty morphine pump, making things a little more manageable.

Mom and I finally made it to my room on the pediatric floor. After the events of the day, all I wanted to do was close my eyes and rest. A hospital may be a place to heal, but it's certainly no place to sleep. People are constantly in and out of your room: nurses, physical therapists, phlebotomy. Just when you've dozed off for a nice little nap, there's another knock on the door. Seriously?

The phone rings. It's dietary. What do I want to eat for dinner tomorrow? Tomorrow? How the hell am I supposed to know? Ask me tomorrow. After the fifth intrusion and disturbance to my peace, I'm done. Mom puts a note on the door for anyone wanting to enter my room. They need to see the nurse first. Finally, some peace and quiet for us both.

After a much-needed siesta, the fun continued: pin care and the lowdown on lengthening. Actually, I was completely okay with this taking place because it was more like social hour involving my person, Pam. It was a private party—invite only.

Pam is a very special person in my life. A calming force amidst the chaos, from the first time I met her in my hospital room on the day I learned to lengthen with the Ilizarov frames, I knew she was special. Three years later, we are still going strong, birthday buddies. Pam has gotten me through some of my toughest moments throughout my lengthening journey. Pin care the first time around—regardless of what kind of external fixator you are dealing with—is something to be wary of. Fresh out of surgery, the surrounding tissue is swollen from all the trauma and thus very sensitive. If I am going to get it done, it is better having someone by my side who I trust 100 percent.

This time around, I have a total of twelve pins instead of the thirty pins during the first phase on my legs. I'll take it. Using the normal saline solution, we began to soak the bloodstained, crusty gauze that was wrapped around the six pins in each leg. Wetting the gauze made its removal less excruciating. Slowly but surely, we unraveled the Kerlix gauze from each leg, cleaned the pin sites thoroughly, and rewrapped them. Through our teamwork and diligence, the whole event didn't end up being as painful as I had anticipated.

Using the same tape and nail polish as we did with the previous two lengthenings, the struts on the orthofix bars were painted and labeled.

It was hard to believe that this would be the last time I would need this tutorial. My Allen wrench and I were all set and ready to make some magic happen; five inches of length, we've got this. During surgery, Dr. Paley had already made an adjustment in my femurs to stop me from walking a little bent over. The nickname I had earned as a little girl—Bubble Butt—was not going to be applicable now.

After two days of laying belly-up on my hospital bed, I was ready to move. With the help of Mom, Pam, and the physical therapist, I was able to get up into the wheelchair and get out of my nasty oversized hospital gown. Prepared with the clothes Mom tailored to accommodate my new fashion accessories, I made some moves. Any more time spent in the smelly condition I was in, and I might start losing friends. Once I was clean, Mom and I went for a walk outside to get some fresh air.

Once we returned to the room, my nurse told us that since I had made leaps and bounds in recovery, I just needed one more night for observation and a physical therapy consult the next morning—and then we were free to go home. Sweet. I was ready, and I know Mom was too. That night, I think we both slept a little better just knowing that home was only an eight-hour drive away.

The next morning, I had one more visit from physical therapy to practice transferring in and out of the wheelchair. It was an art form that I was slowly learning. Then we got our discharge paperwork, and we were free to go. Getting into the car was a little cumbersome, but once I was in and my legs were comfortable, we were all set. My supportive setup involved a cooler and a whole lot of pillows.

44

There is only so much to keep one entertained on an eight-hour drive. After two and a half years of the back-and-forth trips, music and reading got old real quick. Somewhere along the ride, I had to throw some laughs in. Mom was such a good sport.

There are days where I put away the precious white angel wings and put on my glittery red devil horns. It's a voluntary move motivated purely by fun, I assure you. One can only take so much during a lengthy ride in the car, so spicing things up a little bit and having some laughs sounds like a stellar idea—at Mom's expense.

We are halfway home when we stop along the New Jersey Turnpike for dinner and a bathroom break. That in itself is very time-consuming with the wheelchair being involved. Transferring back and forth with pins in my thighs is a bit like playing a game of Operation: out of the car, onto the toilet, off the toilet, back into the car and all without hitting or bumping anything. After relieving my bladder of steel and getting some dinner, we sit in line to get some gas. For whatever reason, Mom needs to run back into the rest area for something she's forgotten—probably some more sugar for her already sweetened tea.

In her absence, I decide to put a little humor into the rest of our drive. Taking her straw, I dip one end into a salt packet and then replace it in her drink. (Insert large grinchy smirk here). After retrieving whatever it was from the rest stop, Mom gets back into the car. We gas up, and I play it cool and help arrange her on-the-go meal so she can eat and drive at the same time. Places to go and family to see, people. On to Massachusetts.

This whole time, I am working extra hard to stifle my laughter at the thought of her taking that first sip, and I am doing an incredible job. I wonder how hard it is to learn how to play poker? With a poker face like this, I have the potential to fool many.

And then it plays out perfectly. Before even taking a bite of her dinner—Roy Rogers fried chicken, of course—Mom grabs her drink. In the middle of her large swig, she makes the most ridiculous, distorted face and nearly sprays her drink all over the car. It is a clear, dead giveaway whodunit. Turning to face me, sitting innocently with my headphones on, trying really hard not to laugh, she yells, "You are brutal!"

I continue to bop my head to the music until I can hold it in no longer and double over in laughter. Soon enough, she gets over her salty sip and joins me in the giggle fest. Muahaha. Daughter wins again.

Adjusting, once more, to being weighted down—literally—was a bit difficult, even though I knew it was all coming. At fifteen years old, my independence coming to a screeching halt was like a slap in the face. Unlike the first two procedures, there was no leeway in being able to walk or even stand up with a walker, due to the lack of all-around support to my broken legs.

Initially, being waited on is nice, having all hands on deck, and Mom, Dad, and Derek at my every beck and call. Sooner than later, though, it gets really old. I needed help with everything: getting my meals, showering, brushing my teeth, and even going to the bathroom. For a small child, it isn't as big of a deal, but for a teenager, it becomes the end of the world—no exaggeration there whatsoever (okay, maybe just a little bit). The best I could do was put forth the effort to be as independent as possible.

With the guidance from my physical therapists, I mastered the ability of transferring from my wheelchair to a chair, the toilet, etcetera without much assistance. Those little accomplishments were huge. The funny part of it all was that my version of transferring in and out of my wheeled chariot was a little bizarre, but it was also genius. Try to picture a reclining wheelchair and a determined fifteen-year-old. Due to the Orthofix bars on either side of my thighs, transferring to the side was extremely difficult. The inability to bear weight on either leg denied me the ability to just stand up and pivot from the chair. The next best thing? Go backward. We discovered that reclining the wheelchair all the way back against the bed, couch, or other destination and sliding up the back of the reclined portion made for an easier transfer and allowed for an added leg rest, especially in the bathroom. A few months into my final procedure, and I was conquering all. Borderline genius, I know.

Stairs. Such a daunting word in the days of fixators. They are avoided at all cost. My bedroom has been moved back into what used to be the dining room downstairs. With a curtain in one doorway and a small accordion-like sliding door in the other, I can hear everything: Derek imitating Jim Carrey from The Mask, Mom slapping a wooden spatula on the counter as a threat to anyone's (not mine) misbehavior, the garage door opening and closing, Dad cursing at the television during a Patriots game, and Mom talking in her high-pitched ... thinking the cat understands ... how many nicknames can one animal possibly have ... please stop now ... voice. Goodbye, privacy. Yet again, this enables a little more independence on my part. Soon you realize that there are certain luxuries that one must let go of in order to gain other privileges. My sanity and privacy for the independence is just one example.

Physical therapy had officially become my home away from home. Since the very beginning, during my Ilizarov days, the ladies at Plymouth Bay Sports and Orthopedic Therapy had become my confidantes and certified ass-kickers. They knew when it was time to get down to business and when I needed a mental break. Only a group of deft physical therapists could keep me from having to go back into the operating room for muscle releases or nerve decompressions. I mean, come on, they get paid to torture people. Three times a week for two hours, I stretched and strengthened with some antics sprinkled in. Had you asked me in the moment, I would have called it abuse. It was anything but easy—it was hard work—but as always, hard work pays off.

My freshman year was completed at home with the help of a tutor. It wasn't ideal, and sitting in my wheelchair for hours on end just wasn't in the books. A reclined position was most comfortable, and I don't think that any of my teachers would have appreciated me rolling into class, reclining my chair and putting my feet up. Not to mention the probability of me falling asleep was greater than that of me paying attention. All of my teachers were very patient with me and sent lengthy explanations of the week's lessons home with my tutor. The work was manageable.

My greatest concern was my friends. A dark component of my mind began to create a universal story that my short stature and surgeries would be the unfair cause of losing some of my friends and inability to make new ones. Getting people to see past my dwarfism and constant medical attention had been a concern since I was a kid. Knowing very well that there was a lot of controversy surrounding limb lengthening, I held true in knowing that my motivation did not lie in becoming taller, blending in, or trying to change who I was. My eyes and my heart were on my future. I was still Kristen, born with dwarfism, the sassy little free spirit who loved spending Friday nights wandering the Independence Mall, hanging out with her friends, and obsessing over NSYNC and Britney Spears. Nothing could ever change that, but was this something my friends understood? I wasn't sure. I wanted them to know I was more than a diagnosis, a label, a condition, or a limitation. As a teenager, it isn't as simple as sitting down and spelling it all out. With my fear outweighing the inquisitiveness, I quieted my thoughts and suppressed the fear.

45

The summer months allowed me to swim. Up in Maine, we—and by we, I mean Dad—found a way to navigate the wheelchair down to the beach and onto the dock so that I could get into the boat. We motored out to the sand bar, and using my sheer upper body strength—careful not to bear weight on my legs—I navigated my way to the back of the boat and down the ladder. The fixators didn't make it easy because I was too wide to just sit on the little platform. I had to angle my lower body and finagle my legs and hardware around the railings. It was not an effortless feat, but where there is a will, there is a way. When swimming was involved, there was always a way. Old Navy was kind enough to sell cute little bikinis with bottoms that tied on the side. Fashionably set, I sure was. Thanks to my weightlessness in the water and the use of an inner tube, I was able to be upright with my feet in the sand for the first time since surgery. What a relief on my hips and back. It wasn't advised, and I was willing to take the risk of infection from floating in the fresh water. As soon as I got out of the lake, using one of those large drink jugs with the little spigot, I doused my legs with warm antibacterial soapy water.

On one trip home from Maine, I had an aha moment. Typically, I was able to fit in the front seat of Mom's Jeep with my legs straight out, propped up on the cooler and some pillows. Not anymore! After three months of lengthening, reclining in the front seat was far too cramped. This particular trip, I decided to forego the blankets under my legs and sit normally, which I had never been able to do. To my surprise, with my knees bent, my heels rested comfortably on a pillow on the floor. Maybe it was only my heels touching and there was a pillow on the floor, but it was a start. The results were obvious, and I was ecstatic.

When I wasn't in Maine, at physical therapy, or down in Baltimore,

I stifled my boredom at home through various activities. The internet was one of them. Through Yahoo! I joined a few listservs designated for individuals with dwarfism or people interested in the limb-lengthening process. My eyes opened to a society divided: those who agreed with what I was going through and those who didn't. People were brutally honest with their opinions, and so was I.

In addition to my presence on the listservs, another opportunity surfaced for me to get my young yet experienced voice heard. An article about Dr. Paley and a lengthening-for-stature patient was published in newspapers nationwide. The article, although shining a positive light on Dr. Paley and his expertise, put the lengthening-for-stature patients in a negative afterglow. After reading it and disagreeing with the adverse slant toward the procedures, I wasn't going to keep quiet. The following week, my letter to the editor in response to the article was published in our local paper. A sense of pride was instilled in me: pride in who I was and what I was going through. I was only one voice, but now I was one voice heard.

> To whom it may concern: I read your article "Growing Controversy" in my local newspaper (August 2001). I am fifteen years old and happen to be a patient of Dr. Dror Paley's. I have been his patient for about three years now. I was born with achondroplasia, and I am also in my last stage of the lengthening procedure, but as I was reading your article I found that I have some very different views on this procedure than many people. First, I did not get this surgery just to become taller. The idea of it was certainly in my mind, but there were more important things that I was looking into and wanted to accomplish. I was not forced to do this in any way. It was my decision and my decision only. When I got the tibial lengthening done, which is the first of the three procedures, Dr. Paley corrected the bowing deformity that I had in my lower legs. When I completed the procedure, not only were my legs much straighter but I was also six inches taller. During my humeral lengthening, Dr. Paley corrected an elbow flexion deformity, which allowed my arms to hang

straight by my side and rest comfortably in my lap. It also eliminated frequent pain that I would get, and I gained four inches in length. Now that I have rounded third base and am on my way home with my femoral lengthening, my hips and back are straighter, I have better posture and I have grown a total of eleven inches. What concerns me is the statement by the LPA: "They want to change how others view them in the everyday quest for jobs, mates, and money." Personally I never really cared about what people who never knew me in public thought of me. I have always known who my real friends and family are. Besides, most of the people who stare are little kids, and I am sure they don't know any better. Many of us would stare at things or people who were new to us when we were little. I know I did. I did not go through all of this just to impress other people or to "blend in." I did it for myself and my future. I also found the comments by the LPA inaccurate. All I have to say is that limb lengthening is not cosmetic. Cosmetic would be getting the procedure done to be as tall as your spouse. Or just so you could be tall enough to be a model. It is not cosmetic to get a procedure done that takes three to five years in order to correct bone deformities. The limb-lengthening procedure has corrected my bowed legs and curvature of my spine, protecting me from possible future complications. Second of all, this is a free country, and other people who oppose the surgery have no right to make judgments toward limb lengthening patients and their decision to go through with the procedures. Limb lengthening does not at all imply that there is something wrong with being a little person. I was thinking about my future and some of the hurdles I would need to overcome when I made the choice to get the surgery done. I am a little person, I always will be a little person, and there is nothing that can change that. I also think that the comments that the LPA made about vascular and nerve damage were stated in the wrong way. This complication can occur during lengthening. Monitoring and nerve testing are performed at every clinic visit to limit the chances of getting any kind of nerve damage. Even though at times it has been painful, I have had extensive physical therapy and spent months in a wheelchair, I am extremely happy with the outcome and do not regret what I have gone through. I consider Dr. Paley a hero to me and many others for the work he does. At this point, I am only going forward and not looking back.

Boom. Take that. And as far as I was concerned, my view wouldn't change. Ever.

Everyone is entitled to their own opinions. I knew that once I expressed my side of the story and made myself 100 percent vulnerable, not everyone was going to agree. In a million years, I couldn't have been more spot on with such an assumption. Some responses I received were indeed congratulatory.

Kristen,

Right on with your comments to the editor and thanks for sharing this with us. I agree with you that one shouldn't be judged by their decision to have this procedure done. As the mother of a daughter who has achondroplasia, if she ever decided to have the procedure done, it shouldn't be anyone else's business or concern. I don't think that the public in general understands that the decision to have this procedure is mostly for assistance with functional ability and not for cosmetic purposes. The fact that the LPA is against this is what surprises me since many of the members have numerous medical and functional difficulties. Good for you, speaking up for yourself and others who have chosen to go through with the procedure. Best of luck as you make it to home plate.

Bravo to you! I hope you will continue talking about your experience to the LPA community. I feel it is important for new parents to know that so much of what is said about limb lengthening by LPA members is exaggerated and/or ludicrous. Keep up the good work!

Can I get an amen please? As expected, other readers did not agree with me so much.

How unbelievably sad! It absolutely breaks my heart to hear about something like this. I find it very scary and disturbing that people are going to further and further lengths to undo all diversity in our society. I'll never forget the day that I asked my mother why she and my dad hadn't at least considered the option of limb lengthening for me when I was younger. She told me that she and my dad thought I was perfect and that the world needed all types of people in order to be interesting. After that, I have been grateful that my family has embraced me for who I am and part of the reason they love me so much is for my uniqueness. If only more people could think this way.

My opinion is this: God put us on the earth the way he wanted us to be. Just because you don't fit in easily, not to say you don't, with the average-size world, does not mean you should go through pain, suffering, and surgery to fit in. It's like half the stuff in the world; it might look good, but what do you want to do or give up to get it? Don't mess with nature, because if you do, you're going to lose the battle anyway. Nature will always win.

46

Early on in my childhood, a longing grew within me to stand up and confront those who spurned me. Despite my urge at the time, I couldn't do it. Some gravitational force held me back. In my mind, I convinced myself that I had no defense. This new experience was beginning to shift my thoughts. Why was my self-defense so futile? As my efforts to justify my decision to undergo the limb-lengthening procedures increased, so did my insecurities.

One of the most terrible things anyone can experience is the indifference of others. As I got older, it became harder to habitually brush off society's ignorance toward my condition and decision to lengthen. I began to lose my self-confidence and ability to laugh at any situation. I was no longer that brave, presumptuous young girl. Society's continual disregard for me as a person began to drown my positivity. In turn, my mind began to create stories. I wondered, believed, and even feared that I may have made the wrong choice. Welcome to my internal battlefield.

As in any situation, there were two sides to this engagement. While the all-consuming thoughts of adversity were nearly deafening, my heart knew better.

Hold up, Kristen. You knew what you were signing up for when this whole journey began. Your reasons for undergoing the procedures have already been voiced. There is no need to stoke the disavowing fires. You made the decision all by yourself, with so much love and support, because you knew that it was in your best interest to do so. You, you, you! No one else is the game maker here, so why are you, all of a sudden, so concerned with what others think about the decision you made? This isn't some kind of game show; you aren't standing in front of a panel of judges waiting for a high score. This is your life. It's hard. It isn't meant to be easy. Defending yourself is not necessary. Choose love for yourself and for others. In those two small hands of yours, you hold a piece of this great big world. Do with it what you choose. Dream you can fly, change how people see different, and never give up.

Times they were a changing. School was about to begin, and that meant homeschooling for a little while. Before the month of August had come to a close, we received notice in the mail that Dr. Paley and his team had outgrown their small clinic space at Kernan Hospital and were moving down the road to Sinai Hospital of Baltimore. I was sad to hear that some of my favorite staff from MCLLR would not be making the transition to the new center at Sinai Hospital, which would be named the International Center for Limb Lengthening and Reconstruction.

Pam was one of those people. My heart felt broken. Clinic appointments would never be the same. Knowing that she would remain at Kernan Hospital was comforting since I could visit whenever I was in town for appointments. Marilyn, thank goodness, would be the child life specialist over at Sinai.

My right leg began to give me issues, and I had to go down for x-rays and nerve testing. The clinic move was going to coincide with our impromptu visit. We were assured that I would be seen by Dr. Paley anyway. With the move from Kernan to Sinai, we nixed the usual stay at the Ronald McDonald House and found a hotel closer to the new hospital.

Sinai Hospital was huge in comparison to Kernan. The new International Center for Limb Lengthening and Reconstruction was doing *big* things, and now they had their own building. We took the elevator to the second floor, and our jaws dropped in astonishment. The clinic had totally transformed. Now, keep in mind, we were there a week before they were actually scheduled to open up to see patients. Things were in a bit of an uproar, but the staff was very accommodating. We were in and out of x-ray relatively quickly and brought back to one of the many exam rooms to wait for Dr. Paley. Not seeing the usual Kernan crew in the clinic was sad, but the new staff at ICLLR were wonderful, and I was so happy to see Marilyn's smiling face pop into my room.

After a fairly decent span of time had passed, the man of the hour made an appearance with his entourage to inform us that everything looked okay with x-rays. His suspicions? The lengthening was beginning to aggravate the muscles and nerves. As the new length in my femur bones was increasing, my muscles and nerves had difficulty accommodating the ever-growing gap. Dr. Paley suggested slowing down the distraction rate. The good news? My femurs had grown four inches of new bone.

Four. Inches.

That meant that I only had one more inch to grow. In that moment, I became all kinds of crazy-happy. Only one more inch! The end really was in sight. The unfortunate news? To be on the safe side, I had to agree to slow down my turn schedule and push myself in physical therapy to keep my tissues from becoming irritated. The last inch was going to take dedication and a little bit more time than initially expected, but I was going to get there—whatever it took.

Upon arriving back home from my impromptu appointment, I found a special delivery on the kitchen table addressed to me. The International Center for Limb Lengthening and Reconstruction at Sinai Hospital had sent me flowers and a little card thanking me for being their first official patient to be seen in the clinic. I had no control over the need to trek back down to Baltimore, but I was honored. What other perks could I expect from being number one at ICLLR?

Just kidding.

47

With the return of back to school, yet again, I wasn't actually going to school. With the regional high school being extremely crowded, we didn't want to risk any injuries getting to and from classes in the wheelchair. Thus, I was forced to be homeschooled—or shall I say "me-schooled." The first portion of my sophomore year, I taught myself all the material for my six or so classes. The only assistance I got was from my books, notes, teacher instructions, and the occasional time with my tutor. Despite my teachers' unbelievable patience and cooperation with my situation, being physically absent from the classroom resulted in school suddenly becoming increasingly difficult. It was a burden. Actually, it downright sucked. Nothing was more frustrating than attempting to teach yourself several subjects without being immersed in the classroom setting.

Alas, I had to realize that learning at home, for the time being, was the right decision. My teachers were only an email or phone call away, and my tutor was willing to do what it took to make sure that I understood all the material. The situation was not permanent. At home, my pain was well managed and if I became uncomfortable, I had easy access to pain medicine and my bed. On the tough days, I rested and then returned to my studies. I might also mention that clothing was optional and I could lounge around in my underwear whenever I felt it necessary.

In addition to the heavy workload of a high school student, my social life was diminishing. Being back in school for the last half of my freshman year was a bit of a tease. My closest friends came over to visit when they could, but in the eyes of a teenager, it wasn't the same. As weeks passed, I began to feel more and more disconnected from my peers and the typical high school drama that every sophomore girl's life revolves around. It was hard not to feel sad, I continued to remind myself that this wasn't forever.

I wake up to the phone ringing and ringing. I turn over and put my good ear on the pillow in the hopes that my deaf ear will stifle the annoyance. I am relieved to hear nothing but my breath. And then it begins to ring again. Mom isn't home to pick it up. With a heavy, drawn-out sigh, I drag myself up, out of bed, and into my wheelchair. I roll over to the wall phone in the kitchen.

"Turn on the television, quick!"

Dad sounds nervous, maybe even a little scared. This never happens. Something is wrong. Hanging up the phone, I wheel myself into the living room and turn on the local news. Still half-asleep, the horrifying visual of a plane crashing directly into one of the twin towers in New York City plays before my eyes. This must be a dream. Only a foot or so from the screen, I stare in disbelief. My heart starts to pound, and tears prick at the backs of my eyes. What? This cannot be real. I'm paralyzed.

Mom walks in from the grocery store, drops the groceries on the floor, and runs into the living room.

"Dad called me," she says. "What is going on?"

We gaze at the live feed on the TV: people running from the crash site with their faces covered, falling debris, and strangers consoling one another. All of a sudden, there is more screaming and yelling as the camera pans to a plane slamming into the second tower. The result is a massive fireball. Our jaws drop, and Mom and I say nothing.

For hours, I sit in my wheelchair—in my pajamas, teeth unbrushed, heart full of sadness—bearing witness to the horrible acts of terrorism. A sick, uneasy feeling settles in my stomach. Over the course of the morning, another plane hits the Pentagon, the twin towers collapse, and a plane crashes into a Pennsylvania field.

What is happening in our world? So much hatred.

I begin racking my brain for a mental list of family and friends in New York and New Jersey. Thankfully, not many come to find, and they are all safe. No one I know was flying today either.

The last thing I want to do is get dressed and go to physical therapy. The morning's events have been emotionally draining. To be sure that everyone at therapy is actually present and able to function during such a tragedy, Mom calls to check in. The crew there is a bit confused. Their only information sources are the radio and word of mouth from other clients. So, what do we do? We cart my little twelve-inch TV to physical therapy so that they can see the news reports. It is eerily quiet, and the mood is somber. There isn't one individual who doesn't feel the heartbreaking effect of today's events.

Why are people taught that violence and hatred are the answers?

The excitement and happiness surrounding my recent lengthening success are quickly overshadowed by the horrible events of that one fall morning. Following the tragedy of September 11, things seemed to head downhill for me. My emotions were rocked, and there was a consistent ache in my heart for everyone affected by it.

With the added emotional stress, the pain and discomfort of the last inch was getting intense. At times, it was unbearable; the demands of physical therapy being downright miserable. My longer legs wanted nothing more than to be bent all the time as a result of the tightening muscles and nerves. An hour a day, I sat with my legs straight out with weights on my knees. At night, I scooted to the edge of my bed and, with assistance, flipped over onto my stomach, letting my legs hang, knees straight. It was a project and extremely uncomfortable but it also gave my butt a break.

For a girl who once loved learning, my studies are borderline intolerable. Notes and instructions from my teachers make no sense. Even having the tutor come to the house to try to better explain my coursework and answer questions is not helpful enough.

Not far along into the school year, I find myself in an ever-deepening hole that I feel unable to climb out of. As my grades on tests and quizzes began to fall, I felt guilty for getting so far behind. The motivation that once drove my academics was now lacking. The only true solution to my problem was to go back to school and physically attend my classes, but I was in too much discomfort to make that possible.

I did the next best thing. After classes were out for the day, Mom drove me to the high school, and I met with each of my teachers to ask questions or have them explain problems I was stuck on. Their assistance and motivation relit the fire under my ass. My mind refueled, I rediscovered the determination to get through the final month of lengthening.

To expedite the process—and without telling a soul—I sped up my turn schedule. One extra turn of the Allen wrench in the morning and another before bedtime.

Even in a wheelchair, I could still be a rebellious teenager.

48

Right before my sixteenth birthday, Dad and I headed back down to Baltimore. The new International Center for Limb Lengthening and Reconstruction was up and running, and it was as crazy as ever. We signed in at the front desk and assumed our seats in the new waiting room complete with a fancy fish tank. All I could think about was how badly I wanted Dr. Paley to tell me that I had reached the five-inch mark. Only the week before, Dad had to extend the footrests on the wheelchair to the longest setting. Gazing down at my legs—my *long* legs—I repetitively thought to myself that it just had to be true.

We moved from the waiting room into our little exam room and waited some more. As I stared at the illuminated but blank x-ray viewing panel, I had the sudden urge to cry. What if I didn't get the news I was hoping for? What if I had another two weeks left to lengthen? Before my mind could conjure up another what-if, the door opened.

Dr. Paley waltzed in and shoved my current scans up onto the wall.

New bone growth was clearly visible.

The man I knew as my hero then uttered two words that actually made me burst into tears: "You're done!"

A very sweet sixteen birthday it turned out to be.

That brought me to tears—tears of complete and utter happiness, excitement, longing, and joy. The release of tension, stress, worry, and frustration was an emotional overload. The ICLLR team probably thought they had a mental psych case on their hands at that point.

Two boxes of tissues to room 3 please.

Dr. Paley was thrilled with my progress and explained that everything looked wonderful regarding length and alignment.

Amen to that!

Now it was time to heal, and the rule of thumb still applied to my femurs: for every inch of length, allow one month of healing.

Yikes. Five more months with the Orthofix bars?

One step at a time, sassy pants. You know that jumping the gun gets you nowhere.

I constantly remind myself to slow down. It is hard to hear that my turns are complete and not to get caught up in the thought of breaking free, walking on my own two feet, ditching the wheelchair, and regaining a sense of normalcy in my almost sixteen-year-old life.

After a month of consolidation, Dr. Paley wants a set of x-rays, and if everything looks good, I can begin putting weight on my legs. For now, he is allowing me to "touch-down" weight bear. Toes on the ground, my upper body strength keeping me upright, and the assistance of a walker is better than nothing. It is an opportunity to be vertical again after five months. My wheelchair and I go together like oil and water right now; we are rapidly approaching enemy status.

With my headphones on in the car on the ride home, I put on my music. Loud. It is a toss-up between "Fallin'" by Alicia Keys, "What Would You Do?" by City High, and "Fill Me In" by Craig David. What I literally need is for the bone in my legs to "fill in." Maybe the song on repeat will spark an internal pep talk with the legs about a necessary, rapid healing process.

Sweet sixteen. Word on the street was that a girl I used to be friends with in elementary school got a car for her sixteenth birthday. I didn't want to sound or feel ungrateful, but if that were me, I just might have been the happiest girl in the world. Waking up that morning of my birthday, I held the tiniest fraction of hope that there would be a car sitting in the driveway with a big-ass red bow on the roof in lieu of balloons, cake, and ice cream. My heart sank slightly when I rolled over in bed to peer out the window at an empty driveway.

My birthday gift that year was not in the form of a vehicle, backstage passes to a concert, or a shopping spree, though all are lovely things to receive as gifts. No, that trip around the sun was more representational than anything else.

Since I was a little girl, rather than allowing myself to express and feel all of my emotions, I chose to hide from them. I saw it as my duty to outwardly act happy, masking the pain and humiliation I felt on the inside. Behind closed doors, I allowed myself to cry, but I wore a bright smile for the world. Gradually, my pent-up feelings surrounding dwarfism led to anxiety, sadness, and fear. Over the years, slowly but surely, my self-confidence dissipated. I started to believe what others said to me. I wasn't beautiful. I wasn't good enough.

In public, I immediately assumed that people were judging me harshly when they looked at me. Kristen was no longer behind the wheel; fear and doubt were. When I looked in the mirror, I felt resentment. In high school, looks are everything. What I wanted seemed nearly impossible: to be accepted for who I was on the inside. It just didn't seem fair. Why was I dealt such a difficult hand?

Life was painful, a little messy, and constantly oscillating with moments of happy and sad. There was nothing to change or fix. The dealing was done, and I was not about to stop playing.

All of that sadness and fear over the past four years had peeled back my layers to reveal an unfamiliar, real me: raw, unfiltered, and authentic. At sixteen, I had endured more than most people would face in a lifetime. A powerful mind-set of "no limitations, no boundaries, and no separation" had evolved, allowing me to remain unstoppable. What many viewed as my disability actually revealed my abilities. The fears I conquered brought forth potential, my failures were lessons learned, and every challenge I accepted to view as a mere road block rather than a dead-end street. It wasn't obvious at the time, but that was the year I crossed the threshold from teenage girl to mature warrior woman. An intangible gift that would gradually begin to make itself known as the hand I was dealt continued to play out.

My physical therapy family did not allow the sweetest of birthdays to go unnoticed. Balloons and cupcakes among hugs with some of my favorite people surprised me upon arrival for my birthday torture session. Now that I was cleared to put two feet lightly on the ground, things were bound to get interesting.

I am facedown on the therapy table, and I pivot myself so the lower half of my body is dangling off the table. Brenda, supports my legs. My arms are stretched the width of the table, hands viscously clutching onto the blue pleather. Oh, my word—nothing has ever felt so wonderful. Inch by inch, I let myself slide farther and farther off of the table until the balls of my feet touch flat on the ground. Due to the newly added five inches in height, my feet touching the floor doesn't take as long as I anticipate. Since it is so early on in the healing phase, my femurs are still fairly fragile. I use caution when resting my feet on the floor, using all of my upper body strength to hold tight to the table. Just to feel my feet on the ground is a high.

Instantly, I have a flashback to standing on the stool at the kitchen counter as a child and looking down to see how far off the ground my feet were. It was a good foot or so, and I thought, Will I really stand this tall someday? Will I really be able to get around the kitchen and help Mom cook without pulling up a chair or the stool?

Yes. Yes, I would. Right now, I am one step closer with the death grip, now on my walker, standing upright, and staring straight into Brenda's eyes. My smile is on crack, and I'm shaking from excitement and my sheer lack of upper body strength.

Every step I take is writing on a page.

That afternoon, after PT, Meaghan and Kate came over to visit. Side by side, I held myself vertical next to them with my walker. All three of us were eye to eye.

'Nuff said, people.

♬ 49 ♬

Ever since my first experience with speaking out about my short stature in third grade, it was something I had become very passionate about, in addition to advocating for limb lengthening. Another opportunity came at the Annual Baltimore Limb Deformity Course, just like the one I had participated in during my first lengthening. This year, I was invited back.

Mom wasn't crazy about making the trek down just for the course. Conveniently, it turned into a checkup appointment, which gave her the opportunity to see the new International Center of Limb Lengthening and Reconstruction. There were multiple reasons why we needed to make the trip to the city I had grown to love, and I made sure to remind her of them all. Mom couldn't say no, and off we went.

Considering it was a last-minute trip, the Ronald McDonald house was full. Mom and I upgraded to a hotel closer to the new hospital that offered a medical rate for Dr. Paley's patients. Even better: there was a Chili's restaurant attached to the hotel. All we had to do was call and order the food, and then Mom walked down to pick it up when it was ready. Dinner in bed after an eight-hour drive was a glorious thing. I knew Mom was with me on that one.

Prior to our travels, we received a letter regarding the time of my case presentation for the deformity course. Dr. Paley wanted x-rays prior to my stage time as well. We needed to be in clinic at eight to get the ball rolling, so that morning, it was up and at 'em bright and early.

After x-rays, Dr. Paley came in for a quick consult. It was short and sweet, but the bottom line was that he was not impressed with the healing in my right leg. *Great.* To help speed things up, he ordered more rigorous physical therapy, allowing me to advance to bear 50 percent of my body weight on each leg, and a bone stimulator.

The bone stimulator resembled a small, rectangular computer with only three buttons. I had to strap a small plastic square around my leg and under the Orthofix bar. There was a hole in the middle of the plastic square that I situated over the osteotomy site on my right femur. After applying some gel—like the kind used for an ultrasound—to the head of the stimulator, it fastened into the hole, and I hit the power switch. That was it. The machine didn't make a sound. The magic was safe, painless ultrasound waves that activated the bone cells at the gap in my femur. The waves stimulated my body's healing cells, speeding its natural repair process. Fingers crossed for success.

Prescriptions in hand, and best efforts to put aside the less-than-stimulating news, we went down to the amphitheater for patient presentations. The lengthening for stature portion of the course was first up. Dr. Paley began with a patient undergoing the first procedure on the tibias. *Been there done that!* Another patient having their arms lengthened was presented, and then there was me.

Using my walker, I stood up for the crowd of doctors so that Dr. Paley could show them how proportionate my arms and legs had become to the rest of my body. Sitting in a chair on stage, my feet actually touched the ground with my back against the chair. Enter happiness and exit bad, worried feelings. Cameras were snapping photos left and right and, I'm not going to lie, I felt pretty damn special. Up on the projector were slides of my x-rays before I started my first phase of the surgery.

Dr. Paley began to describe the methods of lengthening that he used on my legs and arms, and he told the audience that he had begun to make gradual changes in how the process was done. When he clicked forward to my most recent set of x-rays, things became very clear. My left femur was very white, and the gap of new bone was barely visible. On the right side the gap of new bone was still very evident and much darker.

But why?

My happy feeling was dissipating, and worry was beginning to set in. Before I had the opportunity to become consumed by the apprehension in my bones, Dr. Paley asked, "Kristen, can you tell everyone why you chose to go through the surgeries and why you are here to share your story?"

I was caught off guard, and the floor was mine.

I want to offer perspective. What I have learned, no teacher, parent, or friend could have opened my eyes to. When I first began the limb-lengthening surgeries, I was introduced to enormous controversy. The Little People of America deem the procedures cosmetic and claim that those who choose to lengthen do it to blend in with society. Standing up here, I can honestly tell you that my motivation has not been to blend in or simply be taller. Gradually, people are becoming less objective to limb lengthening, and I believe it is because those of us who have gone through it continue to open up about our experiences. Many times, parents of average height who have a child with short stature reach out to me regarding limb lengthening, wanting to pursue it for their child. One thing I always stress is that I made the decision to go through with the surgeries. My parents would have supported me either way. And I would be lying if I said this has been a walk in the park. It's anything but easy. And the successes undoubtedly outweigh the pain and setbacks. In my opinion, it is so important for the individual undergoing the procedures to not only be fully committed but ready for it—to understand everything surgery entails. Limb lengthening isn't for everyone, and that is okay. I would never judge someone for choosing not to do it.

My little internal voice was yelling, "Hell yeah!" Point made and my soul was soaring. It was another successful course for the books.

50

One evening after getting home from physical therapy, Dad informed me that there was a message for me on the answering machine from a television producer in New York City.

The Maury Show. Say, what?

One of the producers for the show, Brooke, told the hospital about doing a piece on limb lengthening; that's how she got my name. The segment is being filmed next weekend, and they want me to come to New York City. Me, on The Maury Show? National television. Why not?

Now, I know what you're thinking: The Maury Show? Really, Kristen? But hold on one second, this is not about some pregnancy gone unnoticed only to surprise the shit out of the baby-daddy months later with the readings of a paternity test. Please, people, that's so not me. This is the beginning of me listening to my heart, truly living my dream, and telling my story. We all have to start somewhere, right? Well, my first national television appearance just happens to be alongside Maury Povich. What is truly important to me is reaching out to a large audience and allowing my voice to be heard.

Dad, Mom, Derek, and I drive to New York City for the filming. The city is still recovering from the terrorist attacks, and the sadness is palpable. Dad and Derek take the subway down to Ground Zero and say that there is still ash and debris everywhere. Mom and I stay behind; getting around with crutches is still a relatively challenging task, and I don't think I can handle the heaviness of the fresh tragedy.

When we arrive at the grand ballroom of the Hotel Pennsylvania, Dad and Derek go into the audience, and Mom and I stay backstage with Brooke, trying to figure out which shirt I should wear on screen. Back in the green room, they were also preparing to film a segment on phobias. Sitting on the couch, talking with Brooke and some of the other staff, I hear a woman begin

187

to howl. I'm talking a bloodcurdling, high-pitched, ear-piercing shriek that you would think was elicited by a horrific looking clown.

My attention turns to the open door and hallway where I hear footsteps bounding toward us. Continuing her auditory assault on my ears, the woman goes thundering by into an adjacent room, slamming the door closed behind her. Another woman casually follows her carrying a large container of cotton balls. Yes—cotton balls. Apparently that is a phobia? People are afraid of those little fluffy things?

Brooke shrugs and grins, and I start to giggle as quietly as I can so the woman in hiding doesn't hear me. In addition to cotton balls, there are individuals with aluminum foil and animal fears. As a behind-the-scenes witness, I am highly entertained.

Being on national television is a little scary. As they begin telling my story to the audience with pictures and video on a big screen, Maury narrates.

I stand behind stage and wait for my cue. Attempting to walk without face-planting, on crutches, with a humongous audience in front of me is violently intimidating. Maury greets me with extremely soft hands and a firm shake. It was rather impressive and unexpected. Our five-minute conversation allows me to look into his eyes and speak directly from my sixteen-year-old heart. Do I regret the decision I had made three years earlier? Hell no. How do I feel about my results? Couldn't be happier. Getting my voice heard feels incredibly empowering. Are people actually hearing what I am saying? Who knows? The most important part to me is making the effort to be heard and knowing that everything I say is the honest to goodness truth.

Bottom line, Maury: I didn't get these surgeries to be taller and blend in. I did it because it was the right decision for me as an individual, and I am now living a happier, healthier life.

51

Another trip to our local medical center for x-rays yielded very interesting results. My left leg was completely healed, but my right leg was still chasing the bandwagon—not healed at all. The email response I received from Dr. Paley was so unexpected that it knocked me off my crutches.

The left fixator is coming off, and my right leg needs a bone graft. A bone graft? Awesome. Of course, rather than focus on the fact that I will be standing with one less fixator, I can't help but feel defeated and sob about the bone graft and mysterious reason as to why my right leg refuses to heal.

All of the removal surgeries I had gone through were a cinch, but the bone graft was new. Questions and uncertainties swirled in my head as Mom and I found ourselves in the Jeep, back on I-95, heading south to Baltimore. The emotions in my body were a toss-up between excitement and stomach churning fear that was all kinds of overwhelming. My cup was running over and spilling onto the floor of the car. Past fixator removals on my tibiae resulted in casts. Was Dr. Paley planning on casting my entire left leg?

Please, God, no.

Sitting in the Jeep, staring out the window, and watching the mile markers fly by, my mind begins to create stories. In case you haven't noticed, this is something I excel in. A full-length cast? A bone graft? Maybe this isn't such a great idea. Could waiting it out for just one more month result in full consolidation of my stubborn right leg? So many questions raced through my mind. As the assumptions and possibilities slowly become all consuming, my eyes brim with tears.

No. Stop it, Kristen. You don't know anything yet. Don't get yourself all worked up. Wait until you talk to Dr. Paley, in person, before you enter a full-fledged panic attack.

The inside of the car seems to be getting smaller and smaller. I don't know what to do. In an effort not to let Mom see me cry, I begin to focus on my breathing. Here I am, deep breath in and a lip-flapping sigh out. How's that for drama? Mom takes her eyes off the road to look at me and I flash her my best, all-teeth smile to signal that everything is peachy on my end. Bringing my Discman and headphones along for the ride helps quiet my racing mind. For the time being, I figured I can spare Mom her sanity and just use my headphones rather than make her jam out to 3LW with me.

See? Teenagers do have respect for their parents' sanity.

The Comfort Inn was a welcoming sight coming off of the beltway outside of Baltimore. Mom and I stuck to our typical ritual of ordering out Chili's To-Go and getting a movie from On-Demand in our room. That was all I was really willing to do knowing—or not knowing—what tomorrow was going to hold. A nurse called later that evening and informed me that I was NPO after midnight. That's right, the good old "nothing by mouth" rule assuming I was definitely headed into surgery tomorrow. Hearing that made me lose my appetite completely.

Knowing that what I needed most was sleep, I tried desperately not to think about my impending surgery. That's like putting a doughnut in front of a child and telling them not to eat it. Seriously. At sixteen years old, I knew too much: the pros, the cons, and the risks that surgery entailed. Rolling into a fetal position, I tried to convince myself to sleep. My body answered with tears. Giving in was my only choice. At that point in my journey, I knew that letting it all out was what had to happen. A fog was slowly rolling in and covering up that once gleaming light at the end of a long and seemingly never-ending tunnel.

It was another quiet morning—until we arrived to clinic. That place was hopping; staff and patients bustling about and kids were screaming their heads off. As terrified for this appointment as I was, it was great to see everyone—my social circle. The greatest clinic visits were those that involved patients I had connected with previously. We would catch up on each other's progress and then talk about completely unrelated topics. Just as we were getting to the juicy gossip, my name was called. It always seemed like I was taken back for x-rays at the most inopportune times: right in the middle of an important conversation or a wheelchair race down the hall.

In the words of Stephanie Tanner, "How rude!"

At this point in the process, getting x-rays, I can pretty much predict every move the technician is going to make: Lift right leg. Slide film under. Check for knee cap positioning. Put on R sticker. Hold breath and hold still. Shoot film. Relax. Wait. Repeat on left side. Wait for clearance. Freedom. At sixteen, I'm confident that I could earn a degree as an x-ray technician with very little classroom education. I know, I'm galloping around on my high horse, but I'm just sayin'.

Rolling back to where Mom was reading her book in the waiting room, my mind once again began to race. I sat and panicked about what the x-rays showed and what news Dr. Paley would have regarding the next step for healing. Waiting always seemed like an eternity when there was anticipated "news." All of that time waiting, wanting, and worrying for one teeny tiny tidbit of information. (Oh, hello, alliteration!) Otherwise, it never bothered me. A typical clinic visit that wasn't to reveal any mysterious complication or potential removal date was, well, just a biweekly appointment and Kristen's extended social hour, which I didn't mind spending time in the waiting room for. Mingling with my kind of people could happen from dawn until dusk as far as I was concerned.

Finally, we were called back into the exam room. My x-rays were already up on the illuminated board on the wall. One look—and I already knew. My left leg looked wonderful. The femur bone was completely filled in where Dr. Paley had made the osteotomy. The right femur? Not even close. Instead of the bone having definite borders and a solid white color on the films, there were several areas of dark space where the new bone growth had taken place. In walked Dr. Paley, and for the first time, as he looked at me, I could see the disappointment in his eyes.

There is a sweet and a sour side to this clinic visit, the obvious sour side being that a bone graft is most definitely necessary. A fragment of bone will be taken from my pelvis on the right side—through a very small incision in my hip crease—and then grafted onto the osteotomy site. Dr. Paley is unsure how long it will take for the graft to actually bond to the existing bone, but he is confident that it will speed up the healing process. The sweet news? The left fixator is coming off. Gone. Goodbye. Forever!

Caught up in the grafting news, for a moment, I forget what is about to go down today. I need to head on down to admitting and do the pre-op paperwork. Paley will see me in the OR in a couple of hours. Wait. What? Holy shit-balls. In realizing that I haven't eaten or drank anything yet today, I am suddenly hungry. Eeesh. I begin to create extensive menus in my head of what I will eat when I wake up after surgery. Ice cream is a definite.

A big sixteen-year-old baby is a fair statement to describe the way I was acting. For my last surgery—to have the fixators put on—I braved the IV placement like a champ, but this time, it wasn't looking good. The nurses reminding me of how it really wasn't that bad of a stick and that this process should be old news by now was not making the situation any better. My growling stomach adding to the stress of everything made the process of an IV give me a very bad taste in my mouth. Since I hadn't eaten or had anything to drink, they wanted to keep me hydrated. Any and all meds would also take effect immediately if they did them through the IV.

Fine.

Mom leaves the scene as two nurses crowd around me like white on rice and attempt to place the IV. I know how silly this sounds. Sixteen years old with pins that could classify as four-gauge needles in both of my legs, and I am crying over a teeny little twenty-four gauge being placed in my hand.

Sorry. Actually, I'm not.

While one nurse held me down and tried to ease my anxiety by telling me how brave and beautiful I was (it may have worked, I'm a sucker for praise), the other poked and prodded until she found a good vein. That is the last thing I remember. I'm willing to bet that they gave me a hefty dose of happy meds as soon as they possibly could so they need not worry about Little Miss Sassy Pants on the gurney in bay two.

Pfft.

By Mom's account, I wasn't taken back into the operating room until four o'clock in the afternoon or so. There is no confirmation on my part since I was completely gallivanting through la-la land in my mind. It's amazing how Valium, Ativan, and all of those happy little drugs can create one cocktail that'll knock the sass right out of a teenager.

Ouch! Ok, I'm definitely awake. I feel something throbbing—my right hip. What was described to me as a simple procedure does not feel like a piece of cake at all. Shocker. It feels like a metal stake has been driven into the right side of my pelvis. Reaching my left hand down to my left thigh—relief.

I can feel that the fixator is gone. My leg is wrapped in gauze. The more conscious I become, the harder the pain hits. Deep breaths are impossible. If my belly expands too much, a harrowing pain sears into my hip. My breaths accelerate and become shallow. For some reason, I don't think the nurses here in recovery are prepared for my breakneck pain level. My pitiful mewling and screeching triggers somewhat of a manhunt for a stronger pain medicine that I am not allergic to. Initially, this was supposed to be an outpatient procedure. Due to my severe issues with pain control, they are shipping me to the pediatric floor.

Oh goodie. Enter sarcasm here.

Transferring from my gurney to the bed for transport to my temporary living quarters is nothing shy of a challenge. Since coming out of the operating room, I have been lying flat with my head propped up on a pillow. The minute I attempt to sit up? All-consuming pain. Like when you hit your tailbone and it takes the wind right out of you. Exasperated, I lay back on the gurney and wave my white flag. These poor nurses. For a hot minute, I feel for them and all the crap they have to put up with. Using the draw sheet, they drag my sorry ass onto the bed, with little help from yours truly.

Entirely not my fault.

Once Mom and I are finally settled in my room, there is a small sigh of relief. Of course, now that the pain from my waist down has subsided a bit, my tummy starts to rumble. Something has to be done before I get hangry. You know when you are so hungry that you're cranky, almost borderline angry? That's hangry. Knowing well that devouring a cheeseburger right this minute is not a solid idea, I opt for some Saltines and water to start. Unfortunately, that doesn't turn out to be a smart choice either.

While chewing on my cracker, somehow I aspirate cracker crumbs and I begin to cough. Much to my dismay, the quick, intense inhales and exhales trigger pain at the grafting sight in my hip. I cannot describe the pain because it involves words not yet listed in the dictionary. My inability to breathe, cracker crumbs flying as I gasp for air, tears pouring down my face, and my hands grabbing at my hip—Mom is yelling at me, asking what she can do to help her hot mess of a daughter. And as I look at the crazed look in Mom's eyes and think about what is truly happening—a fiasco caused by a saltine cracker—I begin to laugh. I am laughing, crying, struggling to breathe, and wincing in pain. Not the greatest combination. Laugh. Wince. Cough. Muffled, cracker crumb *scream. Laugh some more. It is a vicious, ridiculous, unforgiving, hilarious cycle that dies down once a few handy glugs of water enter the picture.*

Sweet Jesus. That was more than I could handle.

The fun wasn't over either. After the cracker incident, I was plagued with an allergic reaction to the pain medicine that they gave me. The list of suitable concoctions that my body agreed with to combat pain was getting shorter and shorter. A girl just can't catch a break. My whole body began to itch. For added effect, my tongue swelled to the point where I thought I was going to suffocate. Okay, maybe that is a little over the top, but in the moment, it was scary. Benadryl saved the day; by a seemingly process of elimination, they found a pain medicine that worked for me. Clearly, Dr. Paley was not going to allow me out the hospital with all the fun I had going on. I can't say I was happy to be spending the night in Sinai Hospital, but I really didn't have a choice.

Mom was thrilled to be sleeping on the hospital chair that rolled out to be a plush, uber-comfortable bed. Not!

Even though all of these unfortunate events were piling up against me, I couldn't help but be elated about my left fixator being gone. One bionic leg down and one to go.

Man, I never thought I would see this day. Now, if only my right leg would just hurry up and heal already. And, oh, the ways we are going to speed that process up. It is time to say hasta la vista to my wheelchair and walker and say hello to a shiny new pair of crutches. The gals in physical therapy are going to have a blast with this newfound mobility.

My first time up on semi-new legs with the assistance of what felt like two toothpicks ready to give way was, um, shaky? My balance was far worse than that of a toddler just learning to walk. For one thing, I was weak. For another, I was also walking another five inches taller. My gait was too short for how long my legs were, and my size 2 pretty princess feet too small for my now taller frame. I needed to retrain myself to walk with a longer stride. With longer steps would come healing, and with healing would come the return of the unhindered Little Sass.

Quite possibly, the other most thrilling plus to being down one fixator was my ability to wear pants. As the weather began to get colder, clothing was becoming a bit of an issue. The thin little pajama pants that Old Navy had graciously stocked their shelves with over the summer were no longer cutting it. Not to mention the fixators: the pins are metal. The metal goes into my bone. When the pins are cold, Kristen is cold. Not just the Not just the "I need a pair of socks and a sweatshirt" kind of cold, either. I'm talking a teeth-chattering, lips-turning-blue, no-matter-how-many-layers-of-clothes-I-put-on cold. Thinking back to my days on the ski slopes, I wondered if a "ski boot warmer" could double as a "fixator warmer?" When I thought about it, I pictured my body overheating or internally combusting. Quite the imagination—and a result I wanted to steer clear of. There was a better solution. Enter Aeropostale running pants. These gems, in a size medium, fit over the one fixator on my right leg. I became proud owner of those babies in every color they made. What could be more glorious? The pants didn't even need to be hemmed! And they were approved by the unappointed high school fashion committee. Due to my being homeschooled, I felt out of the loop most of the time, so it was nice to be with the in crowd on this one.

After a month on crutches, my left femur had healed and my body learned to accommodate the one fixator on my right femur. With permission to ditch the medical grade toothpicks, before long, I was walking unassisted and even riding my bicycle. Most of my pain had subsided, although I still had an off day here and there, which was to be expected. Easing in to a new routine, I returned to school part-time.

With the help of the bone stimulator, lots of weight bearing, and rigorous physical therapy, my latest set of x-rays at the beginning of the new year showed that my femur bone had finally consolidated enough for the fixator to be removed.

Can I get an amen?

52

The light at the end of the tunnel. The same one that seemed to get closer and then disappear again. Burning bright, I was now standing in it, casting a tall shadow over my past. Was this real life? The closing of one door and opening of another, much bigger one. Weeks leading up to the final removal could not possibly have gone by any slower. I found it difficult to focus on my schoolwork. My head was in the clouds. I was thinking about walking upright and unincumbered, a new wardrobe, having no more aches and pains, getting my driver's permit, and everything that came as a result of my impending autonomy. The ladies at physical therapy didn't hesitate to remind me that the real fun would begin once that fixator was gone. I believed them with little hesitation.

We agreed to be safe and allow a few more weeks for extra consolidation. The removal date was scheduled at the end of January. This removal was going to be a little different: it was my last one. Along with the hardware coming off, Dr. Paley and his team were also going to do some releases on my scars. Some of the tissue—from where the bigger half pins had been in my tibias—was actually tethered to the bone and proving to be quite uncomfortable. According to Dr. Paley, that was a quick and easy fix, so I was all for it.

While down in Baltimore for the removal, I found myself in quite the predicament: a situation where I just couldn't say no. *CBS Sunday Morning News* was doing a segment on limb lengthening for short stature, and they wanted me to be a near "finished product." Never in my life had I imagined myself on national television, let alone a second opportunity and I couldn't say no. Not to mention a step up on the daytime television rating scale. Sorry, Maury. They did several takes of Dr. Paley and I walking down the hallway together and talking in the exam room over my fabulous x-rays during my pre-op appointment.

The big day was one that encompassed emotions of all kinds. The end of a long, self-appointed journey and the beginning of the rest of my life. The hardware, the wheelchair, the antibiotics, road trips every two weeks, homeschooling, physical therapy, developing relationship with a wrench, varying degrees of discomfort—all that I had known for the past four years was about to change. From a little caterpillar to a butterfly with its beautiful wings—was I ready? Part of me was hesitant. How would I identify with this newfound freedom, these longer limbs, a body lacking pain and limitations?

Truth was, I would soon find out.

Something told me that I was not going to be let off the hook that easily. The scenario I dreamed of, coming out of surgery and immediately just walking out of the hospital, in slow motion, "Chariots of Fire" playing in the background, was too good to be true. The very logistical Kristen was right. You can't remove an external fixator from a major weight-bearing bone in the body and expect to go bounding out of the hospital.

Initially, when I woke up from surgery, I had a false sense of freedom with no cast on my leg. They just wanted me to be awake for the fun. After an hour or so of admiring my right leg, I was wheeled down to occupational therapy. Brace making was next on the agenda. Due to the extreme sluggishness of my right leg in the healing department, Dr. Paley did not want to take any chances on fracturing post-removal.

I kept my excitement to a minimum.

Just like the splints they made for me post-arm lengthening, the occupational therapist made a mold of my right femur and constructed a brace for my leg. I wasn't pleased. In order to keep the entire thing in place, there was a portion that wrapped around my waist and then connected to the brace on my femur by a large metal hinge of sorts. It was rather bulky and very restricting, and it had to be worn over my clothes. Not appealing to the eye of a fashion sensitive sixteen-year-old—at all.

Waging war against a surgeon, multiple physical therapists, and my parents wasn't worth it. With an embarrassed conscience, I probably rolled my eyes as the "We are only trying to help you" speech went in one ear and out the other. For the next month—with the brace—I was allowed touch-down weight bearing on my right side. That was better than nothing, and it gave my physical therapists a lot to work with in terms of making our time together worthwhile.

Let the necessary physical torture continue.

I hated to love it, and I loved to hate it. Everyone at Plymouth Bay Sports and Orthopedic Therapy had played a very integral part in my healing and recovery process. Whether it was keeping my smart-ass in line, physically stretching my muscles beyond what I thought possible, or wiping away my tears, I had another family who was there for me whenever I needed them.

53

It was the end of an era, for lack of a better term. I was done. It was hard to believe that the procedures I first talked about in third grade had become a thing of the past. My back and tibias were straight. The flexion deformity in my elbows and hips was minimal. At sixteen years old, I was eleven inches taller and wise beyond my years; an empowered young woman with little legs and a big heart determined to fiercely live my life in the face of adversity.

After a month in the brace for my right femur, I regained total freedom of my body and my life, and I was officially deemed as being healed. The feeling of overconfidence is being so sure of something that your heart is about to beat out of your chest. Yes, that feeling. It began in my heart and spread throughout my body. My arms and legs tingling, the corners of my mouth turned upward in a permanent smile.

I felt invincible.

Returning to school, I continued my sophomore year with my friends. Steady on my own two feet, I enrolled in driver's education and began learning the rules of the road. The unofficial Masshole course curriculum had already been mastered, and thanks to Dad, my vocabulary was set with all the necessary expletives for the drivers who did not adhere to said rules.

At the beginning of April 2002, with snow still on the ground and alongside a MA state trooper who could have crushed me between two of his fingers, I passed my driving test on the first try. It was official, I had become an official danger on wheels to everyone around me, depending on who's opinion of the situation you got. That's right—Massachusetts had a new driver on the road.

On my sparkly, brand spankin' new license, my sassy attitude and infectious smile rested atop the numbers: 4'11". Those numbers, simply stating how tall I stood, were, more importantly, proof of a girl who fiercely embraced her individuality and her journey. It was my license to continue living with little legs and a big heart.

Pre-concussion bubbles.

Mom and a very little me looking beautiful as ever.

Apple picking with Derek and Dad which probably involved taking a single bite out of one apple and then immediately moving on to tasting another one.

Water skiing up at Camp.

Swimming with Grammie at The Holiday Inn pool in Baltimore.

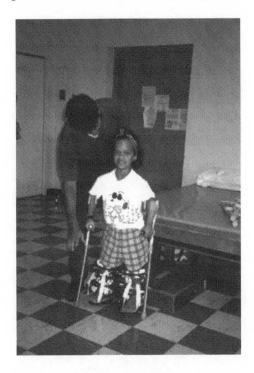

My first time walking on my bionic legs with Greg,
my physical therapist, supervising.

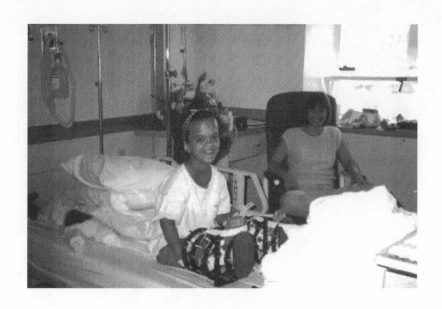

Getting ready to be discharged from the hospital with Aunt Barbie.

Participating in the Baltimore Limb Deformity Course with Dr. Paley.

*Pam Wilson, a true angel, and I, on our birthday following
a very traumatic experience in the adjustment room.*

The very best Child Life Specialist, Marilyn Richardson and I.

Me, in my super fancy white t-shirt cover up, and Derek on the beach.

Pins drilled into my arms didn't keep me from goofing off at a sleepover.

Joey, Derek, Monica, Adrienne and I up in Maine. Monica had just finished her tibial lengthening and I was in the middle of my arms.

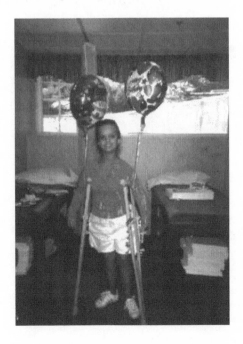

Celebrating my sweet 16 at physical therapy after nearing the end on my final procedure.

Marilyn, Pam and I in clinic during my femoral lengthening.

Riding my bike with my final fixator on my right leg that refused to heal.

Standing up for the first time next to Kate following the completion of all three lengthenings.

Epilogue

Saying goodbye, for the first time in my life, is considerably easy. A far cry from the days when I would melt down leaving Maine, three hours from home, and waving to my Grammie and Grampie Dick, who I was likely to see the following week. I'm ready to spread my wings.

Being 1,004 miles away from home has never felt so good. Mom, however, is having a little bit of a harder time with it; she's been crying since before we even leave my suite on campus. Of course, my emotional ass starts to weep. As Mom and Dad pull away from my dorm on Warren Street, I wave, wipe the sentiment from my eyes, clutch my wallet, and head to King Street. This has been my plan all along. My sassy, rebellious side is about to make a pretty bold move.

I am in Charleston, South Carolina, where hot and steamy doesn't even begin to describe the weather. I am about to begin my freshman year at the College of Charleston. My destination is not the bookstore yet. It's a piercing parlor. Nothing says independence like getting a large needle shoved through my right nostril and then replaced by a shiny stud. Looking at myself in the handheld mirror, with my new bling, I am definitely college ready.

My next stop is the bookstore, which is conveniently situated alongside a Starbucks. It is conducive to my late-night studying and dangerous for my wallet. With my list of books in hand, I carefully select used copies of each. I plan on highlighting the shit out of these bad boys anyway.

Glancing around at the other students, I notice that most everyone is sporting a North Face backpack. This must be the thing these days. Gradually, my arms are growing more and more tired as I select the remainder of the supplies on my list. As I reach the back corner of the store with all the Cougar apparel, I notice a wall full of new backpacks. How convenient! My old, initialed L.L. Bean one will just have to go.

One thing has me utterly confused and borderline perturbed. I have seen a few girls walking through campus with maroon shorts that have the word *cocks* splayed across the ass in large white letters.

Someone, help me out here.

I soon learn that the University of South Carolina in Columbia has a mascot known as a gamecock. Of course, let's all say, "Go Cocks!"

Walking through the Cistern Yard, it dawns on me: I feel like I belong here. In fact, I don't think I have ever experienced such a concrete feeling in my heart and bones. My attention has not been displaced by people staring, laughing, or pointing. This college canvas is far from black and white. Alongside my classmates, I am another brilliant splash of color. This is what I have been waiting for. The vastness of my independence is almost difficult to comprehend. What took more than four years, adding inches and autonomy to my vital spark, seemed like a wrinkle in time—and now the world was mine.

Prepared? I am more than prepared. My class schedule is set, I know where I am going, and all of my books and school supplies have been purchased. I flaunt my Cougar pride and a new backpack; yes, it's North Face. My alarm startles me awake at six fifteen. As excited as I am for this new educational venture, eight o'clock classes every day is not the way to go. College fail!

I have fireworks in my veins, and my knuckles are white as my hands grip the gunnels of the shell. My focus is on the bow of the boat. If I don't maintain proper alignment, we are screwed before even leaving the starting block.

"Two seat, tap down. Everyone else sit ready, blades feathered. Weigh enough two seat. All blades squared."

The air horn sounds, and water begins to fly.

"Half! Three-quarters! Half! Full! One, sit tall! Two, strong legs! Three, four, five, eyes forward! Six, seven, lay back in two! One, two! full strokes here! Send those puddles past stern! Catch, release!"

Immediately, we pull out in front alongside Clemson. This may be the Clemson Sprints, and they might be funded by the school, but we Cougars don't go down without a fight, especially in a mixed eight. This boat is stacked, and I know how bad they all want this win, myself included. Seat-to-seat with Clemson, we have less than a thousand meters to go. Our sprint begins with a ten count at the five hundred mark—that's when shit gets real.

"All right, kids. Here we go. Sprint starts in two! Bump it up! Eyes on the person in front of you. We are at a thirty—let's take it to a thirty-two. Leave Clemson in our wake! Wind it! Last twenty strokes! This is it—all together. Breathe! I have seven seat. Give me six seat! You have ten more strokes! Walk it down the boat! I have five seat! You're doing it! Fuck yeah, Cougars!"

The horn sounds. We did it. Our mixed eight beat Clemson. Gold medals, and for a few of us, clinkage. My crew is spent, and I have no voice left. Fist bumps up and down the boat confirm our satisfaction with the sprint. As we make our way to the docks, someone yells from the bow, "Oh, Kristen! Looks like you're going swimming!" Indeed. And it isn't that warm out, but when you win gold, the crew throws the coxswain in the water—whether we want to swim or not.

Once we get the boat on the trailer, we run down to find out the results of the race. It's confirmed. We beat Clemson by eight-tenths of a second. As soon as all the races have finished, I'm getting tossed in the lake. They'll have to catch me first. Tiny, bossy, and loud. As a coxswain, that is me to a T.

When I joined the rowing team my freshman year, I had no idea what I was in for. Now, I have made the greatest friends, witnessed some of the wildest parties where I learned how to out keg-stand some of my teammates, I'm coaching the high school magnet team, my medal collection continues to grow, and I have been on the Charles River four times in my home city of Boston, for the largest regatta in the world: the Head of the Charles. Love that dirty water.

Confession time. This thing—*yoga*—that everyone is talking about, I'm racking my brain as to why people have invented a new slang word for frozen yogurt. Being from Boston, dropping and adding vowels or consonants isn't unheard of, and I just figure yoga is casual college lingo for a quick trip to TCBY. "Hey, let's go get some frozen yoga!"

No lie. Go ahead and laugh. Silly me.

Finally realizing what yoga actually is—an all-encompassing practice, physical, mental, and spiritual—my interest sparks. I'm all about earning some beer credits to go toward weekend festivities, and in some classes, you sweat your ass off. Maddie convinces me to start easy and take a class with her at Blue Turtle Yoga down on Wentworth Street. Trying new things is my jam, especially with a sweet soul sister.

Our first class is an open flow with Andrew. Maddie and I unroll our mats at the very back of the extremely warm room—as far away from the wall of mirrors as possible. Thank God. Sitting on our mats, as we giggle and gossip about the events of the past weekend, I notice that we are the loudest ones in the room. Taking our voices to a whisper, I do a quick survey. Almost everyone else is either sitting or lying quietly with their eyes closed. Duly noted.

Cracking a smile at each other, Mad and I quiet down. I begin to stretch myself out, still trying to stifle laughter as I catch Maddie out of the corner of my eye. I have a flashback to our stretching circle before rowing practice. I'm not entirely sure what is in store for the next hour. As an automatic response to the unknown, my body begins mass-producing sweat.

Thank God I remembered to put on deodorant this morning.

My first down dog is a sight for sore eyes. I am already slipping and sliding all over my mat. My hamstrings are tight, and I cannot stop giggling, especially when I catch Maddie's gaze.

Andrew says, "Right foot forward," and I step with my left.

Get your shit together, Kristen.

I barely survive the heated flow. Walking out of class I feel dehydrated, confused, and convinced that yoga is not for me. I'd prefer a trip to TCBY, thank you very much. And yet, for some reason, I feel compelled to go back again and again and again. To be honest, I'm not sure I can tell you why in the moment. It just feels right.

As a child, I pushed my body to the limits. Challenges, limitations, disability—those words did not exist in my vocabulary. Short stature was a part of who I was, but it never kept me from doing what I loved. All of a sudden, I am in a room with twenty other strangers moving their bodies, and the comparison begins.

During another class, it dawns on me that, as I have gotten older, I unknowingly have begun to give society the authority to tell me what I can and cannot do. My capabilities are solely based on my stature and how I think others perceive me. The outside world's potential to make me something I'm not has exceeded my aptitude for greatness. In an ocean prominent on perfection, this little water droplet is screaming imperfection. Yikes.

Then, one day, I wake up. Literally. Lying next to Maddie in savasana, my hand rests in hers as I listen to the teacher talk. She is open, raw, and exposed. A shiver runs down my spine as every word that she speaks resonates with my bruised being. Pain, acceptance, body image issues—I wasn't alone. Tears roll down my cheeks and pool uncomfortably in my ears. As if Maddie knows, I feel a gentle squeeze on my hand. Yes, I am different. So what? We are resilient beings with enormous capacity for change and rebirth. The more we understand ourselves, each other, and our differences, the faster the wall of discrimination crumbles. Our differences lose their prominence, and we see each other as beautiful individuals. Yoga is bringing me to my senses; it is my gateway to self-love and acceptance. Slowly but surely, it is peeling back the layers, bringing to light the real me.

My asana practice continues to play a huge role in my authentic healing. Who would have thought that a full-blown transformation begins on a foam mat in a heated room full of strangers? A place of safety, freedom, and self-expression—a place I know that I am free to be me. There is no judgment, no harsh words, no staring, no laughing, and no pointing. Here, I am fully present, grounded by my decisions and guided by love. Every time I step onto my mat, I become vulnerable and can express that vulnerability without having to use words.

There is a lot of beauty that comes from knowing my strengths and dropping the urge to push myself over the edge. Physically, my asana teaches me to respect my boundaries and honor my body—whatever that looks like. Modifications and props are my best friend. Some days my body craves a sixty-minute heated vinyasa flow, and other times, I simply need to lay flat on my back with my legs up the wall. Allowing myself to find child's pose when my body needs it is what makes me a strong yogi. Love is the fluidity and core of who I am, and in my practice, my intention is to love myself, honor my body, and recognize my breath without comparison. I am a yogi who is far from the mainstream individuation of a practitioner seen on present-day social media. These days, I have perfected savasana and the art of patience. I know that on my mat I am free to be me. Some days, there is a lot of underlying discomfort in that; it is a reflection of the uncomfortable feelings I hold onto surrounding my story. When that shit bubbles up, I allow it.

No one else in this world is walking in my shoes, and they don't have a yoga practice that looks remotely similar to mine. When you think about the enormous complexity of such a phenomenon, that everyone has their own inimitable journey, it is beautiful. My physical practice and constant progress erase the boundaries I once created for myself and that others continue to create for me based on my dwarfism.

The outside world has the potential to make us something that we are not. From my experience, there is nothing worse than being outed or unheard. Society, at times, has lead me to believe that I am not enough, but society is wrong.

My yoga has taught me to forge meaning and build identity. Forging meaning through changing myself. Building identity by committing to make an impact and change the world. This grand adventure I am on is expansive. I have drawn—and I continue to draw—strength from my practice on and off the mat.

Walking down Corinne Street, the Charleston humidity settles on us like a hot, wet blanket. Why I even bother to put time into getting ready for the day is beyond me. The second my big toe touches the front step, I am covered in sweat—and my hair resembles Rod Stewart's signature 'do. One of the many things to love about summer in the lowcountry.

Making our way to the end of the street, I see it scrawled in large capital letters on the side of the last house on the block. My heart sinks as I continue to walk alongside my roommate who has yet to notice. Her voice trails off, and she stops dead in her tracks. I know why. Her eyes found what I have already seen. "Midgets Suck" is big and bold enough to see a mile away.

"Kristen ..." she starts, and then I can tell that she doesn't even know what to say.

"C'mon, let's go," I say, not wanting to make a big deal out of it.

As much as I want to say that something like that doesn't cut deep, I can't. I would be lying. It hurts—some days worse than others. Why can't we change the discourse? Anyone who is different, disabled, living with a medical condition … we should have the same respect as everyone else. We are of value, and we have so much to give this world. Ironically, our gifts reside in our suffering. It's part of our learning and growth as humans.

The next morning, on my way to work, the malicious mural has been painted over, by whom, I'm not sure—and it doesn't matter. It doesn't cover up the fact that ignorance is the greatest disease that plagues our society. From this day on, you have my word, I will fight to the end.

Everyone says they have life-changing experiences. It is so cliché yet so true. I truly believe that all I have gone through is what has shaped my personality and beliefs about myself and how I fit into this crazy, different world. I still see my differences as positive, as something good and distinctive, despite the prejudice that I continue to experience.

Living little is all I have ever known, but it has not stopped me from dreaming big—and it won't. What I didn't see coming was the unrelenting fight for acceptance that I would be up against with society. Wanting nothing more than to be loved and accepted by others, the formidable task of unconditionally loving myself stood before me.

It does not matter how long your legs are—you can only take one step at a time. The story of a little girl who wanted to make little huge continues.

Afterword

The controversy surrounding limb lengthening is a considerable one. Back in the day, most people would say, "What the hell is that?" But limb lengthening was and still is a very hot topic within society today, specifically, with the Little People of America. Not only has the cosmetic controversy proven to be a touchy subject matter with the LPA, but while going through all three of my surgical procedures, the subject seemed to be popping up in nationwide newspaper articles, on the internet, and even on television.

I recall watching a *CSI* episode where they visited an LPA convention, and the victim of the crime they were attempting to solve was a dwarf who had undergone a limb-lengthening procedure. Grisham and the CSI team immediately frowned upon it. It was impossible not to have heated feelings toward their discrimination. As I watched the episode, it threw me for a loop. What did they know anyway? Why didn't they go and criticize the other little people at the convention for deciding against the procedure? Who wrote the very slanted episode?

Obviously, I have never been afraid to speak out about the debatable subject. People don't always see both sides of a story or refrain from jumping to conclusions. It has never crossed my mind to judge another little person for deciding not to lengthen their limbs. To each his own, right? So why is it necessary to single the individuals out who have chosen to undergo the surgeries? Limb lengthening is a radical procedure—yes, there is no denying that, but let me reiterate and make a few things very, very clear.

First of all, my parents did not pressure me to make this life-changing decision in any way. In the beginning, Dad was actually very hesitant about the whole idea. He feared premature arthritis, among other complications, but when it came down to it, both of my parents would support me in whatever I decided to do. At twelve years old, I was fully capable of understanding the risks and the long road that lay ahead. However, I was concerned about my future. My lower legs were severely bowed, and sooner or later, that was going to have to be corrected. The moment I heard about limb lengthening and met Dr. Paley, I knew that it was the right decision for me. And when you know, you know.

Enter the Ilizarov fixators—say that five times fast. The frames straightened both bones in my lower legs, and there was also the added bonus of increasing my height by six inches. Six inches! I was initially told that the only solution for my bowed legs was to have surgery that involved shaving or removing part of the bone to make it straight. No, thank you; that was an immediate pass. The growing pains I constantly suffered in both arms were a result of the flexion deformity in the elbow joint. With the lengthening surgery, that disappeared—and four inches were added to my humeri.

My spine was a whole different story. Starting at the age of three, I was braced for kyphosis. Also known as "swayback," it caused significant discomfort when I sat for long periods of time. I also was diagnosed with lordosis which caused my little tushie to stick out like a bubble, hence my notorious nickname: Bubble Butt. As I got older, I walked slightly bent over because of this. The last thing I was worried about at twelve was the way my bum looked—okay, maybe not the last thing—but the pain certainly had to go. The third phase of lengthening lessened the lordosis of my spine. Unfortunately for Mom, Bubble Butt became an insufficient nickname. My back isn't perfect, and that's ok. My back pain is minimal, and in addition to correcting the hip flexion deformity, my posture became noticeably straighter, resulting in an added inch in height. That's on top of the five inches I gained in my femurs.

Do the math: that is more than eleven inches added to my height.

A major issue of concern for me and both of my parents was proportion. People with dwarfism have normal-sized torsos with shorter limbs. My goal was not to end up with abnormally long limbs for my body. As long as my arms and legs were in proportion to my torso, I would be a happy girl—and that I am. My body, which I now refer to as my 'soul suit' is not perfect, but then again, whose is? My soul suit is mine, and I love it just the same.

My height was the least of my concerns going into these procedures, but it was a big bonus. The biggest argument in the dwarfism community is that limb lengthening patients just want to be taller and blend in with society.

Blend in? Oh, please.

To this day, I couldn't blend in with a crowd if I tried. Genetically, physically, emotionally, spiritually: every which way you look at me, I am still a little person. I have lived and continue to live every day of my life with dwarfism. Being little is part of what makes me who I am, and there is absolutely nothing that I, or anyone else, can do to change that. It is not something I desire to change. Yes, I still deal with staring and ridicule from children and those who choose to remain ignorant and immature, and I have come to understand that the thoughts and actions of others are not a reflection of me but of themselves. Of course it stings, and sometimes I find myself spending the day making myself small to feel more accepted. Several people have taught me that the opposite is true. In reality, I am a lot bigger person than most people I encounter in my everyday life. In fact, I have more reasons to be happy and love life rather than belittle myself. Height is just a number, and I am proud standing at just under five feet tall: a straight, proportionate, pain-free, independent, and loving four feet eleven inches tall.

Limb lengthening is cosmetic, they say. I think not. Funny how some think that what I went through over the course of four years is considered to fall under that category. Until the day I die, I will fight to defend what I believe. Rather than undergo corrective procedures alone, I chose a road that corrected most of the deformities I suffered from and added inches to my stature. That road—three very invasive procedures—did not improve my looks, but it did improve the way my body functions. That is not the definition of a cosmetic procedure.

You know what else? Limb lengthening does not "undo" diversity or mess with nature. I am still me. A woman. A daughter. A sister. A friend. I'm more than a statistic, one in forty thousand. I am a woman living with dwarfism, a condition that some see as basis for ridicule. There's more to me than people know. I'm a lover. A fighter. A rule breaker. A woman determined to change how the world views different.

My scars tell a story. Superficial proof of perseverance. When I'm feeling rebellious, an extravagant tale of how I was attacked by a great white might become my explanation to a stranger's very concerned question, "What happened?" All in good fun, of course. What really happened is the story of a girl who began fighting for her future at the age of twelve.

By sharing my experience, I strive to motivate people, no matter what their story is, to stay positive in the face of adversity. A true story, one of authenticity, has the potential to heal as much as modern medicine and that is why I have shared and continue to share mine. Connections are best made by revealing our weaknesses, challenges, and failures; we all have them. My insatiable curiosity and desire for authentic connection are what fuel my love for friendship and helping others.

Defining people instills limitations, putting them in a box and giving them a label.

Yuck.

I am beautiful, not in words or looks but by simply being. So are you. There are as many shades of different as there are of people.

I am learning to ignore the harsh words, stares, and laughing. I choose to embody an un-fuck-with-able, compassionate, and loving spirit. I am dropping the judgment and embracing the now—what is.

Achondrolplasia and all that I have endured does not define me. We are limited only by what we think our boundaries are. My little legs have carried me through a lot in my life: meeting people, sharing stories, giving hugs, shedding tears, absorbing wisdom; all forms of love and all reasons why my heart is bigger than my legs are long.

This book started coming to fruition when I was twelve years old and ever since then I have felt lead to share it with the world. The people throughout these pages have shaped me. They have lifted me up and kicked me down. Regardless of how they impacted my life, I am grateful to each and every soul because they have contributed to my growth in one way or another. And this is what my story is about: acceptance, perseverance and growth. In talking numbers, I am one; one person and one experience. Sometimes another person's perspective is all it takes to change someone else's life.

My name is Kristen. I have little legs and a big heart. Height is simply a measurement. At the end of the day, it doesn't matter how long your legs are—you can only take one step at a time.

About The Author

Kristen DeAndrade is a writer, speaker, and advocate for those living in the face of adversity. Born with dwarfism, and believing that disability is only a state of mind, Kristen shares her journey of living in the face of adversity with anyone who needs reminding of their own indomitable will. Whether that means appearing on national television programs/networks, such as The Learning Channel and CBS Sunday Morning News, or speaking at local schools and events, Kristen is passionate about pushing herself out of her comfort zone and into your heart. Aside from writing and speaking about her life, she is a dedicated yogi who currently resides and shines her light in West Palm Beach, FL.

Made in the USA
Las Vegas, NV
30 November 2021

35626323R00139